The Short Oxford History of Italy

General Editor: John A. Davis

Liberal and Fascist Italy

1900–1945

Edited by Adrian Lyttelton

OXFORD
UNIVERSITY PRESS

OXFORD
UNIVERSITY PRESS

Great Clarendon Street, Oxford OX2 6DP

Oxford University Press is a department of the University of Oxford.
It furthers the University's objective of excellence in research, scholarship,
and education by publishing worldwide in

Oxford New York

Auckland Bangkok Buenos Aires Cape Town Chennai
Dar es Salaam Delhi Hong Kong Istanbul Karachi Kolkata
Kuala Lumpur Madrid Melbourne Mexico City Mumbai Nairobi
São Paulo Shanghai Singapore Taipei Tokyo Toronto

with an associated company in Berlin

Oxford is a registered trade mark of Oxford University Press
in the UK and in certain other countries

Published in the United States
by Oxford University Press Inc., New York

British Library Cataloguing in Publication Data

Data available

Library of Congress Cataloging in Publication Data

Data available

ISBN 0–19–873197–3 (hbk)
ISBN 0–19–873198–1 (pbk)

10 9 8 7 6 5 4 3 2 1

Typeset in Minion
by RefineCatch Limited, Bungay, Suffolk
Printed in Great Britain by
T.J. International Ltd., Padstow, Cornwall

General Editor's Preface

Over the last three decades historians have begun to interpret Europe's past in new ways. In part this reflects changes within Europe itself, the declining importance of the individual European states in an increasingly global world, the moves towards closer political and economic integration amongst the European states, and Europe's rapidly changing relations with the non-European world. It also reflects broader intellectual changes rooted in the experience of the twentieth century that have brought new fields of historical inquiry into prominence and have radically changed the ways in which historians approach the past.

The new *Oxford Short History of Europe* series, of which this *Short History of Italy* is part, offers an important and timely opportunity to explore how the histories of the contemporary European national communities are being rewritten. Covering a chronological span from late antiquity to the present, the *Oxford Short History of Italy* is organized in seven volumes, to which over seventy specialists in different fields and periods of Italian history will contribute. Each volume will provide clear and concise accounts of how each period of Italy's history is currently being redefined, and their collective purpose is to show how an older perspective that reduced Italy's past to the quest of a nation for statehood and independence has now been displaced by different and new perspectives.

The fact that Italy's history has long been dominated by the modern nation-state and its origins simply reflects one particular variant on a pattern evident throughout Europe. When from the eighteenth century onwards Italian writers turned to the past to retrace the origins of their nation and its quest for independent nationhood, they were doing the same as their counterparts elsewhere in Europe. But their search for the nation imposed a periodization on Italy's past that has survived to the present, even if the original intent has been lost or redefined. Focusing their attention on those periods—the middle ages, the *Renaissance*, the *Risorgimento*—that seemed to anticipate the modern, they carefully averted their gaze from those that did not; the Dark Ages, and the centuries of foreign occupation and conquest after the sack of Rome in 1527.

Paradoxically, this search for unity segmented Italy's past both chronologically and geographically, since those regions (notably the South) deemed to have contributed less to the quest for nationhood were also ignored. It also accentuated the discontinuities of Italian history caused by foreign conquest and invasion, so that Italy's successive rebirths—the *Renaissance* and the *Risorgimento*—came to symbolize all that was distinctive and exceptional in Italian history. Fascism then carried the cycle of triumph and disaster forward into the twentieth century, thereby adding to the conviction that Italy's history was exceptional, the belief that it was in some essential sense also deeply flawed. Post-war historians redrew Italy's past in bleaker terms, but used the same retrospective logic as before to link Fascism to failings deeply rooted in Italy's recent and more distant past.

Seen from the end of the twentieth century this heavily retrospective reasoning appears anachronistic and inadequate. But although these older perspectives continue to find an afterlife in countless textbooks, they have been displaced by a more contemporary awareness that in both the present and the past the different European national communities have no single history, but instead many different histories.

The volumes in the *Short History of Italy* will show how Italy's history too is being rethought in these terms. Its new histories are being constructed around the political, cultural, religious and economic institutions from which Italy's history has drawn continuities that have outlasted changing fortunes of foreign conquest and invasion. In each period their focus is the peoples and societies that have inhabited the Italian peninsula, on the ways in which political organization, economic activity, social identities, and organization were shaped in the contexts and meanings of their own age.

These perspectives make possible a more comparative history, one that shows more clearly how Italy's history has been distinctive without being exceptional. They also enable us to write a history of Italians that is fuller and more continuous, recovering the previously 'forgotten' centuries and geographical regions while revising our understanding of those that are more familiar. In each period Italy's many different histories can also be positioned more closely in the constantly changing European and Mediterranean worlds of which Italians have always been part.

John A. Davis

Contents

List of contributors

RICHARD BELLAMY is Professor of Politics and International Relations at the University of Reading.

EMILY BRAUN is Professor of Art History at Hunter College, City University of New York.

PAUL CORNER is Professor of European History in the Faculty of Political Science at the University of Siena.

MARCELLO DE CECCO is Professor in the Department of Public Economics at the University of Rome 'La Sapienza'.

EMILIO GENTILE is Professor of Contemporary History in the Faculty of Political Science at the University of Rome 'La Sapienza'.

ALICE A. KELIKIAN is Associate Professor of History at Brandeis University.

MACGREGOR KNOX is Stevenson Professor of International History at the London School of Economics and Political Science.

ADRIAN LYTTELTON is Professor of European History, Johns Hopkins University Center, Bologna.

THOMAS ROW is Resident Assistant Professor of History, Johns Hopkins University Center, Bologna.

BRUNO P. F. WANROOIJ is Professor of History and Social Sciences at the Florence Program of Syracuse University and at Georgetown University, Villa le Balze (Florence).

J. R. WOODHOUSE is Fiat-Serena Professor of Italian Studies and Fellow of Magdalen College, Oxford University.

Abbreviations

ACI	Azione Cattolica Italiana
	Catholic Action
ANI	Associazione Nazionalista Italiana
	Italian Nationalist Association
BCI	Banca Commerciale Italiana
	Italian Bank of Commerce
CGL	Confederazione Generale del Lavoro
	General Confederation of Workers
CLN	Comitati di Liberazione Nazionale
	Committees for National Liberation
CREDIOP	Consorzio di Credito per le Imprese e le Opere
	Pubbliche
	Credit Consortium for Enterprises and Public Works
CSC	Centro Sperimentale di Cinematografia
	Centre for Experimental Cinema
FIAT	Fabbrica Italiana Automobili Torino
	Italian Automobile Factory: Turin
FUCI	Federazione Universitaria Cattolica Italiana
	Italian Catholic University Federation
GIL	Gioventù Italiana del Littorio
	Italian Youth of the Fasces
GUF	Gruppi Universitari Fascisti
	Fascist University Groups
ICIPU	Istituto di Credito per le Imprese di Pubblica Utilità
	Institute of Credit for Enterprises of Public Utility
IMI	Istituto Mobiliare Italiano
	Italian Institute for Securities
IRI	Istituto per la Ricostruzione Industriale
	Institute for Industrial Reconstruction
ISTAT	Istituto Centrale di Statistica
	Central Statistical Agency
MDRF	Mostra della Rivoluzione Fascista
	Exhibition of the Fascist Revolution
MIAR	Movimento Italiano per l'Architettura Razionale
	Italian Movement for Rational Architecture

MVSN	Milizia Volontario di Sicurezza Nazionale
	Voluntary Militia for National Security
ONB	Opera Nazionale Balilla
	National Balilla Organization
OND	Opera Nazionale Dopolavoro
	National Afterwork Organization
ONMI	Opera Nazionale Maternità e Infanzia
	National Foundation for the Protection of Maternity and Infancy
OVRA	Fascist secret police: meaning of initials uncertain. Probably Opera Vigilanza Repressione Antifascismo Organization for the Surveillance and Repression of Anti-Fascism
PCd'I	Partito Comunista d'Italia
	Communist Party of Italy
PNF	Partito Nazionale Fascista
	National Fascist Party
PPI	Partito Popolare Italiano
	Italian People's Party
PSI	Partito Socialista Italiano
	Italian Socialist Party
PSU	Partito Socialista Unificato
	Unified Socialist Party
RSI	Repubblica Sociale Italiana
	Italian Social Republic
UIL	Unione Italiana del Lavoro
	Italian Union of Labour
USI	Unione Sindacale Italiana
	Italian Syndical Union

Introduction

Adrian Lyttelton

An era of growth: Italy 1900–1914

The new century in Italy brought a fresh start, in the economy, in society, and in politics. Italy benefited more than most nations from the international economic upswing which began in 1896. Until the crisis of 1907, the pace of Italy's economic growth was faster than that of any other major state. Industrial production grew at around 7 per cent a year between 1896 and 1908. After the financial crises of the 1890s, a reformed banking system proved efficient both in managing the currency and in channelling funds to industry. It was possible for the state to return to a policy of actively promoting economic growth without, as before, incurring dangerously large budget deficits. For important sections of Italian liberal opinion, this role of the state was an anomaly, a distortion of the natural course of economic development. But in fact difficulties in mobilizing private capital and the need to modernize infrastructures made the increased intervention of the state indispensable for sustaining growth and making possible the beginnings of a modern, diversified industrial economy. There were still many complaints about the use of the public administration as a source of patronage; but interventionist policies were carried out with a new competence thanks to men like the governor of the Bank of Italy, Bonaldo Stringher, the railway manager Riccardo Bianchi, or the experts in land reclamation linked to the southern economist and politician Francesco Nitti. In the private sector, the new industrial culture which Giuseppe Colombo and the Milan Politecnico had

worked to create now bore fruit. Well-prepared and ambitious entrepreneurs were ready to seize the opportunities provided both by the
state and the market. As Paul Corner mentions, many of the famous
names which dominated Italian industry during the rest of the century appeared in this period. Italy developed one of the leading
hydroelectrical industries in the world, which allowed the economy at
least partially to overcome the obstacle of dependence on foreign
sources of energy. Economic growth temporarily assuaged the violent
social conflicts which had put liberal institutions at risk in the nineteenth century. The resistance to a progressive fiscal policy was still
too great to be overcome, but by announcing the neutrality of the
state in strikes, the progressive governments of Giuseppe Zanardelli
and Giovanni Giolitti allowed the labour movement to make important gains. The real wages of industrial workers rose by approximately
40 per cent between 1900 and 1913, although the large mass of poorly
paid women workers in the textile industries benefited less than most.
The labour movement acquired a new confidence and a degree of
legitimacy. In general, the state allowed more room than before for a
vigorous civil society to express itself through the formation of all
types of association. The press, too, benefited from greater security
from government interference. By the eve of the war, the *Corriere
della Sera*, though firmly linked to its base among the Milanese bourgeoisie, had become a genuine national newspaper in both its readership and its coverage. In a long-term perspective, the expansion of
civil society and of freedom of expression provided an indispensable
base for the democracy which eventually took root after 1945. The
political socialization of workers and peasants through the strong
regional subcultures of the Socialist movement (in the industrial
north-west and Emilia-Romagna), and the Catholic movement (in
the Veneto and the north-east), had consequences that outlasted their
violent extirpation by Fascism.

However, economic growth also posed new problems. The deep
fissures in Italian politics and society were papered over rather than
truly closed. Rural overpopulation, unemployment, and poverty were
still enormous problems, even if they were alleviated by mass emigration. The organization of the landless labourers of the Po Valley by
the socialist Federterra was an achievement unique in Europe, but it
set in motion processes of class conflict and local power struggles
which the Liberal state in the end proved unable to control. By the eve

of the war, employers in modern agriculture and to a lesser degree in industry were openly questioning whether social conflict could be contained within democratic structures. On the Left, ideological extremism fed on both territorial inequalities and on the difficulties of long-term reformist strategy in a poor, developing country.

Industrialization widened the gap between north and south. Dissidents on both the Left (Gaetano Salvemini) and the Right (Sidney Sonnino) denounced the protectionist, pro-industrial policies of Giolitti for favouring minorities of northern industrialists and workers at the expense of the majority of peasants, and of the Mezzogiorno. These denunciations of Giolitti's policies as responsible for the South's growing relative impoverishment no longer look convincing. Not all critics have taken to heart Albert Hirschman's warning that economic growth in developing countries is always unbalanced. The accusation that southern interests were sacrificed to the policy of tariff protection designed to favour northern industry does not take account of the efforts made by Italian negotiators to secure favourable terms for southern agricultural exports in commercial treaties with Germany, Austria, and other countries. The special laws in favour of the industrialization of Naples (1904), and for the development of the Basilicata and Calabria, marked the beginning of purposive state action to address the causes of southern backwardness. The first serious steps were taken to combat the scourge of malaria, with the free distribution of quinine. The take-over of elementary education by the state from the local communes in 1911 demonstrated the state's increasing concern with the persistence of illiteracy, although on the eve of the First World War unacceptably high levels still prevailed throughout most of the South. The vision of an immobile South, unable to share in the benefits of progress, has been substantially revised by recent studies. Mass emigration was certainly a sign of the continued lack of equilibrium between population and resources, but it also brought important benefits. Wage levels rose as labour became scarcer, and returning emigrants (one in two of all those who left) brought a new spirit of independence and new horizons of expectation. The *americani* invested their savings in new, substantial houses of stone or brick, which stood out against the wretched hovels of the other peasants. Purchases of land by peasant cultivators increased markedly, a process which culminated after the war.

It is harder to dismiss the accusations made against the workings of Giolitti's political system in the South. The failure of liberalism to win a mass base, or even to develop a national political organization, had serious consequences. With the rise of the Socialist Party and of Catholic political groups in the north and centre of Italy, the liberals became increasingly dependent on the parliamentary support of the southern politicians and their local clienteles. Governments, independent of their political leadership and programme, could count on a bloc of obedient deputies, the so-called *ascaris* (named after African mercenary troops). Giolitti was particularly successful in manipulating them through a judicious mixture of patronage and heavy intervention by the prefects and police in key constituencies. Certainly Giolitti did not invent these methods. They had been used by all governments since unification, and it was Francesco Crispi, the first prime minister from the south, who had taken the decisive steps in co-opting the southern political class, formerly often in opposition. Fraud and intimidation in elections were serious, but they did not, as in Spain, fundamentally vitiate the whole electoral process. Still, the skill and ruthlessness with which Giolitti 'made' elections became increasingly offensive to a more aware public opinion. Gaetano Salvemini's famous book *Il Ministro della malavita* portrayed the methods of Giolitti's electoral machine in the south with biting sarcasm; particularly damaging were his demonstrations of the collusion of government agents with the Mafia and other criminal groups, like the *mazzieri* of Apulia. The introduction of universal suffrage did not, as Salvemini had once hoped, put an end to government manipulation of elections in the south. It merely made it necessary to use force and fraud on a larger scale and more visibly, and the correspondents of the *Corriere della Sera*, edited by the austerely honest conservative Luigi Albertini, publicized the abuses.

Giolitti had won a respite for liberalism, but he had not solved its fundamental problems: an incapacity to create a nationwide political organization with mass support, and an inability to elaborate a persuasive ideology to legitimate its practices of mediation. It was the 'anti-system' movements of the Socialists and the Catholics, instead, who were able to build national networks of associations. They did more: they created cohesive political subcultures which embraced welfare, sociability, leisure, and adult education.[1] They outmatched the liberals not only in the extent but in the density of the associative life which they promoted. An all-inclusive system of associations was matched by an equally all-inclusive ideology, and each reinforced the other. The lesson was not to be lost on the Fascists, who drew on the experience of the earlier mass movements and often directly absorbed their organizations in order to create their totalitarian political apparatus.

In the more conservative areas of northern and central Italy, Catholicism did not pose a head-on challenge to the liberal state, as socialism did in the Po Valley plains. In part, as Alice Kelikian shows, this was thanks to the decision of Pope Pius X to halt the growth of Christian Democracy and to offer the support of Catholic organizations to the liberals for defence against socialist expansion. But the first universal suffrage elections of 1913 made it evident that outside the south liberal electoral victory was underpinned by Catholic mass organization. When the Catholic political movement resumed its independence with the foundation of the Popular Party in 1919, the hollowness behind the Liberal political façade was fully revealed. So much attention has been paid to the defects of the strategy of the socialist *massimalisti*, whose ineffectiveness as revolutionaries was matched by their success in vetoing any alliance for reform and democratization, that the question of why Catholic-Liberal coalitions in the post-war period failed to achieve stability has been relatively neglected. It is clear that the legacy of mutual distrust left by the conflicts of the Risorgimento, and crystallized in the Roman Question, were decisive.

Italy and the European crisis

The weakening of international financial constraints and Italy's ability to exploit great power rivalry to its own advantage in an increasingly polarized Europe gave the Italian state a much greater degree of true independence after 1900. Economic growth made the high costs of maintaining great power status more sustainable.

---

[1] Emilia-Romagna, the region of greatest Socialist strength, was also the region which showed the most rapid increase in literacy.

However, these achievements also brought their dangers. Increasing numbers of intellectuals, businessmen, and members of the policy-making élites became impatient of the restrictions on foreign and colonial policy which a poorer Italy had reluctantly accepted. They wanted to be players in the new world of imperialism and *Weltpolitik*. Giolitti felt himself unable to resist the public clamour for the conquest of Libya in 1911, an enterprise which was decisive in frustrating his ambitious plans for an 'opening to the left' to include the Socialists in his majority. It was particularly significant that Milanese business interests, which had been hostile to Crispi's Abyssinian venture during the 1890s, now backed colonial expansion. By the eve of the First World War, Italian businessmen were reaching out for new opportunities abroad, and expecting government backing in securing new markets and new opportunities for investment. One unfortunate side effect of the key role of state intervention in the economy was the disproportionate political influence wielded by those groups who were most dependent on state support: the shipping companies, the shipbuilders, the armaments firms, the steel makers, and the sugar manufacturers. Because of the patriotic imperative so forcefully described by Marcello De Cecco, industries linked to national defence were particularly well placed to exploit public opinion and élite concerns with national power to advance their own interests. Although the *Corriere*, with its large circulation, was able to remain independent, these pressure groups acquired an increasingly strong hold over the newspapers. The strong links between heavy industry and nationalism were a feature which Italy shared with the other 'latecomers' to the great power system, Germany and Japan.

As Richard Bellamy makes clear, the shortcomings of the Giolittian political system were interpreted through the conceptual schemes of an already well-established anti-parliamentarianism. In a revealing exchange with the economist and sociologist Vilfredo Pareto, the young intellectual Giuseppe Prezzolini wrote that, while Pareto might see the theory of élites as a contribution to science, 'I see in it instead a scientific justification of my present political needs.'[2] The composition of the Italian political class, formed in the majority by lawyers and professors, seemed increasingly inadequate to the needs of

---

[2] *La cultura italiana del novecento attraverso le riviste*, Vol. VII. *Leonardo-Hermes-Il Regno*, ed. del novecento D. Frigessi (Turin, 1960).

an industrializing society. Many intellectuals were ready to conclude that a new state and a new *classe dirigente* could only be created by a violent upheaval. This was one of the sources of inspiration for the politically variegated bloc of 'interventionists', who saw Italy's entry into the First World War as a way of destroying the Giolittian political system. They included sincere democrats, who saw Giolitti as responsible for the persistence of corruption and clientelism, as well as revolutionaries hostile to the culture of reformist compromise, and nationalists who were impatient with his caution and the primacy he assigned to domestic over foreign policy. Even the modernist aesthetic revolt of the Futurists against bourgeois traditionalism and bad taste served the interventionist cause by inventing a new style and symbolic expression for the radical nationalism of the streets.

A number of the chapters in this volume insist on the crisis of 1914–15 over Italy's entry into the First World War as a decisive turning point. In domestic politics, the success of interventionist groups in controlling the piazza in May 1915, although in reality it only confirmed a choice for war which had been made by the government and authorized by the king, was a critical precedent for Fascist action in the post-war period. In any case, parliament was effectively excluded from the decision-making process. Italy's most famous poet, Gabriele D'Annunzio, used his rhetorical skills to incite the interventionist crowds to violence against those who were trying to 'strangle the nation'. This foreshadowed his mobilization of nationalist sentiment in 1919 against the Versailles peace settlement with his slogan of the 'mutilated victory'. Equally important as a premiss for the invention of Fascism was the new ideological synthesis of revolutionary nationalism elaborated by Mussolini and others. If one looks, instead, at the interaction between foreign and domestic politics, it is worth pointing out that Italy paid a high price for the diplomatic flexibility and freedom of manoeuvre which it had enjoyed in the pre-war period. When it came to war, foreign policy, strategy, and public opinion were all at odds. In both world wars, in spite of the radical difference in their ideological justifications, Italian policy-makers cultivated similar illusions. Both Salandra and Sonnino in 1915 and Mussolini in 1940 believed it possible to fight a 'parallel war' without concerting strategy with their allies. Certainly, Mussolini's illusions were far more disastrous because his aims were far more ambitious. But even in the First World War, policy and strategy between 1915 and 1917 combined to produce the maximum effort for the minimum result. Only in 1917–18, after the disaster of Caporetto, did the imminence of total defeat force the Italian military and governing élites to concert policy and strategy with their allies. Unfortunately, in the peace negotiation Italy's statesmen, the prime minister, Vittorio Orlando, and the foreign secretary, Sidney Sonnino, returned to a policy of short-sighted 'national egotism', which took little account of Italy's financial weakness and the new dominant position of the United States.

Many of the ideologists of intervention, like the philosopher Giovanni Gentile, hoped that war would forge a new and broader national consensus. Yet, again, in the first years of the war the government did singularly little to bring this about. Propaganda was neglected and so were measures to maintain the morale of the fighting troops. The network of private patriotic associations, in which women played a major role, took more effective action than the state. After Caporetto, the government adopted a more active propaganda policy, but this did not prevent a further polarization between opponents and supporters of the war.

In many ways, as both De Cecco and Row point out, Italy's effort in mobilizing for the war was remarkable. Starting out badly prepared, Italy's industrial economy rose to the challenge. But both the financial and the institutional costs were high, as the state failed to maintain control over the pricing of government contracts and autonomous agencies proliferated. In its use of coercion, in the increased power given to producers' associations, and in the development of 'para-state' agencies, the wartime economy foreshadowed the 'organized economy' of Fascism.

Fascism

The post-war crisis confirmed the depth of popular opposition to the war. The victory of the Socialists and the new Popular Party in the 1919 elections, who together took half the seats in parliament, was a decisive blow to the Liberal ruling class. The rising expectations of all classes conflicted with the need to reduce government expenditure.

Inflation destabilized the middle classes, the only social group on whom the Liberals could rely for support.

The explosive growth of industrial action was characteristic of all the former belligerent nations, not least Britain. Italy was no exception in this respect, although the pro-Soviet revolutionary stance of the Socialist Party leaders undoubtedly made class conflict politically more menacing. But the scale of agrarian agitation was something unknown elsewhere in Western Europe in the post-war period. Both Corner and Gentile make clear the primary role of agrarian Fascism in propelling Mussolini into power. It was a phenomenon which he did not organize or control, although his rhetorical skills and political astuteness were essential for the Fascist movement's success.

Both Knox and Gentile insist on the need to take Fascism's totalitarian ambitions seriously. In consequence, they argue that the foreign and internal policies of Fascism cannot be separated. The drive towards foreign conquest and the drive to eliminate the institutional, social, and religious constraints on the totalitarian re-education of the Italian people were intimately connected. The creation of a militarized political movement was not only the indispensable prerequisite for Fascism's seizure of power, but a model for the intended militarization of the nation. The Fascist regime created a formidable network of organizations which were involved in all phases of its subjects' lives, from birth to death, and in all their activities, from work to sport. The new techniques of mass communication, especially the radio, were put at the service of a 'secular religion' with its own rituals and calendar of commemorations. Fascism, as Emily Braun shows, preserved a notably greater degree of tolerance towards different forms of artistic expression than other totalitarian regimes, but this did not mean that artists and architects failed to contribute to Fascist propaganda. Particularly in the 1930s, when the economic crisis had much reduced the opportunities for obtaining private patronage, many artists willingly met the requirements of the state. Their cooperation was essential to the success of the *Mostra della Rivoluzione Fascista* in 1932.

Gentile points out that it is not altogether satisfactory to describe Fascism as an 'imperfect totalitarianism', since totalitarianism is an ideal type, which has fortunately never been realized in its entirety, not even in Mao's China or Stalinist Russia. And Fascist regimes, because they preserved private property, even if they greatly increased the economic role of the state, were unable to control the life chances of individuals to the same degree as Communist regimes. However, it is difficult to avoid the conclusion that Fascist totalitarianism was more imperfect than others. In some ways, in the absence of mass terror and the general atmosphere of suffocating conformity, it had a greater resemblance to the post-Stalinist regimes of Eastern Europe. Certainly, there was also a marked difference, in the much greater degree of active enthusiasm which it could arouse among the younger generations, who still believed that Fascism was the wave of the future.

Knox suggests that even Mussolini's 'totalitarian will' and the creation of a secular religion which inculcated the absolute primacy of politics did not compensate for the lack of a coherent, elaborated, and dogmatic ideology which provided clear directives. Some of the other contributors suggest that the social and cultural consequences of this weakness were evident. The internecine conflicts within the regime between modernists and traditionalists, and Mussolini's own relative lack of interest in the regulation of high culture, left open spaces of autonomy which artists and writers could exploit, as both Braun and Woodhouse show. Young writers, some of whom had believed in the revolutionary potential of Fascism, turned to American literature for inspiration, and in the long term this had an insidious political effect. The *Enciclopedia italiana*, under the direction of Giovanni Gentile, the regime's most distinguished philosopher, allowed the participation of anti-Fascist experts. More surprisingly, even the PNF's own *Dizionario di politica* (1940), failed to develop a distinctive Fascist interpretation of history and was forced to make use of the services of eminent independent scholars such as Walter Maturi, Federico Chabod, and Arturo Carlo Jemolo.[3] Certainly intellectuals were compromised by their collaboration with the regime; but in many cases one could argue that Fascist ideology was compromised by collaboration with the intellectuals.

Even at the level of mass culture, where the intervention of the regime was undoubtedly much more purposeful and effective, the appeal of the 'American way of life', transmitted above all through the movies, challenged Fascist orthodoxies. American products, as Bruno Wanrooij writes, invaded the Italian market and set the

---

[3] See A. Pedio, *La cultura del totalitarismo imperfetto* (Milan, 2000).

standards for a new consumer culture, although its reach was still limited by mass poverty. The regime's own efforts to organize women and promote female participation in sport paradoxically conflicted with the traditionalist, patriarchal messages about the place of women which it purveyed, in alliance with the Church. A minority embraced the model of the new Fascist woman, modern and activist. In the sphere of family and sexual morality, however, the influence of the Church remained paramount. The alliance with the Church which Mussolini established through the Lateran Pacts of 1929 was a political triumph which vastly extended the regime's area of consensus. Many clerics served Fascism with enthusiasm, and blessed Mussolini's 'crusades' in Ethiopia and Spain. Yet the alliance with the Church was never without its tensions, and it imposed perhaps the gravest of all the constraints on Fascist totalitarianism. Pius XI might be willing to make any number of practical compromises, but he was firm and clear in his condemnation of the doctrine of the totalitarian state. The Vatican's fears about Fascist totalitarianism were much increased by the passage of the Racial Laws in 1938. Although many leading Catholic personalities failed to follow the Pope's lead in condemnation, like the founder of the Catholic University of Milan, Padre Agostino Gemelli, who referred to the Jews as 'the deicide people',[4] racist propaganda and the alliance with Nazi Germany were profoundly at odds with the mentality of popular Catholicism.

The regime was largely successful in stifling Catholic political dissent and in restricting the sphere within which Catholic Action was allowed to operate. But, as Kelikian shows, the competition of Catholic organizations in the fields of philanthropy and education remained formidable. Women in particular had good reasons for preferring the old-fashioned, protective paternalism of the Church to the aggressive, militarist culture of the Fascist organizations.

The Fascist regime thrived on ambiguity, as Wanrooij points out, appealing simultaneously to defenders of traditional family values and the rural way of life, on the one hand, and to youth's desire for a modernist revolution, on the other. Yet this ambiguity may in the long term have been a drawback. It inevitably made Fascist action in changing social structures and cultural attitudes less incisive. *Ruralismo* failed to check the flight to the cities, as rural poverty worsened.

[4] R. A. Webster, *Christian Democracy in Italy 1860–1960* (London, 1961), p. 160.

The regime's demographic campaigns were almost equally unsuccessful in checking the fall in the birth rate. Rather than creating a more homogeneous society, Fascism accentuated social divisions. In the end, under the stress of the European crisis of 1938–9 and the war which followed, the ambiguities were exposed. The divisions within the Fascist *classe dirigente*, which in large part reproduced the earlier conflicts between party extremists, on the one hand, and moderates and *fiancheggiatori*, on the other, were dangerously aggravated by the split between supporters and opponents of the alliance with Nazi Germany. Young believers in the Fascist revolution began to turn towards Communism as an alternative. Popular consensus began to unravel as Mussolini's commitment to Nazi Germany became ever more evident. However, many Italians retained an almost magical belief in his ability to score diplomatic triumphs without involving Italy in a major war. Italy's 'non-belligerence' in September 1939, which Mussolini accepted only with great reluctance, confirmed this illusion. In June 1940 it seemed to many Italians as if Mussolini had backed the winner and that the war would be short and relatively painless. For both leaders and followers, this was the worst possible intellectual and psychological preparation for the realities of the Second World War.

The interpretation of Fascism as simply the personal dictatorship of Mussolini is profoundly mistaken, as both Knox and Gentile show. Mussolini was certainly gifted with extraordinary natural talent as an orator, but nevertheless his was in large measure a 'manufactured charisma'. However, the totalitarian regime of Fascism, like that of National Socialism, focused its ideology and propaganda on the cult of the infallible leader. It was a 'totalitarian Caesarism' (Gentile). This made it inherently vulnerable to the loss of belief in the leader's charisma. In addition the Fascist Party notably failed to meet the challenge of war. One particularly serious aspect of its loss of control over the 'home front' was the failure to check the growth of a flourishing black market, in which, indeed, many *gerarchi* were notoriously involved. Another was the breach in the monopoly of communications, as Italians became totally sceptical of the regime's information and turned to the BBC and other foreign radio stations for news.

Mussolini's legendary skill in manoeuvre soon revealed its disastrous limitations, as the war was protracted and extended. Worse still, the hollowness of the regime's claims to have created a new, powerful Italy were revealed by a series of humiliating defeats. 1941 already saw the beginning of the loss of Italy's independence, as Italian military efforts and war aims became subordinate to those of Germany. These developments marked 'the ideological death of the regime' (Knox). In part, they stemmed from the inherent mismatch of Mussolini's ambitions with Italy's industrial potential. But they were also due to the regime's failure to modernize Italy's notoriously inefficient systems of planning, command, and coordination between the armed services.

Conclusion

The story of the years 1900–45 ended in what seemed to be an unmitigated national tragedy. Not only was Italy's independence lost, as rival armies with their dependent regimes fought over the peninsula, but war left behind a terrible legacy of destruction and impoverishment (see Epilogue). In 1944 per capita national income was lower than at any time since the beginning of the century.

However, Italy's post-1945 economic recovery, its creation of a functioning democracy, and its cultural achievements (see Patrick McCarthy's concluding volume in the series), cannot be understood without taking into account the longer term continuities of the preceding period. The same is true of many of the limitations on these positive developments: a lack of transparency in the relations between large firms, shareholders, politicians, and the state administration; a 'blocked democracy' with a strong 'anti-system' opposition and a consequent lack of any legitimate alternative to the dominance of the party in power; the reliance of that party on the use of state patronage and clientelism; a university system which produces a large number of poorly qualified and unemployable graduates, and a restricted reading public.

Much of the history of the post-war Republic was dominated by the alliance between the United States and the Catholic Church. The strength of both partners was in part a result of the situation created by the fall of Fascism. The United States was by far the most powerful and the most popular of the allied nations who liberated Italy. The

Catholic Church was the only domestic organization which had preserved a nationwide network of associations which could fill the political and social void left by the fall of Fascism. For a drastically impoverished population, often lacking the basic necessities of food and shelter, both offered vital resources of charity and reassurance. But the emergence of these two victors had more long-term roots. A famous passage in Carlo Levi's *Christ Stopped at Eboli*, tells how, even at the height of Fascism, it was very rare to find an image of the Duce in the houses of the peasants in the village of the Basilicata where he had been confined. But instead two images were never lacking: the Madonna and President Roosevelt. In the case of the Catholic Church, the antiquity and profundity of its roots obviously do not need emphasis. But Alice Kelikian's chapter makes clear that the eventual triumph of the Church over its political rivals was due not just to a maintenance of its traditional hold over rural society, but to its intelligent adaptation to the new problems created by industrialization and, with more hesitation, to mass political organization. And from the 1890s onwards there was a persistent strain of democracy among the Catholic laity, which survived the disapproval of the ecclesiastical hierarchy. The hold which the United States acquired over mass culture, and even over younger intellectuals, during the 1930s has already been described. But America had captured the imagination of the Italian masses much earlier than that, with emigration. An intense current of exchanges linked the emigrants to their *paesi*; savings flowed back not only into family savings but to repair churches and embellish the statues of patron saints. The First World War already brought home to the more open-minded of Italy's political and economic élites the decisive weight of the United States' economic power, and its ideological inventiveness. In the 1920s, industrialists joined Rotary Clubs and founded institutes of scientific management to bring American economic methods to Italy.

A cultural coda

During this period the gap between most forms of high culture and popular culture remained wide. As in the nineteenth century, the most obvious exception was opera, which remained a genuinely popular art form. Among composers, no one emerged to rival the great names of the nineteenth century, and only Puccini added to his reputation, with *Tosca* and *Turandot*. But perhaps the most famous Italians of the period were performers: the conductor Arturo Toscanini and the tenor Enrico Caruso. However, a comparison reveals the tension between modernity and popularity. The successful tenor had a status as a popular hero which can be compared in some respects with that of the champion bullfighter in Spain. It was the most spectacular way in which a poor boy could achieve fame and fortune. The difference was that in the case of the Italian tenors, their fame could be worldwide. Both Caruso and Toscanini were greatly assisted by the existence of an Italian world beyond Italy in the United States and Latin America, which helped to make them international stars. But whereas Caruso was unreservedly popular, Toscanini's relationship to the Italian public was more complicated. They did not always appreciate his stylistic innovations and the rigid discipline which he imposed. When he threw out the traditional scenery and costumes from Verdi's *Trovatore*, or banned encores, he was hissed by the galleries. An intelligent commentator remarked, instead, on the analogy between Toscanini's methods and those of the manager of a modern industrial enterprise: the imposition of a discipline which was based on the strict measurement and use of time.

The taste for the 'operatic', of course, was not just musical. It involved lavish costumes and scenery, and until the rise of *verismo* in the late nineteenth century, it typically depicted conflicts of passion played out against the background of epic historical events. These characteristics may help to explain the rapid, if brief, primacy which Italy enjoyed in the new medium of film, through the invention of the spectacular historical epic. Films like Giovanni Pastrone's *Cabiria* (with titles by D'Annunzio) inspired D. W. Griffith and foreshadowed Cecil B. De Mille. One of the film's characters, Maciste, played by the actor Bartolomeo Pagano, became the archetype for all the 'strong men' of the cinema, from Johnny Weissmuller's Tarzan to Schwarzenegger's Conan. During the 1920s, Maciste became identified in the popular imagination with Mussolini. In Europe at least, the great divas of the Italian screen like Lyda Borelli and Francesca Bertini set new standards for sexual allure and female stardom. Many Italian intellectuals rejected film as a vulgar mass entertainment, but D'Annunzio and later Pirandello were actively involved in film making. War and American competition put an end to the first flowering of Italy's film industry, which was brilliant but financially fragile, like so much of Italian enterprise. As Emily Braun shows, the Fascist policy of economic and cultural autarchy, whatever its sinister totalitarian overtones, at least had one good result. The foundation of Cinecittà in 1937 and the restrictions on the import of foreign films, though they did not destroy the hegemony of Hollywood, were a successful example of a policy of import substitution, which laid the foundations for Italy's second great period of film making after 1945.

Even under Fascism, cultural innovators found ways of escaping the suffocating embrace of the regime and of profiting from the opportunities which it afforded. But the damage done by totalitarian controls and policies was real. Even if the loss was incomparably less severe than in Germany, racial discrimination and persecution took its toll. Two of Italy's greatest geniuses, Toscanini and the physicist Enrico Fermi, both went into exile as a result of the Racial Laws (neither was Jewish, although Fermi had a Jewish wife). Fortunately, writers like Giorgio Bassani and Primo Levi survived to tell the tale of persecution and to contribute to the foundation of a new culture of freedom.

State and society, 1901–1922

Paul Corner

Optimism and reform, 1901–1907

The two decades which straddle the year 1900 present remarkable contrasts in Italy. Before the turn of the century, Italy had seen banking and corruption scandals in which government was directly implicated, disastrous and humiliating colonial adventures in Africa, continued acute civil unrest culminating in the Milan bread riots of 1898 (ruthlessly suppressed by artillery), an assault on the functions of parliament when it seemed for a while as though Italy's fragile democratic structure might succumb to an authoritarian backlash, and finally, in 1900, the murder of King Umberto I at the hands of an anarchist. Small wonder that it is usual to speak of the 'crisis of the end of the century'. For many contemporary commentators the persistent atmosphere of emergency appeared almost to threaten the continued existence of the unified Italian state; it began to look as though the hopes of the new nation had been disappointed and the challenges too great. Yet, within a matter of months, between 1900 and 1901, the crisis passed and Italy found itself back on an apparently even keel. The elections of 1900 returned a more progressive chamber, government was relatively stable, and social protest, if it continued at a high level, seemed somehow to be once again controllable. In the political comment of the time the transition is almost tangible. If the 1890s had given rise to a wave of national pessimism, even desperation, the first years of the new century were to provide grounds for a considerable degree of optimism.

This optimism was based, first and foremost, on a rapidly expanding economy. Between 1899 and 1907 national income rose by almost 38 per cent, between 1907 and 1914 by a further 20 per cent[1]—a total increase which has earned for the period the title of Italy's 'industrial take-off'. The principal heavy industries, iron and steel, grew substantially, benefiting from state protection and from state orders (armaments, shipbuilding, steam locomotives), but the more significant expansion was realized in the newer industries—the chemical, mechanical, and electrical industries, which did not enjoy protection and depended to a greater degree on the conditions of the open market. Famous names were born in the course of this expansion—Pirelli, Olivetti, and, in the new world of motorcars (where newcomers could compete on equal terms with the rest of Europe) Fiat, founded in late 1899, followed within a few years by Lancia (1906), and Alfa Romeo (1910). Agricultural production also grew very rapidly, reflecting new techniques and an increasing industrialization of agriculture in certain areas of northern Italy. After 1900 there were very significant increases in the production of wheat, maize, and rice (all for home consumption), while the typical export crops—citrus fruits, wine, and olive oil—realized very high levels of sales right up to the outbreak of the First World War. These last tended to compensate to some extent for the fact that industrialization sucked in large quantities of raw materials, with a negative impact on Italy's balance of trade, only partially redressed by the invisible earnings of emigrant remittances, tourism, and payments for shipping hire.

Rapid economic development encouraged the perception that, in many ways, liberal Italy was finally moving closer to general European patterns of life. Indeed, it is interesting to note that the period 1901–13 was the only moment before 1950 in which the tendency of British and Italian per capita incomes to diverge was halted, even inverted.[2] This seemed to signify that the new nation was well on the way to realizing one of the objectives of the Risorgimento, that is, of making Italy a full and respected member of the industrial nations. Certainly many Italians were convinced that Italy was finally catching

---

[1] Istituto Centrale di Statistica (ISTAT), *Sommario di statistiche storiche italiane, 1861–1955* (Rome, 1958), p. 212.
[2] G. Carocci, *Storia d'Italia dall'Unità ad oggi* (Milan, 1975), p. 105.

up. This conviction was rooted less in military strength (although defence expenditure remained extremely high) than in the social developments which accompanied economic expansion and which mirrored changes elsewhere in Europe. Before the First World War Italy was still a predominantly agricultural country from the point of view of production and working population,[3] but rapid industrial development and the great expansion of the public administration was producing a society which, at least in the north, increasingly resembled those of other European states. Urbanization had begun in earnest after 1880 and accelerated after 1900. By 1911, 56 per cent of Italians lived in centres with more than 20,000 inhabitants. After Rome, which virtually doubled its population between 1881 and 1911, the principal cities of the north grew most rapidly, with Milan, Turin, Genoa, and Bologna registering great increases, while in the south, Naples (still the biggest Italian city in 1911, with almost 700,000 inhabitants) and Palermo grew more slowly. Typically, however, Italy managed to remain the country of the hundred cities; more precisely, in 1911 there were 140 centres with a population between 20,000 and 50,000, making up around one-third of the total national population. The larger towns had seen developments analogous to many other European centres, with important (if sometimes debatable) works of clearing and rebuilding in the last two decades of the nineteenth century, producing cities with new districts broadly comparable to areas of Paris, Vienna, or Berlin.[4]

In many ways comparable were also the inhabitants of these districts—the growing urban bourgeoisie. At a time when landed proprietors had begun to lose influence under the impact of the agrarian crisis of the 1880s and of electoral reforms which lessened their hold over local politics, the increase in economic activity produced a rapidly growing professional bourgeoisie, formed of lawyers,

---

[3] Around 59% of the active population was still employed in agriculture in 1911, which produced 46% of GNP. This compared with 24% in industry (24% of GNP) and 17% in other activities (30% of GNP). See, for population, ISTAT, *Sommario di statistiche storiche dell'Italia 1861–1975* (Rome, 1976), p. 14; for contribution to GNP, ISTAT, *Sommario 1861–1955*, p. 213.

[4] F. Socrate, 'Borghesie e stile di vita', in G. Sabbatucci and V. Vidotto (eds.), *Storia d'Italia, Vol. III. Liberalismo e democrazia* (Rome, 1995), pp. 398–99. The population of Rome in 1911 was 522,000; corresponding figures for other European capitals were Paris 2,888,000; London 7,256,000; Berlin 2,071,000; and Vienna 2,031,000; B. R. Mitchell, *European Historical Statistics, 1750–1970*, (London, 1975), pp. 76–8.

bankers, engineers, doctors, and university teachers—some linked to central or local government jobs, some active in the private sector. This was very much the representative class of the Italian *belle époque*—well educated, well housed, used to domestic servants, measuring status less by absolute wealth than by the ability to maintain that dignified and decorous style of life which clearly distinguished it from that of artisans, clerks, or manual labourers. It was the class of the café, of the theatre and the opera (Giuseppe Verdi died in 1901), of the literary society and the charitable organization, and of the holidays *in collina* and, increasingly after the turn of the century, at the summer villa by the seaside in expanding resorts like Rimini or Viareggio, now served by the very extensive railway network. It was also the cosmopolitan class, reflecting the fact that, before the First World War, Italy was culturally very much part of Europe (Italy had four Nobel prize winners between 1901 and 1914),[5] something which would be destroyed by the cultural autarchy of Fascism and regained only with great difficulty after the Second World War. Finally it was the class which set the tone for the petty bourgeoisie, increasingly prominent after 1900 and particularly keen to copy habits and uses which would accentuate that short distance which separated it from the new working class. Thus, as the war approached, there was a gradual trickle-down of the customs and manners of the bourgeoisie to an army of minor administrators, school teachers, shopkeepers, and public employees who also began to experiment with sport, holidays and popular imitations of the latest fashions.[6]

Yet, while Italy might be catching up in certain respects, in others there was still a long way to go. Poverty remained a major problem, particularly among the landless agricultural workers of the north (the *braccianti*) and more generally in the south. Industrialization served only to increase the distance between north and south in economic terms. This was reflected in patterns of emigration. Whereas in the period 1881–90 more than 41 per cent of emigrants had come from the north-east of Italy and slightly less than 27 per cent from the south, by 1912–13, when the outflow reached its height (1.5 million in

[5] Giosue Carducci (poetry) and Camillo Golgi (pathology) in 1906, Ernesto Moneta (peace) in 1907, and Guglielmo Marconi (physics) in 1908.

[6] State employees (including military personnel) rose from 98,000 in 1882–3 to 286,000 in 1914. G. Melis, *Storia dell'amministrazione italiana 1861–1993* (Bologna, 1996), pp. 184–7.

two years), the situation was inverted with almost 44 per cent coming from the south.[7] The same division appeared in the figures for literacy. In 1911 more than half of the population of the south was still unable to read and write. In Calabria some 70 per cent were illiterate, compared with a national average of 38 per cent (Piedmont had 11%). The figures for Basilicata (65%), Apulia (60%), and Sicily and Sardinia (both 58%) were not far behind.[8] Poverty was also clearly a factor in illness, again affecting the poorer south more than other regions. Tuberculosis and malaria were the great killers, and, despite medical improvements, they would remain so until the mid-1930s. Poor nutrition, contaminated water, and unsanitary living conditions contributed principally to the persistence of disease. Infant mortality was high; around 40 per cent of all deaths registered in this period were those of children less than 5 years old.[9]

Bad—often appalling—living and working conditions inevitably produced political protest of the kind which had seemed in the 1890s to threaten the very foundations of the Italian state. By the last decade of the nineteenth century, it was obvious to most intelligent observers that social protest and established institutions were on a collision course. Industrialization had provided few, if any, benefits for the mass of the population; the standard of living of both peasants and workers remained very low—probably little better than it had been at the moment of unification. The large number of peasant 'massacres' (when the *carabinieri* would simply shoot demonstrators) testify both to popular anger at food shortages, unemployment, and high taxation of basic necessities and to the repressive nature of the authorities. This circuit of protest, repression, and further protest served almost to institutionalize what was, even at the time, seen as the division between 'real Italy' and 'legal Italy', between the people and those who governed them.

Liberalism, unlike the rapidly growing socialist movement and a more slowly developing political Catholicism, had no mass base in the country. This was of little consequence when few could vote; even after the electoral reform of 1882 fewer than 25 per cent of Italian

---

[7] ISTAT, *Sommario 1861–1955*, p. 65.

[8] Associazione per lo sviluppo dell'industria nel Mezzogiorno, *Un secolo di statistiche italiane: nord e sud, 1861–1961* (Rome, 1961), p. 795.

[9] ISTAT, *Sommario 1861–1955*, pp. 69–71 for fatal illnesses, pp. 56–7 for infant mortality.

males had the vote. Before 1900, government and the governing class, always uncertain of its capacity to control the new kingdom, was inclined to consider popular opposition to be 'subversive' and tended increasingly to confuse its own interests with those of the nation as a whole. As a result, popular protest against harsh government often turned into protest against the Italian state itself; disorders which, in many other European countries, would have been seen as simply anti-government, often took on a revolutionary complexion in Italy, first at the instigation of the anarchists and subsequently, in the 1890s, stimulated by revolutionary socialism.

The severe political crisis of 1899–1900, which in certain moments had threatened a return to even more authoritarian government in order to meet the challenge of popular protest, produced a political polarization which saw the emergence in early 1901 of a rather uncertain progressive majority. The central figure of the new government, headed by the leader of the left-liberals, Giuseppe Zanardelli, was in reality the Minister of the Interior, Giovanni Giolitti, already noted in the previous decade for his considerable political acumen. The Piedmontese statesman, who was to dominate the political scene between 1901 and 1914, understood very clearly that the progress which Italy had made in many areas would be at risk if anti-systemic protest were not controlled and brought within the institutional framework of the state. This meant ensuring that Italy's political institutions were an adequate channel for the expression of a gradually emerging popular opinion. In part this rested on an enlargement of the suffrage—something Giolitti would realize only in 1912—but success also depended, inevitably, on the formation of alliances with new groups, both Socialist and Catholic, and it was to be around his capacity to achieve some kind of popular alliance—to form a progressive coalition—that the subsequent history of Italy was to turn.

Giolitti's strategy was, fundamentally, that of replacing exclusion by inclusion, at least for some. In its ultimate aim this was a conservative operation, designed to render the state more stable and less subject to disorder, but the methods proposed were for the time very radical. The decision to legalize strikes and to guarantee government neutrality in labour disputes derived from the conviction that it was better to resolve conflicts through mediation rather than through confrontation. But the key to successful mediation lay in the capacity of government to win the confidence of its opponents and this was far from easy. Reformist socialist leaders, like Filippo Turati, who were ready to cooperate with government, had to see positive results, otherwise they risked replacement by more radical leaders who argued, along conventional revolutionary lines, that there was no room for accommodation with the bourgeois state. At the same time, Giolitti, always walking a tightrope between the conservative and progressive components of his own majority, was heavily conditioned in what he could offer.

In 1901 government proposals turned essentially around the question of fiscal reform, intended to permit some highly overdue redistribution of wealth and to remove, or at least to reduce, many of the taxes on essential articles of consumption (flour, bread, pasta) which were the cause of so much resentment among the popular classes. Giolitti had previously distinguished himself as a strong supporter of fiscal reform (he described the existing system as 'inverted progressive taxation'), seeing it as a way of both dampening protest and reinforcing the process of social integration required by accelerating industrialization. But the proposals of the young finance minister, Leone Wollemborg, which envisaged a reorganization of communal taxation, particularly on food and services, and the imposition of an income tax for the rich, were defeated by largely agrarian conservative interests in parliament, formally on the orthodox liberal grounds of the need to balance the budget (and at the same time maintain a high level of military expenditure), while in reality those interests feared (correctly) that fiscal reform would increase the tax burden on themselves. In broad terms, this was to be the fate of all subsequent attempts at tax reform before 1914.

In the immediate circumstances of 1901–3, the problem was partially circumvented by the fact that, given freedom to organize and to strike, many northern workers did gain wage increases as a consequence of a wave of successful disputes. This had some limited redistributive effect, but while it drew the sting of some labour protest, it did not really represent a coherent alternative to fiscal reform. One very significant limit of the policy was that to leave the improvement of living conditions to the results of agreements between employers and *organized* labour might favour the industrial workers of the north but did little to help the *braccianti*; nor did it assist the workers of the south, given the absence of an organized working or peasant class on any significant scale. The lavish public works projects which were undertaken to drain marshes and improve water supplies could hardly compensate in the long run. As important, a policy that relied on the formula 'higher profits–higher wages' to produce agreements between capital and labour was predicated on a favourable economic cycle, which disappeared with the world crisis of 1907 and was not restored during the subsequent years of relative economic stagnation.

Fiscal reform apart, important social legislation was passed in the early years of the century. Measures were approved which controlled female and child labour in factories and mines and which extended the number of categories of worker for whom insurance against accidents was compulsory. This last was to be a forerunner of the much more comprehensive state social insurance scheme, introduced by Francesco Nitti in 1912. There was also considerable special legislation which aimed to improve the condition of the south. Perhaps most significant, however, was the legislation which gave greatly increased powers and responsibilities to the communes, permitting municipal government to intervene more directly in fixing levels of some local taxes and in the provision of essential services. This extension of 'municipalism' was to be important because it permitted socialism to assert itself at a local level while it remained excluded from power at the centre, a fact which many large landowners (whose position was eventually to become exactly the opposite) first resented and then came to fear.

Such reforms served only in part, however, to reduce popular distrust towards the state. For much of the first decade of the century, socialism oscillated unhappily between the temptations of reformist collaboration with government and the rigidities of revolutionary intransigence. Dissatisfaction with Giolitti culminated in a general strike in 1904, which, although successful from an organizational point of view, achieved little more than thoroughly terrifying the petite bourgeoisie of office workers and shopkeepers who watched helpless at socialist revolutionary posturing. Never one to miss a chance, Giolitti responded to the strike by calling an election, which saw the Socialists lose four deputies (although they polled more than 300,000 votes, around 20% of the total vote). The 1904 elections also saw the first overt participation of Catholics in politics since 1871, with the tacit suspension by Pius X of the *non expedit*. Catholic opinion represented a possible source of support for Giolitti's politics of mediation, although the division between the so-called Christian Democrats, who attempted with some limited success to emulate socialist workers' organizations, and the more conservative Catholics reduced the potential of Catholic participation. And the bitter hostility between socialism and political Catholicism meant of course that they were cards which Giolitti could play against each other if necessary but which he was unable to play together.

The widening of divisions, 1907–1914

Reformism foundered not only on the hesitations of the Socialist leadership but, more significantly, on the iron resistance of the conservative majority within parliament, intent as always on protecting rents and property (and military expenditure). In times of economic expansion, as between 1901 and 1907, this majority could at least be put under ministerial pressure to accept some aspects of reformism. But with the onset of economic crisis after 1907, the margins for concession were dramatically reduced, provoking a renewal of hard-line resistance on the part of landowners and industrialists alike, a fact that was reflected in parliamentary attitudes. It appeared that, far from realizing a broader social base for liberalism, the Giolittian experiment had succeeded only in promoting expectations and in improving the organization of popular opposition, while at the same time that opposition increasingly questioned the authority of the Liberal state. The political struggle became ever more intense and increasingly bitter. After 1907 strikes and lock-outs were common in much of the north. Rather ominously, divisions began to appear within the organizations of industrialists and landowners, with a new more dynamic group of capitalist businessmen gradually undermining the authority of the more traditional élites and replacing the paternalist and deferential politics of these with a much more aggressive anti-socialist stance. In their declarations these new men were often explicitly anti-Giolittian, anti-parliamentary, and advocates of direct action against labour protest.[10]

[10] A. Cardoza, *Agrarian Elites and Italian Fascism* (Princeton, 1982), chs. 3 and 4.

The formation of such positions was not necessarily disastrous for Giolitti; such people remained a minority even within their own categories. But the unhappy irony of Giolittian politics was that the attention dedicated to the domestication of socialism, an attention which had a fundamentally conservative objective, produced a reaction to the right from many who might otherwise have been strong supporters of the Liberal state. In particular, certain components of a rapidly emerging urban petty bourgeoisie became increasingly alarmed by the growth of organized labour and began to question Giolitti's priorities. Disillusionment in international affairs, combined with a general crisis of positivist and liberal beliefs, produced a gradual rejection of parliamentary and democratic values which eventually crystallized around dynamically expansionist nationalist sentiments. The Italian Nationalist Association (ANI), formed in 1910, was to remain a relatively small movement before 1914, but its imperialist ideas found at least partial resonance among people drawn from very disparate political groupings—Liberals, Republicans, Catholics, syndicalists, and even some dissident socialists—as well as among bankers and the new men of industry and agriculture. Hierarchical and élitist, anti-parliamentary, anti-bureaucratic, anti-socialist, the nationalist movement rejected the language of class conflict and from the start claimed to speak in the name of producers rather than workers. Integration of the masses into the nation was also an objective for the nationalists, but 'the proletarian nation' was to be a new Italy, very different from the nation built around liberalism and compromise with socialism. Although novel, this message accorded well with certain traditional patriotic themes. For some middle-class intellectuals, it was almost a religious conviction that Italy should in some way rise up above what seemed to them to be the mediocrity of *giolittismo* in order to fulfil the national mission which Mazzini had stressed so strongly.

Recognizing the tendency, in 1911 Giolitti embarked on a war against the Ottoman Empire for the control of Libya, concluded only partially successfully in 1912 after a long and excessively costly campaign. But the war, because of its signally uninspiring conduct, inflamed rather than satisfied nationalist aspirations and worsened rather than improved his situation. In the short term, however, Giolitti, having looked to the right, could now look to the left; if war was one option, reform was the other. Reformist socialism remained a considerable force, particularly in urban areas and among the professional middle class, and in 1911 Giolitti once again attempted to attract this force to his side, first by inviting the reformist leader Bissolati to join his cabinet (an offer which was refused after hesitation) and then by championing the old reformist cause of universal male suffrage. Extension of the suffrage appeared to offer the possibility of a stable majority, partly through the support which the grateful socialists would give to government and partly through the votes of the peasantry which could be relied on to be relatively conservative. Yet, although the proposal was passed in 1912 (taking the number enfranchised from 3.3 million to 8.7 million), the immediate political fruits were disappointing. At the 1912 congress of the PSI in Reggio Emilia, the revolutionary socialists, by now ostentatiously dismissive of parliamentary politics and riding a wave of popular indignation against the Libyan war, gained the upper hand and expelled both Bissolati and his 'right-wing' reformist colleague Bonomi. Achieving national notoriety for the first time, the young republican Benito Mussolini was elected to the new directorate of the party.

Faced by mounting opposition on both left and right, the Giolittian 'system' built on mediation and compromise appeared by the end of 1912 to be in pieces. The increasing polarization of politics was evident as economic crisis strengthened the appeal of revolutionary socialism and syndicalism, on the one hand, and the worsening international situation provoked ever-more overt expressions of nationalism, on the other. Between 1912 and 1914, Italy was to witness some of the most bitter strikes in its short history, costing more than five million working days, with agricultural labourers and industrial workers expressing open hostility towards the state which had become synonymous with misery and repression. The circuit of violent protest and violent repression was resumed, but with a new ferocity. In the elections of 1913—the first with universal male suffrage—Giolitti was able to gain a majority only through the massive intervention of the Catholics on his behalf. What became known as the 'Gentiloni Pact', after its Catholic proponent, promised the support of Catholic voters to liberal candidates only after these had formally undertaken to uphold a series of pledges drawn up by the clerico-moderate electoral association. This reflected the degree to which Catholics had mobilized politically since the elections of 1904 and the extent to which, despite a formal papal ban on participation in politics, the Church had once again become an important factor in political life. While Catholic intervention in 330 of the 508 electoral colleges helped to produce a majority for Giolitti, the price paid was high. The Radicals withdrew their support and liberal anticlericalism expressed its grave doubts about government's complicity with Catholicism. In March 1914 Giolitti resigned, designating as his successor Antonio Salandra, a conservative southern landowner.

Judgements on the Italian situation in the months before the outbreak of the First World War vary markedly. Some continue to endorse the optimism of the first years of the century and argue that, despite severe problems, Italy had made remarkable economic progress and that the realization of universal male suffrage and the entry onto the political scene of long-excluded Catholic opinion represented major steps towards the democratization of the political process. At a formal level this can hardly be questioned. Yet, while so many of the elements of a democratic society were either present or developing, they were doing so in a political context which appeared to have ever less space for a democratic consensus. The clear exhaustion of the politics of compromise apparent in Giolitti's resignation reflected a radicalization of the political scene which, if it would only become totally explicit after the war, was already threatening stability even in 1914. Salandra's appointment as prime minister implied that the reformist road had been abandoned in favour of a return to a more authoritarian stance on the part of government. Thus, the formation of some kind of popular liberal-reformist socialist coalition—on the lines of the British 'lib-lab' pact of 1906—which might have permitted a radical transformation of Italian politics and brought Italy more into line with many other European states where socialism, for all its anti-collaborationist dogma, was slowly being drawn into often informal involvement with government, was not to be realized. This was of great importance, because the realization of such an alliance could have meant that Italy would have met the challenge of the First World War with a very different political countenance. Even more crucially, it might have laid the basis of some kind of Weimar-type coalition for the post-war period, permitting a more effective expression of popular aspirations at the institutional level.

In part, it has to be said, the incentives to the formation of such an alliance were less than they might have been in a more developed

democratic political system. As long as majorities could be manufactured through the clientelism of political notables, by electoral
corruption and by ministerial manipulation and as long as peasants
did not have the vote—and this was the case until the elections of
1913—government had little motivation to broaden its electoral base
and to play for the popular vote. Equally, Giolitti was always very
aware that moves towards the left were likely to cost him support in
the centre and on the right and that what were manifestly the needs
of the country did not always correspond to parliamentary percep-
tions. Universal suffrage may have seemed a way out of this impasse,
but in fact it served as a further destabilizing factor; liberal politicians, distrusting political parties for ideological reasons, had no real
answer to the formation of mass electoral blocs. In this sense there
was a marked hiatus between parliamentary politics and those of the
country, where parliament was frequently depicted as corrupt and
irrelevant—a symbol of the state to be superseded. And, for all his
efforts, Giolitti's social reforms had succeeded only partially in
weakening anti-state sentiment; their effects had been felt principally
in the towns and among the northern working class and not in the
rural areas. Possibly the greatest failure of the period was the failure
to draw the sting of rural protest, where the struggle between aggres-
sively capitalist commercial farmers and the *braccianti* intensified in
bitterness and violence in a way which completely overrode the limits
set by liberal government.

In fact, by 1914 it seemed that what was essentially a crisis of
legitimacy of the Italian state had become more rather than less
acute. Divisions had become deeper; anti-parliamentary, anti-liberal,
and anti-state sentiments made themselves heard with increasing
vigour. In June a wave of social unrest culminated in 'Red Week', an
open insurrection against the state during which large areas of central
Italy were taken over by anarchists, republicans, revolutionary socialists, and syndicalists. Described as 'the dress rehearsal for revolution',
Red Week shocked moderate opinion; it required the intervention
of the army to restore the authority of the state. This suggested very
strongly that, behind the façade of increasing democracy, many very
pressing problems of state and society had still to be resolved.

The First World War: internal politics by other means

The outbreak of the First World War in August 1914 did nothing to reconcile divisions within Italy, although to some it appeared to offer the opportunity to do so. Italy's initial declaration of neutrality reflected uncertainty, lack of preparedness after the exertions of Libya, and even embarrassment (Italy was a member of the Triple Alliance, although not obliged, under the terms of the agreement, to support Austria-Hungary unless it was attacked). There were no immediate reasons for Italian participation in the conflict and neutrality undoubtedly had the support of the majority in the country, even if for different reasons. With the exception of certain intellectual groups, moderate, middle class, liberal opinion favoured neutrality, as did most representatives of Catholic politics. The socialists, following internationalism and pacifism, also argued against intervention. In fact, throughout the autumn and winter of 1914–15 workers and peasants once again increased their protests against inflation, shortages, and rising unemployment, adding to the protest their hostility to any Italian involvement with the war.

An exception to this position was provided by the young Mussolini, one of the leaders of revolutionary socialism and editor of the socialist newspaper *Avanti!*, who broke with the party line in November 1914 by calling for intervention. The reasons for this about-turn remain far from clear. Mussolini very probably thought that the war would result in a general European cataclysm, from which revolutionary change might spring, and feared that the neutralism of the Socialists, a fairly passive and defensive position, would simply result in their isolation from events. He was expelled from the party and became almost overnight one of the most vociferous proponents of intervention (and one of the most violent enemies of the PSI), utilizing funds from France and from certain interventionist industrialists to publicize his views in his newspaper, *Il Popolo d'Italia*.

The minority campaign for intervention reflected many different currents of opinion, ranging from the extreme left to the extreme right. Like Mussolini, syndicalists and anarchists thought the war would be 'revolutionary', although it was not always clear in what ways, while democrats, republicans, radicals, and certain reformist socialists wanted war against what were judged the authoritarian and militaristic central powers and called for the conquest of the *terre irredente* of Trento and Trieste, a demand which the Nationalists also supported once they had abandoned their initial support of the Triple Alliance. Such a heterogeneous movement had difficulty in finding a focus, but one factor which helped to unite the diverse viewpoints was a generalized desire for aggressive participation on the European scene after a decade of Giolittian moderation and mediation. The revolt against what many considered an *Italietta* of mundane wage negotiations, dull social legislation, and corrupt political practice sought the realization of a different Italy—an Italy which, through victorious involvement in the war on the side of the Entente, would undergo spiritual and cultural regeneration and take its rightful place among the great powers. Democratic ideas and expansionist Nationalism could all find common ground in their ambitions for a *new* Italy, even if that Italy was often significantly different.

The decision to denounce the Triple Alliance and to intervene on the side of the Entente—a decision which was communicated to the country in the 'radiant days' of May 1915—probably owed a great deal to the promises made to Italy in the secret Treaty of London (April 1915). However, the decision to abandon neutrality had other, more fundamental, motives linked to questions of internal politics. Prime Minister Salandra, the representative of the agrarian interests of the conservative right, saw Italian participation in the war as an opportunity to realize a restoration of social discipline and hierarchy in an Italy which, by 1914, appeared to be near to tearing itself to pieces. War would provide the justification for repressive legislation and permit an authoritarian solution to Italy's divisive social and political problems, thus realizing a national recomposition on con-servative lines. And victory would ensure that no questions were asked about the methods which had been used to achieve it. It was a project which promised, moreover, to destroy the reformist alliance which had hovered uncertainly around the figure of Giolitti and, through a greater reference to the powers still held by the king, to reduce the influence of parliament in the decision-making process.

It was only after enormous pressure that parliament was persuaded to give full war powers to government. Parliament had, in any case, already been overshadowed by the *piazza*. Throughout the first half of May 1915, interventionist groups, recruited mainly from the urban petty bourgeoisie and among students, held highly vocal demonstrations in favour of war in many of the cities of Italy, on occasions clashing with neutralist counter-demonstrations in violent street-fighting. When intervention was eventually announced, it seemed that decisive action by a relatively small élite had changed the course of history. This was, of course, not the case. Salandra, a few of his ministers, and the king (the military were not consulted) had taken the decision, as was their constitutional right, but the impression of a victory for extra-parliamentary agitation remained, and was to be important in later years. Many interventionists, particularly students and other young people, would eventually find their way to Fascism, and for many of them the apparent triumph of the *piazza* in 1915 provided a precedent for political action which they would not forget.

Excitement at the prospect of combat which interventionists expressed so vividly at this point could not conceal the fact that Italy had entered the war against the wishes of the majority of the population (the only Western belligerent nation in which this occurred) and that war had not produced any kind of immediate national cohesion as in France or in Germany. Salandra, in fact, made no effort to achieve any national consensus for war; in his view, a short victorious war would bring consensus for government in its wake. In the meantime special wartime legislation and repression would deal with disaffection.

The history of Italian participation in the war is, in effect, the history of a gamble which did not pay off. If one of the government's principal objectives of intervention had been that of creating some kind of unifying national consciousness, albeit under the aegis of authoritarian politics, that objective was disappointed. On the contrary, the effects of the war on a society already fragmented by social conflict, in which the very authority of the state was often questioned, were devastating. The many tensions present at intervention, far from disappearing as the war dragged on, were accentuated by the first experience of 'total' conflict. At the front, the war quickly became a stalemate, characterized by 'useless slaughter'. By late 1916, discontent with harsh conditions, poor commanders, and pointless frontal attacks on enemy machine guns provoked indiscipline and mutinies among an army made up largely of peasant conscripts who had little clear understanding of what they were fighting for or why (the Italian war was, after all, technically a war of aggression). The response of the Supreme Commander, Luigi Cadorna, was to invite his officers to repress dissent through all means available. This produced numerous field executions and the frequent use of decimation against undisciplined units. Military tribunals were responsible for over 4,000 death sentences—proportionately far more than among any other Western army—passed on soldiers for desertion or other acts of alleged indiscipline.

On the home front, tensions were equally high. The vast economic expansion required by the war (certain armament and other war-related firms grew tenfold in the course of the conflict) pulled a large number of first-time factory workers (many of them women) into war production. Under the terms of the industrial mobilization legislation, which subjected factories within the ever-growing war zone to military discipline, workers were put on the same level as soldiers and could be sent to face military tribunals in cases of unsatisfactory behaviour. Hours of work were increased and strikes declared illegal, although there was, in fact, little that the authorities could do when workers (with women often to the forefront) downed tools in protest against working conditions, rampant inflation, and food shortages, these last a consequence of disastrous provisioning policies on the part of the government. The failure to provide almost any kind of assistance to families adversely affected by the war increased resentment, as did the refusal of government to move towards progressive direct taxation in order to finance the war effort. As always the authorities preferred to increase indirect taxes. The growth of a flourishing black market, where only money counted, helped to fuel the belief that the war was being fought by the poor and that the rich were hidden in safe office jobs and suffered few hardships. This sense of injustice, the idea that necessary sacrifices were not being shared equally (an idea which had considerable basis in fact) did much to increase social tensions, as was made evident in Turin in August 1917, when workers demonstrated en masse against food shortages and the continuation of the war, and some even called for revolution. In suppressing the riot, the army killed more than fifty protestors.

Military and civilian discontent with the authorities was especially significant in Italy because mass mobilization of the population—the first really national effort in the history of united Italy—was anything but a positive 'nationalizing' experience for the great majority of Italians. Letters from the front, stopped by the military censor, reveal the desperation of many of the soldiers and their bitterness towards their officers and commanders. Similarly, for many civilians, the first experience of factory work was under the harsh and repressive militarized conditions imposed by the industrial mobilization. By itself, this did not particularly distinguish Italy from other belligerents. There were despairing soldiers in all armies and heavily disciplined workers in all economies. But, while British soldiers might want to shoot General Haig and French factory workers riot about work rates, they did not often put the war effort itself in question; some cohesion of purpose was maintained throughout. What was significant in the Italian case was that mounting discontent was very rapidly directed at the *state* itself rather than exclusively at the generals or the bosses. Conversely, government considered popular discontent in both the army and the factories to be a treasonable subversion of the state and reacted by increasing repression rather than by attempting to redress justified complaints. Thus, those tensions which were present in all other Western combatant countries, which governments were able to deal with by negotiation and mediation, became in the Italian case potentially revolutionary, and were seen as such by government. This perception was, of course, heightened as news of events in Russia began to arrive in early 1917.

The situation came to a head in October 1917, with the rout of the Italian second army at Caporetto. The Austrians took more than 300,000 prisoners and looked for a brief moment to be on the point of capturing Venice. Many Italian soldiers, convinced that defeat meant a welcome end to the war, began the long walk home. It took several days before the disbanded were rounded up and sent back to the front, where a defensive line along the river Piave eventually held. Low morale among the soldiers had not been the cause of defeat, which was to be attributed to poor communications and lack of foresight among the general staff, but it undoubtedly helped to turn defeat into rout. Predictably, Cadorna put the blame on the soldiers, speaking of a 'military strike' inspired by subversive propaganda, and interventionist opinion began to look for a scapegoat. This was found, not in the deficiencies of the Supreme Command (something which would have undermined the whole war effort), but in the activities of the so-called 'defeatists' of the PSI. From the first, the Italian Socialists had refused to vote war credits and had maintained their anti-war stance throughout the conflict, declaring (rather passively) that they would 'neither support, nor sabotage' the war effort. The panic of October 1917 produced a hysterical witch-hunt against the 'internal enemy', accused of all kinds of anti-national and anti-patriotic activities and many Socialist leaders were arrested and imprisoned.

The response to Caporetto is extremely instructive of the way in which war had both widened and consolidated divisions within the country. Interventionist opinion, which had been extremely hetero-geneous at the outset of the conflict, united in the face of possible defeat and, more important, united along patriotic, nationalist, and violently anti-socialist lines. Left-wing, democratic, and moderate liberal opinion tended to become assimilated to the more extreme views of the right. Many who had been, in one way or another, sym-pathetic to socialism before 1915, now distinguished themselves for their vitriolic attacks on the party of alleged defeatism. Fear of defeat generated hatred of the 'defeatists'. Often, of course, the lines of hatred also corresponded to class division. The socialists, forced onto the defensive by the fury of the attacks against them, became very much the pariahs of the situation, but precisely for this reason were confirmed in their hostility to the authorities and to the state.

The long experience of war produced other consequences as well as further political polarization. What little authority parliament had enjoyed before the conflict was almost completely lost; parliament was called very infrequently during the war (ministers did not want to hear criticism of the conduct of hostilities) and became something of a government cipher. Government ruled by decree, thus avoiding control by the legislature. At the same time, the whole governmental process had been revolutionized by the totally novel requirements of the mass mobilization of population and production. Responsibility for the provision of arms and munitions was passed to administrative organisms in which the industrialists and the military themselves played the leading roles, often far removed from any kind of govern-mental oversight. The massive requirements which total mobilization made on the state greatly enhanced its role, therefore, but at the same time produced a fragmentation of the functions of the state. Public responsibilities were entrusted to private hands, something which resulted in the creation of autonomous administrative 'satrapies' virtually exempt from government supervision.[11] In one sense it worked. The Italian economy did meet the challenge, if somewhat belatedly, but the institutional cost was enormous. Farming out the authority of the state without retaining strict government controls was to gravely weaken the (already very uncertain) authority of the state in relation to private interests. It established a complicity between government and industry which industrialists would not forget, obviously welcoming freedom of movement in respect of production and prices in a regime of state regimentation of the workforce. It was no accident that, after 1925, fascist legislation in respect of industry and labour would be directly inspired by the legislation of the First World War.

In broad terms, therefore, the consequences of mass mobilization appear to have been quite the opposite of those envisaged by the authorities at the outbreak of hostilities. Government had seen war as an opportunity for imposing social discipline and reducing internal division. Yet, at both military and civilian levels, popular response was negative and hostile. Instead of the realization of a patriotic apotheosis, the sufferings and injustices of war had accentuated feelings of mistrust in respect of the government, whose incompetence, both at the front and at home, was bitterly resented, even by that officer class whose patriotism had been taken for granted. Total war had imposed heavy burdens on the whole population, but there seemed little government recognition of this fact, and little apparent desire on the part of government to compensate for popular sacrifice. For the majority of Italians, the war was something to which they submitted. If it made peasants more aware of belonging to a nation called Italy, something of which many had been largely unaware before the outbreak of the war, it did so on terms which did anything but consolidate patriotic sentiment and reinforce a positive sense of national identity.

[11] Giuliano Procacci, 'Appunti in tema di crisi dello Stato liberale e origini del fascismo', in *Studi storici* (1965), vol. ii, pp. 221–37.

The *biennio rosso* and the advent of Fascism

Victory, after such a close run, was of course the realization of a dream for many among the bourgeoisie, for whom the traditional liberal patriotism had become increasingly infected by rampant nationalism. But, beyond the glory, victory seemed to bring few benefits. Certainly Italy was a different country from that of 1915. The war had seen an enormous acceleration in industrialization and in urbanization, with a corresponding increase in the size of the working class, even if many of the new industrial workers—particularly the women—would have difficulty in retaining their jobs after demobilization. But the most significant shift, in part a response to the experience of the trenches, in part a consequence of the dramatic challenges posed by economic expansion, was in attitudes. The horrors of the war had provoked a generalized expectation of radical change; at the same time, the very heavy (but novel) state intervention in all aspects of civilian life during the course of the war had increased resentment against the liberal state on both the right and the left, but had also promoted the idea that the road to the new world lay inevitably through the action of the state. On the left, this suggested that the liberal state should be superseded by socialism; on the right, ideas of the restoration of hierarchies, of a world of social discipline and class collaboration under the aegis of a new state, began to seem increasingly attractive. Liberalism was left isolated and seemingly outdated.

This dividing of the ways was not immediately obvious in 1919, when, quite naturally, there was initially an attempt to return to business as usual. But the depth of class divisions became apparent very rapidly. Industrial workers, *braccianti*, and peasants, numerically much stronger than in 1915, better organized, and with the example of the Russian Revolution before them, moved to the attack in an unprecedented popular onslaught on power which would turn 1919 and 1920 into the *biennio rosso*. Initially, demands were economic— for higher pay in the face of galloping inflation and for a shorter, eight-hour, working day. These, employers conceded without too much difficulty, no doubt convinced that what was given away today could always be recouped tomorrow. Much more alarming were those demands which implied the loss of employers' control of farms and factories. In the Po Valley, with its large capitalist farms, socialist leagues finally managed in early 1920 to win a monopoly control of the hiring of labour. They were thus able to dictate the number of workers needed for any particular job and to refuse this labour if employers protested. This, effectively, gave them control over the whole process of production.[12] Similarly, in the northern towns, industrialists found themselves facing mounting pressure for workers' control from the factory council movement—pressure which culminated in the spectacular but ill-fated occupation of many northern factories in September 1920.[13] In other areas of Italy, notably in Lazio and the south, there was a strong, almost spontaneous, movement to occupy uncultivated lands, something which seemed to many to put property rights in question.

Liberal Italy was unable to find any adequate political response to this challenge. In a sense, the pre-war chickens came home to roost in 1919 and 1920. Popular sentiment, never integrated into the political framework of the state before 1914, again asserted itself as a massive anti-state movement. In the November elections of 1919, both the PSI and the newly-formed Catholic party, the Partito Popolare Italiano, made great gains at the expense of the liberal establishment, to which, for differing reasons, both were openly hostile. This meant more than a simple electoral turn-around provoked by an enlargement of the suffrage and the introduction of proportional representation. It represented a decisive defeat for the old liberal politics, dominated by local notables, with their traditional methods of patronage and persuasion. Indeed, it was the irony of 1919 that the urban bourgeoisie, which had emerged from the war undoubtedly strengthened by victory and by economic development, found itself without the political means or the necessary direction to assert that strength. In reality it was a bourgeoisie economically stronger, but far more fragmented, than it had been before the war. That enlightened bourgeoisie of the professional classes which had been at the heart of the *belle époque* had lost ground to new groups of industrialists and to a petty bourgeoisie greatly reinforced by the wartime expansion of public

---

[12] P. Corner, *Fascism in Ferrara, 1915–1925* (London, 1975), pp. 89–90.
[13] P. Spriano, *The Occupation of the Factories: Italy 1920* (London, 1975); M. Clark, *Antonio Gramsci and the Revolution that Failed* (New Haven, 1977).

administration and the return of demobilized officers. This shift corresponded to changed political allegiances, with a serious weakening of democratic liberalism and a reinforcement of nationalist, anti-socialist opinion, reflecting fears provoked by inflation and social conflicts within Italy and bitter resentment at the 'mutilated victory' handed out to Italy at the Versailles peace conference.

Post-war Italian governments were all characterized by weakness. This was partly a consequence of the presence of Socialists and Catholics in parliament in numbers large enough to have a determining effect on majorities; as long as both PSI and PPI remained hostile to each other, the parliamentary system risked partial paralysis. But it was also a result of the economic situation governments found themselves facing. Victory had been achieved at enormous cost. Italy had incurred massive debts during the course of the conflict, mainly to Great Britain and the United States and also had to face the extremely expensive process of conversion to peace. The possibility of repaying debts (and raising essential fresh international loans) was dependent on curbing rapid inflation, raising taxation, and following policies of austerity. Politically, for liberal governments, this was almost impossible. Taxing the rich (something which had not even been done during the war) was likely to offend that one remaining group on which the liberals could rely for support, while repressing consumption, reducing wages, and pursuing austerity ran directly against all popular expectations for reform at the end of the war and was likely to provoke serious civil disorder. This was a dilemma which Liberal governments were unable to solve; in the end it was Fascist violence and intimidation towards workers and peasants which solved it for them.

Fascism was at first an irritated response to government weakness and later a further cause of that weakness. The first Fascism—of Milan in March 1919—reflected the generalized radicalism of the moment (combined with a deep hatred of neutralist socialism, which continued to denigrate the war effort) and Mussolini's own personal desire to find himself a new political constituency after his clamorous breach with socialism in 1914. It attracted a very disparate group of urban deracinés—journalists, writers, artists, out-of-work union organizers, students, and former soldiers. These had little in common beyond a virulent hostility to socialism (but not always towards the working class) and a belief in the patriotic 'values' which had been saved by victory. Initially the movement was a failure, heavily over-shadowed by Gabriele D'Annunzio's melodramatic and highly sub-versive occupation of Fiume (denied to Italy in the peace treaty) in September, and humiliated in the elections of November. Essentially the Fascism of 1919 fell between two stools. Most radical opinion still looked to the left and to socialism, while more conservative opinion still expected government to reassert itself in the face of popular protest (and also remained profoundly sceptical about both Mus-solini and the Fascist movement). Recognizing his weakness and probably scenting the likely exhaustion of socialism, Mussolini changed his stance in the spring of 1920, abandoning much of the early radicalism and accentuating the element of anti-socialist 'pro-ductivism' which proposed collaboration between all producers, regardless of class—a clear enough message to the right. This drew some attention, but Fascism still remained one movement among many.

The situation changed dramatically in the autumn of 1920. With the huge agricultural strikes of the spring and summer of that year, northern agrarians—in particular the capitalist farmers of the Po Valley—finally understood that government, led once again by an ageing Giolitti, was not going to intervene on their behalf in the ongoing confrontation with the socialist unions and began to look to their own resources. A sense of panic was accentuated by the onset of economic crisis and the proximity of local administrative elections, in which the socialists seemed likely to consolidate their dominance. The response was—as it had been on occasions before the war—to attempt to use urban anti-socialist groups to break the stranglehold of the rural socialist leagues. These groups were found in the very small *fasci di combattimento* of the provincial centres—*fasci* inspired by Mussolini but often with little real contact with the Milan-based movement. Formed largely by students[14] and former soldiers, the *fasci* began to organize systematic attacks on socialist leaders and union organizers, beating and killing with apparent impunity. The strategy was immediately immensely successful. In the province of Ferrara, for example, the socialist leagues, deluding themselves that they would be

---

[14] The number of university students doubled between 1911 and 1920 (from 27,783 to 53,239, of whom 9% were women). Most of the increase occurred between 1916 and 1919. ISTAT, *Sommario 1861–1955*, p. 78.

protected by the police they had spent so much time vilifying, were forced to capitulate within a matter of weeks. An organization which boasted more than 70,000 members in the autumn of 1920 had virtually ceased to exist by the spring of 1921, when the newly-formed Fascist unions claimed 40,000 enrolled.[15]

The success of agrarian fascism was based in part on the complicity of the authorities, who in many cases aided and abetted the violence of the squads.[16] It was also facilitated by the uncertainty of revolutionary socialism, which had achieved so much at a provincial level but had no idea how to proceed to the revolution. But it was based fundamentally on the support which Fascism gained from the large commercial farmers, who gave money to pay the *squadristi*, provided transport for the military-style 'punitive expeditions', promised to defend sharecroppers and to give land to land-hungry peasants, and gave work to those *braccianti* who abandoned the socialist organization. This last was, of course, the decisive factor in consolidating Fascist dominance. Once the socialists had lost their control of the labour market, defenceless labourers faced either starvation or, if they wanted to work, adherence to fascist unions and the acceptance of drastic wage reductions.

Agrarian fascism proved to be the launching pad for a movement which, up to that point, had decidedly failed to take off. At first dismissing agrarian fascism as a pure reaction of the landed proprietors, Mussolini quickly changed his tune when he realized the opportunity offered him. In fact, as Fascism spread—beating and burning—through much of northern and central Italy, Mussolini rose rapidly to the level of a national figure. His status was confirmed when, with colossal misjudgement, Giolitti invited him to enter the government list in the political elections of April 1921. The Fascists returned 35 deputies to the Chamber and were given a legitimacy which, up to then, their violent methods had always denied them.

Electoral success alongside Giolitti was a very clear indication of both the weakness of liberalism and the novelty of Fascism. In some respects what had happened in Ferrara and Bologna in late 1920 was not new; it had happened in other places before the war. The best

---

[15] Corner, *Fascism in Ferrara*, chs. 6 and 7.

[16] See G. Neppi Modona, *Sciopero, potere politico e magistratura, 1870–1922* (Bari, 1969), pp. 215 ff.

example is provided by events in Parma in 1908, when groups of middle-class students, armed and protected by cavalry, intervened against strikers to defend what they defined as liberty. In fact, before 1914, despite government policies of non-intervention in labour disputes, piecemeal local repression of certain kinds of organized protest had been common. What was different about Fascism was less the violence used against opposition than the fact that the violence was no longer episodic or restricted to one or two localities. Instead it was highly organized around the squads, was systematic in its operations, and moved very quickly from being a local to a national phenomenon. This was a measure of the change in politics and society in the two decades since 1900. Liberal governments had relied on a succession of single, isolated acts of repression in order to retain control; but, just as the elections of 1919 had seen the defeat of the locally-based politics of liberalism in the face of nationally organized parties, so reaction to socialism was also forced to move to the national level. If the war had failed to realize a 'nationalization of the masses', it had certainly seen a nationalization of political problems. The political spaces which were opened by mass politics were beyond the control of liberalism and, to the right, they were filled by Fascism. Agrarian Fascism was initially a local response to a local problem, but, in the circumstances of 1920–1, the Fascist conquest of one or two provinces would have been pointless. From the start of agrarian Fascism, which tolerated no opposition, there was an inbuilt mechanism of all-or-nothing which pushed the movement towards the conquest of whole regions and, thereafter, of the state.

If Giolitti's intention was to try to control the Fascists by drawing them into some kind of collaboration with government, the result was simply to open the way to further Fascist triumphs. In fact, more slowly and less securely, Fascism began to make greater inroads in the large cities of the north where it collected ready support among an urban petty bourgeoisie exhausted by inflation, strikes, and socialist revolutionary rhetoric. Disillusioned and unemployed ex-soldiers found Fascism appealing, as did the unemployed in general, while shopkeepers[17] and white-collar workers also rallied to the Fascist cause in large numbers. In particular, Fascism appealed to young

---

[17] See J. Morris, *The Political Economy of Shopkeeping in Milan, 1886–1922* (Cambridge, 1993).

people, with its military dynamism, its promise of national renewal, and its role as the 'anti-party' of the new generation. And, if the large industrialists remained cautious and hedged their bets, many small industrialists welcomed the methods of Fascism in dealing with a restless workforce. Urban Fascism was less openly violent than that of the rural areas—industrialists valued their skilled workers—but intimidation by *squadristi* outside the factory gates was a weapon which proved extremely effective in breaking union solidarity and permitting the reduction of wages.

Victorious at the local level in much of northern and central Italy, Fascism liked to present itself as the movement capable of reconciling widening social and ideological divisions through the creation of a society founded on the idea of the nation. The national solidarity which had not been realized by participation in the war was to be achieved through the all-embracing message of Fascist nationalism. That this operation was premised on violence and class repression made many doubt the prospects of success, but, with a parliament hopelessly divided between Liberals, Socialists, and Catholics, it proved impossible to stem the tide of the new movement. The March on Rome—more choreography than *coup d'état*—simply confirmed at the centre a victory already completed in the provinces. From that point on, and for the next twenty years, those divisions in Italian society which had grown since the beginning of the century and which the politicians of the period had so signally failed to bridge would be suppressed by force, by regimentation masquerading as class collaboration, and by the flimsy promises of Fascist propaganda.

The Church and Catholicism

Alice A. Kelikian

The Roman Question

On 6 June 1861, in a malarial delirium, Count Camillo di Cavour uttered Montalembert's formula, 'a free church in a free state', to the priest who had come to administer last rites to the excommunicated prime minister.[1] Subsequent premiers of Italy would share his fixation and frustration with the Roman Question, which remained a thorn in the side of all liberal regimes. The Vatican did not acknowledge the reality of the united Kingdom until 1929. Papal disaffection from high politics perforce limited the nature of representative democracy in a predominantly Catholic country, and it underscored the narrowness of the Italian political class.

Other European nations came to blows with the Church over secularist legislation. Still, the schism between cross and crown placed the Piedmontese monarchy in a predicament without parallel elsewhere. Only Italy was home to the bishop of Rome and the turf of his temporal domain. The architects of unification differed in their sentiments towards the spiritual authority of the papacy: democrats and freemasons clung to their arch anticlericalism, while observant Catholics constituted the majority in the moderate stream of

---

[1] William Roscoe Thayer, *The Life and Times of Cavour*, Vol. II (Boston, 1911), p. 491; S. William Halperin, *The Separation of Church and State in Italian Thought from Cavour to Mussolini* (Chicago, 1937), pp. 7–8.

liberalism. But the Pope's crusade against the putative laicism of the Risorgimento and his reluctance to abandon political power compelled opinion in most governmental circles to make the campaign against the institutional influence of the Holy See their creed.

From this anomalous situation in relation to the Vatican nineteenth-century liberalism would never recover. The conflict exhausted governing coalitions. The unsettled claims of the Apostolic See meant that battles over education, charity, and the regular orders would be revisited for decades to come. The Roman Question framed the debate on matrimonial jurisdiction and divorce. Church precepts and papal pronouncements on family, morality, and domestic virtue overshadowed lay attempts to create a national conscience through public schools and law codes. The Holy Penitentiary conditioned Catholic voting habits in municipal and parliamentary elections. The religious issue split the political temperament of the bourgeoisie into a left and a right. Anticlericalism became the acid test of progressive parliamentarians.

Catholicism cast in stark relief other problems that cursed the new nation. The economic and social power of Church beneficence exposed the poverty of public provision for the poor. Patterns of sacerdotal organization and voluntary alms-giving laid bare the division between a prosperous North and an ill-developed South. The diocesan clergy in upper Italy could rely upon a close and moneyed network of pastoral, educational, and charitable agencies to attend to the everyday concerns of the faithful. The former Kingdom of Two Sicilies, on the other hand, accounted for only one-fifth of the parochial districts in all of Italy. In the Neapolitan and Sicilian provinces, parishes were scattered, bishoprics penniless, and priests insubordinate: more than half the ecclesiastics convicted of felonies in 1874 served the cross in the Mezzogiorno. Superstition more than prayer and piety characterized popular religiosity there.[2]

The Roman Question hamstrung liberal patriots. The extreme assertions of the papacy left them little room for manoeuvre. Not one concession from King Victor Emanuel II seemed to satisfy the Curia. If the Piedmontese constitution recognized Roman Catholicism as the sole faith in the land but accepted the private observance of other

---

[2] Leone Carpi, *L'Italia vivente: aristocrazia di nascita e del denaro—Borghesia—Clero—Burocrazia* (Milan, 1878), pp. 390–3.

beliefs, then the Vatican interpreted this freedom of worship as a threat to religious unity and demanded civil penalties for those of other persuasions. Objections to toleration aside, Pius IX had for some time been averse to the nationalist ambitions of the House of Savoy. Only the mercy of foreign troops kept the pontifical state intact. After the Austrians lost Lombardy in 1859, they withdrew their regiments from the Papal Legations. The Kingdom of Italy seized Romagna, and the next year it annexed Umbria and the Marches. All that remained of the 'patrimony of St. Peter' were Rome and its vicinity. The Pope excommunicated king and cabinet, and these repeated ecclesiastical censures muzzled any patriotic stirrings among the clergy. In 1864 he issued the *Syllabus Errorum*, which upheld the temporal power of his Holiness, denounced liberalism as an anathema, and made Catholicism incompatible with nationalism. The promulgation of the infallibility of the Pontiff and the universality of his episcopate reinforced this ultramontane dogma at the First Vatican Council. The synod of nearly seven hundred bishops came to an ominous end when the French garrison left at the outbreak of the Franco-Prussian War. In September 1870, with foreign troops repatriated, the Italian army at long last took Rome and negotiated terms of surrender.

The Church found its abundant recompense for the loss of temporal authority in the rediscovery of its spiritual primacy. Alongside the many political and diplomatic reversals endured by Pius IX came significant ecclesiastical and devotional achievements, including the elaboration of Marian dogma, the definition of the Immaculate Conception, and the extension of the feast of the Sacred Heart to the universal church. The intimate life of Roman Catholicism flourished during his pontificate.

Inevitably, the Vatican's influence forced the state to take a tougher stance than it had originally intended, especially on education. Teachers in parochial schools needed to get professional certification, although standards improved as a result. The university system abolished all theological faculties. The Church exploited to the full the political implications of anticlerical legislation. It used electoral abstention as a weapon to impugn the legitimacy of representative government and undermine the foundations of the franchise. In 1871 the Penitentiary Tribunal instructed Catholics to boycott parliamentary elections. The *non expedit*, restated by the Pope in 1874, kept ultramontanists away from the polls and postponed the formation of a clerical party. The ban did not obtain to municipal races: the faithful participated fully in local politics, usually through the establishment of clerico-moderate alliances with right-wing liberals.

In February 1878 Pius IX died but one month after allowing Victor Emanuel II to receive the viaticum during the king's final bout with malaria. Liberals expected that the Pope's passing would signal an end to the stand-off between Church and state. They miscalculated. During his long pontificate, half the Sees of Italy had been staffed with clerics on the side of intransigence. When the conclave at the third scrutiny elected Gioacchino Pecci to the tiara as Leo XIII, the schism between the papacy and the Italian government widened. He converted the recommendation that Catholics stay away from polling booths into an outright prohibition against voting in national campaigns. He gave fresh stimulus to worship of the Blessed Virgin and consecrated all mankind to the Sacred Heart. He called for a return to the doctrines of St Thomas Aquinas as a defence against the errors of the modern age. The Leonine revival of Thomism stressed the primacy of divine over natural law and gave the clerical reconquest of Christian civilization a philosophical rationale.

The Church, the orders, and Catholic welfare

Early in his first premiership, Francesco Crispi changed an 1859 compulsory education law mandating that students take lessons in Scripture and catechism. The 1888 royal decree made religious instruction an after-hours option rather than a requirement in the elementary grades. About one-tenth of those who taught the final truths at the turn of the last century came from the clergy, the vast majority of whom lacked public certification. At the centre of the prime minister's anticlerical programme stood the overhaul of the Opere Pie. The 1890 reform touched indoor relief and placed all private benevolent institutions under state control. Bishops throughout Italy denounced the legislation, which allowed lay overseers to disregard donors' bequests and redirect the flow of endowments and gifts. Leo XIII countered this unparalleled assault on the autonomy of Catholic beneficence with an unprecedented admonition of his own. The 'economist Pope' implored laity and clerics alike to address the social question. His New Deal, put forward in the 1891 encyclical *Rerum Novarum*, proclaimed private property a natural right but condemned laissez-faire capitalism as well as socialism. This pronouncement united all shades of clerical opinion. The bull moved the Church agenda away from anachronistic apologetics and into the industrial age, but it also reminded women of their natural place in the home as guardians of the faith.

The last decade of the nineteenth century saw the entrenchment of regional subcultures in Italy, and social Catholicism prevailed throughout much of the North. When anticlerical legislation sought to curb the power of the clergy institutionally, nuns and priests made pastoral work welfare work. The Opere Pie reform inadvertently turned the Church into a nursery for local activism, since it compelled lay almoners to gain control of town councils in order to administer charitable funds vested in religious trusts. *Rerum Novarum*, which spoke of rights and justice, beseeched the faithful not only to commune with the less fortunate but also to supplement conventional religiosity with social responsibility.

As traditional property relations unravelled in the aftermath of the agricultural crisis, parish priests defended the flock against the encroachments of the market and clerical town councillors. The Opera dei Congressi, which began as part of Catholic Action in 1874, took off after *Rerum Novarum*. The lay association first undertook to reclaim youth through parochial schools but then addressed the predicament of the impoverished tenants unable to get collateral loans. A network of 588 land banks, mostly in the North, helped sympathetic peasants secure low interest rates on a personal basis. Small farmers from religiously observant homes could look forward to cheap credit and stable leases. By 1897 nearly 4,000 committees had been set up to run rural syndicates, coordinate municipal electoral alliances, and found mutual-benefit societies. Faced with the formidable economic and civic endowment of the Christian social movement, premier Antonio Starabba di Rudinì that same year ordered prefects to crush it completely. Many of the clubs and circles reemerged with the change of prime minister, but the persecutions left Church activists debilitated and the episcopal hierarchy looking elsewhere. The Opera dei Congressi never rallied after this reverse. When in 1903 Leo XIII died and the Patriarch of Venice ascended to St

Peter's throne as Pius X, the Vatican dismembered the political arm of the organization for good. The credit unions and cooperatives alone survived the trampling of 1904.

Reform-minded clerics did not disappear altogether. The congregations sought to give practical demonstration of their belief by assisting and moralizing the working masses. Even though government had formally dispersed monks in cloisters, clerks and canons regular survived after unification. The number of brothers and priests dropped from 103,161 in 1882 to 89,329 by the turn of the century. The fall in the number of candidates for the ordained ministry accounted for this decline. The secularization laws, by and large, did not affect female religious, a national resource for the care of the sick and the poor. Anticlerical regimes found few alternatives to their professional force. The state removed the Daughters of Charity of St Vincent de Paul from lying-in hospitals only to invite them back to work the wards. In 1909 nearly 60 per cent of nurses in Italy still wore the habit. Nuns also provided cheap personnel for preschools, infirmaries, sanitariums, asylums, soup kitchens, and orphanages, especially in the North. Their ranks jumped from 28,424 to 40,564 during the pontificate of Leo XIII, who inspired a generation of postulants in social welfare. This phenomenal growth continued until the Second World War. By 1921, 71,679 women had joined communities, and in 1936 over 100,000 belonged to sisterhoods.

Unlike monks, who fell under the direct authority of the Pope, the female orders answered to the episcopate and had the approbation of the local curate. Proximity to the parish brought conventuals closer to the everyday concerns of churchgoers. Their vocational and pastoral activities formed an integral and intimate part of diocesan life. Nuns in welfare orders moved down the social ladder as the female orders progressed into the twentieth century. The Ursulines, the Society of the Sacred Heart, and the Canossian Institute drew their novitiate from the urban and small-town bourgeoisie; the Daughters of St Vincent de Paul, the Salesians, and smaller congregations attracted postulants from a variety of backgrounds.

By 1936 Italy had little over 41,000 diocesan clergymen. Seminarists were rewarded with a small stipend from the public ecclesiastical fund, the renunciation of marriage, and an isolated presbytery to call home. They depended upon contributions from the congregation to make ends meet. A freethinking parish might represent a pastoral challenge but it also meant sacerdotal indigence. Small wonder the number of priests declined. Women saw commitment to the religious life in different terms. For many, service to Christ constituted the only creditable alternative to matrimony and childbed. Their vows of chastity, poverty, and obedience gave them a moral authority and a spiritual standing that others of their gender, regardless of social and marital status, did not command. Convents produced cadres of female professionals in nursing, teaching, and welfare provision. These nuns brought devotional fervour to their secular vocations and laid the groundwork for the Catholic revival in the twentieth century.

The Ursulines, who had traditionally dominated education and childcare, and the Daughters of Charity of St Vincent de Paul, who specialized in nursing, expanded at the turn of the century. Newer congregations thrived, especially those focused on devotion to the Blessed Virgin, the Eucharist, and the Sacred Heart. Local sisterhoods with social commitment proliferated too. In 1828 Saint Magdalene of Canossa, a Veronese aristocrat, opened the Institute of the Daughters of Charity in Milan, and then one in Venice, to give succour and solace to the needy. The order expanded throughout smaller centres in Lombardy and the Veneto in the late nineteenth century. Saint John Bosco, the son of Piedmontese peasants, chartered the Society of St Francis of Sales to educate poor boys. In 1872 he transformed an apostolate started by St Mary Mazzarello, a seamstress, into a Salesian congregation under the appellation the Daughters of Our Lady Help of Christians. Don Archangelo Tadini, a priest who saw himself as 'God's weaver', built a spinning mill in 1895 near Brescia. Five years later, he established a house of worker nuns, the Suore Operaie della Santa Casa di Nazareth, to toil alongside adolescents in the manufactory and to supervise the boarders at the dormitory next door. Female religious had nothing to fear on the shop floor. Factory labour, he claimed, sanctified women.

Priests and nuns alike sought to revive Catholicism through the instrument of the charitable organization, but this often meant dependence on the business community. The valleys of the North hid grey textile towns, where local convents operated schools and hostels for management. Manufacturers bankrolled confessional welfare schemes to avoid the spread of socialism in the labour force, and the religious obliged them in order to reclaim the alienated poor for the Church. Paternalistic employers wanted obedient, God-fearing workers, while the Marian missions hoped to impose religious practice and inculcate popular piety among those on the margins of industrial society. Catholic virtues became company values: conformity, deference, and patience.

Thus, the Church attack on modernity and progress did not dissuade industrialists pushing conventional religiosity on the working class. Textile manufacturers in the North first underwrote confessional welfare schemes, but their efforts were inconsistent and intermittent until the twentieth century. Alessandro Rossi, the leading proponent of protectionism for the wool industry in the 1880s, pioneered a distinctively Venetian model of industrial development, and organized religion came as part of the package. Rossi, a personally observant but politically liberal Catholic, entered parliament as a deputy in Italy's first legislature and became a senator in 1870. His close ties to the episcopacy in Vicenza gave him autonomy from the clerical establishment and allowed him to ignore the *non expedit*. The entrepreneur attended seminary before proving his worth in the family firm, his brothers served the cross, and his daughter, who took the veil, set up the Salesians in their hometown of Schio. He himself helped to reconstitute the local congregation of Augustinian nuns after the law of the land had suppressed them, and he protected the convent when an 1886 decree threatened to evict the sisterhood once again.

Rossi transformed the artisan organization of his father's firm into the most advanced textile concern in Italy by seizing the opportunity to modernize and mechanize. He deplored the mentality of the merchant-manufacturer but still maintained the exclusiveness of the local wool aristocracy. He relied upon his close-knit clan not only to manage the business at auxiliary plants but also to oversee the company crèches and schools. When he turned to the orders, rather than the state system, to provide instruction to the children of his employees, the female religious in charge of academic administration came from families related to the industrialist by marriage. Three young nuns, all sisters-in-law of his sons, superintended the staff of twenty-five teachers on the payroll, and they took his surname as theirs under vows. The senator's influence seemed without bounds, even in Rome. In 1888, just as Crispi undertook to make anticlericalism a plank of his governmental platform, Sister Maria Kechler Rossi, Sister Nina Garbin Rossi, and Sister Maria Bozzotti Rossi received top honors for excellence from Professor Paolo Boselli, the minister of education and future premier.[3] Concerned that working mothers commuting from the countryside might leave toddlers alone at home during the day, he showcased infant care as a major perk of company employment. Exercises in the lower grades incorporated the precepts of Friedrich Froebel, the originator of the kindergarten system who insisted on the importance of play, and Ferranti Aporti, the Catholic pedagogue. Although Rossi opposed juvenile labour legislation in order to preserve the prerogatives of management, he refused to hire adolescents who had not finished fourth grade. Illiterate adult operatives could attend evening classes.

Rossi attempted to manufacture a company culture by combining traditional piety with reverence for rurality and veneration for labour. He built housing in the new quarter of Schio on the model of Verviers in Belgium, and by the turn of the century the neighbourhood grew to accommodate about one thousand residents. There, workers could avoid the alienation of the Manchester masses or the estrangement of the Parisian poor by living in detached homes with vegetable patches and front gardens suggestive of their peasant origins. At the border of the company development and the old town centre stood the parish church, which had as its titular St Antony Abbot, the father of urban flight and patron saint of animals and basket weavers.

An avatar of entrepreneurial autonomy in Italy, Rossi fought against the interference of both Church and state in affairs of management. He saw no room for religion in the settlement of industrial disputes and therefore came to blows with Christian Democrats, who envisioned a role for the cross in labour relations. But he encouraged devotional practice among his employees, and this included time out for morning mass and feast days even though the cults and catechisms of conventional worship seemed antiquated to him. Rossi hoped for a new brand of Catholicism. Indeed, he wanted to capture for Rome the spirit of Protestantism. Inspired by the ideology of perfectionism and by the gospel of self-help, Rossi viewed popular piety in the United States as more attuned to the exigencies of industrial culture. The *soi-disant* Christian paternalist penned the preface to the

---

[3] Biblioteca Civica di Schio, Archivio Alessandro Rossi, Copialettere, May 1887 to Jan. 1889, p. 384, A. Rossi to P. Boselli, 1 Sept. 1888.

Italian edition of William Ellery Channing's *Personal Education* and handed out the conservative Unitarian tract to workers at his mills.

Rossi's grandiose elaboration of the Christian industrial community disappeared with his death. Orthodox Catholicism, with its dogmas and devotions, presented problems to other manufacturers. If some employers sought to avoid the spread of Marxist materialism by using the clerical establishment as an instrument for social control, they failed to understand the importance of grounding a company culture in the heritage of indigenous spirituality. Carlo Caprotti, a freethinking Lombard cotton producer, saw little compatibility between religious life and the commercial ethic, but his irreverence turned to repugnance when his sister became a bride of Christ. The Cotonificio Cantoni opened a hospice near Lake Como in the 1870s and another, decades later, not far from Varese; nuns worked as guardians, but management refused to let their charges observe Church feasts and holidays not recognized by the state. With the help of a local convent, the firm operated a shelter for orphan girls, who laboured for free in return for room, board, and evening classes in home economics. The pastoral visits completed by the bishops showed no signs of shop-floor surveillance by the orders in the late nineteenth century. That rural industrialists did not encourage obligatory piety figured as a common lament of diocesan priests throughout the North.

During the last years of Leo XIII's pontificate, religious houses tried to win over the poor for Catholicism. They did not canvass the streets in search of business but rather proffered their services to industry. Company boarding-houses began to dot the landscape of Lombardy, the Veneto, and parts of Piedmont, as the female congregations sought to preserve the virtue of young women living at the edge of urban society. First the Ursulines and the Canossian sisters, then the Daughters of Charity of St Vincent de Paul, and finally the Salesians involved themselves in protecting working girls from worldly temptations. This trend continued after Pius X became Pope. During his tenure, they resurrected the teaching and charitable orders and contributed to the Catholic revival.

Rapprochement between Church and State

After his election to the tiara in 1903, Giuseppe Melchior Sarto distinguished himself from his predecessor. Unlike Leo XIII, Pius X made it clear that the promotion of piety rather than social engagement would represent the hallmark of his tenure. He recommended daily Communion, began the codification of the new canon law, and restored the authentic Gregorian chant. But circumstances, both in Italy and in France, forced him to engage in affairs of state. A patriot and a conservative, he cultivated a positive rapport with Giovanni Giolitti, the prime minister. He enjoyed good relations with the House of Savoy, and Victor Emanuel III officially received him just months before the college of cardinals voted him Pope. He had no use for the restoration of temporal power to the Holy See, and he considered Rome capital of the Kingdom. The new Pontiff's conciliatory attitude towards the liberal regime adumbrated the policy of accommodation between cross and crown that became law with the Lateran accords during Fascism.[4]

The new style of papal politics became manifest on two fronts. The Pope opened the door to collaboration with liberal officialdom in secular affairs but closed off all possibility for change within the Kingdom of Christ. Little after a year on the throne, he relaxed the *non expedit*, encouraging the faithful 'to do what your conscience tells you' in elections with church interests at stake. This counsel, meant to solidify clerical-moderate coalitions against 'subversives', inadvertently made way for the formation of a national Catholic party. The vague language encouraging participation in anti-socialist voting blocs left the door open to subsequent interpretation by a less conservative Curia. By contrast, the Vatican's attack on the religious reform betrayed no ambiguity. The Pontiff set out to defend dogma and to strangle doctrinal Modernism, the movement that turned away from neo-scholasticism in favour of an activist philosophy and a critical reading of scripture. Pius X condemned such ideas as 'the synthesis of all heresies' in his encyclical letter *Pascendi Dominici Gregis*. He instituted an anti-Modernist oath for all aspirants to the

---

[4] D. A. Binchy, *Church and State in Fascist Italy* (London, 1941), pp. 54–5.

priesthood, excommunicated clergy associated with the new errors, and pushed Thomism as the intellectual weapon to discredit the 'gainsaying of knowledge falsely so called'.[5]

When in July 1904 Pius X disbanded the Opera dei Congressi, a number of Christian Democrats defied the Vatican and set up a National Democratic League with an eye towards starting a Catholic party. The Holy See forbade clerics to join the new organization, and it implored prelates to observe vigilantly all sacerdotal activities in order to secure the subservience of priests and to rout out rebels and rogues. Don Romolo Murri, the Modernist clergyman who had led the revolt, found himself defrocked and excommunicated. *Il Fermo Proposito*, an encyclical promulgated in 1905, confirmed the relaxation of the ban on parliamentary participation but made voting subject to episcopal authorization. The papal letter also reconstituted Catholic Action. The apostolate now divided into four separate unions and made the social and political mission secondary to the restoration of Jesus Christ 'to the family, the school, and society'.[6]

The dismemberment of the Opera and the crusade against doctrinal unorthodoxy put Catholic militants on the defensive during the pontificate of Pius X. But placing lay activities under the control of bishops made room for closer and more centralized collaboration between the episcopacies, sympathetic businessmen, and the charitable orders. In Lombardy, the Daughters of Charity of St Vincent de Paul and the Apostles of the Sacred Heart appeared on the bankrolls of silk manufacturers, and they supervised company orphanages and dormitories. Shelters for single girls in employment at cotton mills proliferated in the North and especially in Lombardy after 1910. The secular clergy from nearby parishes recruited maidens from needy or troubled homes. Both nuns and the ecclesiastical establishment insisted on purity, piety, and obedience as conditions for bed and board: after the factory bell chimed at sundown, residents returned to their hostels to attend chapel, recite the rosary, and sing hymns. By the eve of the First World War, textile entrepreneurs

[5] Pius X, *On the Doctrines of the Modernists, Pascendi Dominici Gregis*, 3 July 1907; Giovanni Spadolini, *Giolitti e i cattolici (1901–1914): con documenti inediti* (Florence, 1960), pp. 68–70; Christopher Seton–Watson, *Italy from Liberalism to Fascism, 1870–1925* (London, 1967), pp. 272–5.

[6] Pius X, *On Catholic Action in Italy, Il Fermo Proposito*, 11 June 1905; Bolton King and Thomas Okey, *L'Italia d'oggi*, 3rd edn. (Bari, 1910), pp. 547–8.

had accommodated the practice of orthodox Catholicism into the package of their paternalism. The Vatican did not condone work for matrons outside the home, but in 1908 Pius X did graft a female section onto Catholic Action to rouse the ladies of the laity to spread the word. During the years of his pontificate, women assumed pride of place in confessional beneficence. They doled out and received propaganda and welfare.

When the Pope died in August 1914 one week after the outbreak of war, the conclave elected Cardinal Giacomo Della Chiesa, the archbishop of Bologna, to succeed him on the throne. Benedict XV was heir to the universalist tradition of Leo XIII rather than the pastoral patrimony of Pius X, even if he did widen the worship of the Sacred Heart and promulgated the new canon law. He preserved the Holy See's neutrality even after Italian intervention in the European conflict. While reaffirming the campaign against Modernist heresy, the 'Prince of Peace' had no patience for integralist diehards and showed unusual toleration for divergence of opinion among the faithful. He reorganized Catholic Action, restoring its autonomy as well as its vitality, and he welcomed Christian democrats back into the fold. The Roman Church accepted the novelty of women's work outside the home and did not regard the development as necessarily detrimental to the integrity of the Christian family. After the Armistice, the Chamber of Deputies voted to abolish *autorizzazione maritale*, which had established the juridical authority of the husband over his wife in the civil code. *Civiltà Cattolica*, the Jesuit journal that often spoke for the Vatican, heralded the legislative change and recounted the arguments against the inferior legal position of the female sex.[7]

Open in the matter of women and the law, the Society of Jesus put back on the blinders for the subject of the Church and parliamentary politics. In January 1919, Don Luigi Sturzo, a Sicilian priest and a Christian Democrat who had never flirted with Modernism, founded the Partito Popolare Italiano. Benedict XV saw the civic future of Catholics in a non-confessional lay party, and he took pains to keep the new movement independent of the Curia. His quiet liquidation of the *non expedit* allowed laymen and clergy alike to participate fully

---

[7] Civiltà Cattolica, 19 Apr. 1919, cited in Paolo Ungari, *Storia del diritto di famiglia in Italia* (Bologna, 1974), p. 217.

in the life of the nation. The Popolari drew voting strength from peasants in the North and emerged in the elections that year as the only grass-roots, mass-based alternative to the socialist challenge; in 1920 and 1921, they supported the Giolitti ministry and received two cabinet positions. But before long *L'Osservatore Romano*, the official voice of the Vatican, began to distance itself from the party and push Catholic Action as the appropriate organization for confessional activism. In municipal races the clerical conservatives entered into local alliances with liberal candidates and thereby doomed the development of a coherent anti-Fascist platform. Small wonder that popular Catholicism came to grief by 1922, when squabbling between rightist, centrist, and radical factions enervated the national leadership.

Roman Catholicism and Fascism

In January 1922 Benedict XV died unexpectedly of pneumonia, and the sacred college crowned Cardinal Achille Ratti, a former vice-prefect at the Vatican library, to succeed him as Pius XI. The new Pope broke with the modern custom upon his election: for the first time since Rome's occupation, the Pontiff returned to the old proto-col and imparted *Urbi et Orbi* from the loggia above St. Peter's. A signal of rapprochement between the Papacy and the Kingdom of Italy, the solemn blessing pointed to a change in the Holy See's understanding of temporal authority. Church diplomacy turned to resolving the breach with the liberal regime, and this spirit of appeasement grew with Mussolini as prime minister.

Like the Pius before him, Ratti disassociated the Vatican from Christian democracy. When squads in black shirts destroyed the white cooperatives and unions, no recriminations came from the Holy Father. As Catholics retreated from politics, the new govern-ment brought the crucifix back into schools and courthouses. Milan's University of the Sacred Heart, which showcased neo-Thomism in the philosophy curriculum, received state accreditation. The regime raised the stipends of clergy and restored a number of ecclesiastical properties to the orders. Italian officialdom incorporated the celebra-tion of mass in public ceremonies. The Fascist security ordinances, introduced soon after the establishment of the dictatorship in 1925, borrowed from the 1850 police regulations of the Papal States measures that banned transvestitism and other forms of personal camouflage; the legislation survives to this day as Article 85 of the republic's security laws. The Popolari went underground during 1926, as did the other opposition parties, with hardly a murmur from the Primate of Italy. That same year, negotiations began between 'the Vatican and Mussolini to settle the Roman Question once and for all.

The Holy See and Mussolini signed three protocols at the Lateran palace in February 1929. A treaty awarded the papacy temporal sovereignty of the Vatican City and confirmed Roman Catholicism as the 'sole' faith of the nation. A financial convention gave the Church cash and bonds to make amends for properties confiscated between 1861 and 1870. Finally, the conciliation stipulated a concordat, whereby the state recognized the civil validity of sacramental marriage performed according to canon law and acknowledged religious instruction as the foundation for public education. The Fascist regime appeared to occult its ideological interests and totalitarian ambitions in order to gain prestige abroad and consolidate consensus at home.[8]

Even if the Curia had no time for political Catholicism, the Sovereign Pontiff did seek to bring about a *reconquista* of civil society. Already in 1922, he called for 'the restoration of all things in Christ' by way of marriage, education, and the social order.[9] Much the same as Pius X, he spurred on the laity through the apostolate of Catholic Action, which he had reorganized in 1923 and purged of party intrigue. Article 43 of the Concordat guaranteed the independence of this pliant and ostensibly non-partisan organization, with youth, student, and adult sections promoting the religious mission of the Church.

But two years after signing the Lateran accords, the Holy See saw fit to protest against the persecutions endured in Mussolini's Italy by the Pope's followers. In 1931, when it came under brutal attack by Fascist youth and university students, Catholic Action had grown to include 250,000 adherents with 4,000 male chapters, and 5,000 branches for boys and girls. The political potential of the vast lay movement,

[8] Richard A. Webster, *Christian Democracy in Italy, 1860–1960* (London, 1961), pp. 109–11.
[9] Pius XI, *On the Peace of Christ in the Kingdom of Christ, Ubi Arcano Dei Consilio,* 23 Dec. 1922.

which fell under the direction of 250 diocesan committees through-out the country, dismayed the regime and forced the government to curtail its activities especially among the young. Pius XI responded to the campaign of violence in *Non Abbiamo Bisogno*, the encyclical that decried the 'pagan worship of the state' and the snatching of children from Christ.[10] Even after the conclusion of a formal compromise, the subterranean conflict between Catholic Action and the authorities gave the association a semi-official yet insubordinate status as the only legal alternative to Fascist organizations; by 1939 it had 388,000 members. Federazione Universitaria Cattolica Italiana (FUCI), the university federation attached to the apostolate, became a kind of secrete society, not unlike freemasonry during the second half of the nineteenth century. From its inner circle emerged the leadership of the Christian Democratic Party after 1945.

For the most part, the dictatorship staked its ideological claim on war, sport, and youth. During the 1930s, issues surrounding family and faith remained the domain of the Church. On New Year's Eve 1929 with *Divini Illius Magistri*, Pius XI held forth on chaste love, condemned sex education in schools, attacked motion pictures, and advised against immodest athletics for adolescent girls. One year later the septuagenarian librarian promulgated *Casti Connubii*, the first encyclical since Leo XIII's pontificate to deal with conjugal rela-tions and the sanctity of life. The papal missive denounced abortion, divorce, contraception, sterilization, female emancipation, and other errors of the modern age but also suggested gender equality of a sort by insisting on the importance of premarital virginity and spousal fidelity for both women and men. The Fascist penal statutes, which went into effect on 1 July 1931, delivered a similar message to Italians in order to bolster the regime's demographic policy. Title X of the Rocco Code outlawed the practice of birth control; it also inter-preted the termination of pregnancy, the procurement of 'pro-creative impotence', including vasectomy as well as tubal ligation, and the transmission of venereal disease as offences against the integrity of the race. Only with the liberalization of abortion in 1978 did this category of crime fully disappear from the law books of the republic.

In 1931 the Pope revisited the social question with *Quadragesimo*

---

[10] Pius XI, *On Catholic Action in Italy, Non Abbiamo Bisogno*, 29 June 1931.

Anno, a letter that confirmed the evils of free competition, 'collectivism', and the 'gainful occupation' of mothers outside the home. Four decades after *Rerum Novarum*, the Vicar of Christ on earth preached as his only response to the Depression cooperation between management and labour through the resurrection of medieval guilds.[11] His remedy, however, differed from Fascist corporatism because it did not envisage the patronage of the state. Mussolini's regime may have claimed credit for introducing leisure facilities and appropriate housing to workers during the depths of the economic crisis, yet outside the great cities nuns oversaw recreational activities and vocational training. They resuscitated the welfare orders, and membership in convents catering to indoor relief soared. In the 1930s, when deflation and dictatorship circumscribed the strategies of light industry, employers in wool, cotton, and rayon reverted to a familiar form of company paternalism with the help of sisters on the payroll. Female religious still provided social services on behalf of management, but they also reported back to the headquarters of their congregations. They undertook supervision and surveillance to keep their charges safe more for Christendom than for capitalism. The teaching orders thrived too, with enrollments in parochial secondary schools climbing from 31,000 in 1927 to 104,000 in 1940.

When in 1938 the dictatorship fell under the sway of the Third Reich and adopted anti-Semitic legislation, tensions flared again between the Vatican and the Fascist regime. In the summer Catholic Action once more came under attack. During the autumn the government gave alien Jews six months to leave the country. A decree-law of November defined Judaism in biological rather than religious terms and prohibited intermarriage with Aryans. In open violation of the Concordat, these nuptiality restrictions encroached upon the authority of canon law in the sacrament of matrimony and deprived the Christian wedlock of converts from Jewry of civil effects. The Pontiff, gravely ill with heart disease and diabetes, grew concerned about the 'exaggerated nationalism' of the Duce. He commissioned a letter to denounce racism but never published it. Pius XI died on 10 February

---

[11] Pius XI, *On the Reconstruction of the Social Order, Quadragesimo Anno*, 15 May 1931; Pius XI reiterated the 'holy crusade' against the abuses of film in the encyclical *On Motion Pictures, Vigilanti Cura*, 29 June 1931.

1939, just one day before an audience he had arranged for the Italian hierarchy on the tenth anniversary of the Lateran accords.

Cardinal Eugenio Pacelli, the Vatican's secretary of state who in 1933 negotiated the Concordat between the Roman Church and Hitler, succeeded the dead Pontiff as Pius XII. The new Pope came from a diplomatic rather than a scholarly background. But his experience as nuncio to Germany, together with a personal tendency towards equivocation, did not stand him in good stead as universal pastor during the Second World War. The Holy Father stayed silent on the Final Solution. Although, in his Christmas Eve homily of 1942, he condemned state worship as well as the atrocities, he did so in generic terms: not once during the broadcast did he single out anti-Semitism or the Third Reich. The Primate of Italy maintained his reticence when the Nazis rounded up Jews in the old Roman ghetto and deported them from the Eternal City.

Pius XII, like his predecessor, encouraged the growth of Catholic Action, perhaps as much to fight communism as to spread the word of Christ on earth. The apostolate still benefited from the special status guaranteed by the Concordat; two years after the war, it boasted over a million and a half members, giving the Church an organizational infrastructure and mass following with which to launch a national party. Mussolini had also afforded the regular and secular clergy an opportunity to introduce religion into classrooms, dormitories, hospices, and recreational clubs during the dictatorship. This evangelical revival ensured the allegiance of a whole generation after the fall of Fascism. The years of authoritarian rule allowed the Roman Church to return to Leo XIII's strategy and appropriate civil society for the cross. Finally, in 1948, the Lateran accords were incorporated into the constitution of a republic run for three decades straight by the Christian Democrats. One hundred years after the Risorgimento began the campaign for unity, Catholicism claimed its place in the apparatus of the secular state.

The economy from Liberalism to Fascism

Marcello De Cecco

Italy became a nation at a time when the presence of the state in economic development and the importance of markets, national and international, were both on the rise. The historian Alberto Caracciolo has noted the most salient points of Cavour's intervention policies, and remarked how these had come at the end of a whole century of greater involvement of the state in the economy in all Italian pre-unitary states, whether constitutional or absolutist. The experience of Piedmont was the most important example, but by no means the only one.[1] If we look back at the modes of state intervention in the economy in the forty years following Italian unity, we can identify a trend that was destined to prevail even in future decades, especially after the Second World War. Starting with the construction of infrastructures, the state would then realize that private capital was not following its lead, and would replace it by direct intervention in straightforward industrialization.

With unification, Italy became a great power only in territory and population, but it definitely lacked the economic strength that was required for it to be considered an effective great power. The élites, who had made unification possible by their skilful action in world politics, knew full well that economic power was indispensable. If the

---

[1] A. Caracciolo (ed.), *La Formazione dell'Italia industriale* (Bari, 1963).

free working of the market could guarantee rapid industrialization, they would embrace laissez-faire. But when they saw that, with laissez-faire, the process would have been too long, and the involvement of foreign capital, with the political ties it implied, too great, they rejected laissez-faire without many qualms and embraced the doctrine of state intervention. The protagonists of the Italian Risorgimento had rebelled against the view which saw a subject and weak Italy as part of the natural order of things. Their liberal agenda could not prevail over their foremost priority, which was to see Italy return to what they considered to be its natural state, that of a protagonist in European affairs. Economic ideology took a decidedly secondary place, with respect to what they considered as an overriding historical imperative.

This could not be fulfilled without problems. Direct incentives to industrialization were inaugurated while the world economy underwent what has been called the first great world depression, which lasted from the mid-1870s to the mid-1890s. An important part of that depression was the crisis of European agriculture, and Italian agriculture was no exception. This was all the more serious as Italy was still a prevalently agricultural country. Following a trend prevalent everywhere in Europe, the Italian ruling class tried to weaken the effects of the world depression by introducing tariff protection for agriculture as well as for industry. We now know that what went under the name of the Great Depression was in fact a powerful case of world economic integration, involving the creation of a truly international market for goods, services, capital, and labour. While previously the state had been in charge of each national economy, in those twenty years the world economy began to dominate individual national economies. The reaction, almost everywhere, was to resurrect state intervention, to guarantee national élites a sufficient political space.

Economic policies of the 'Destra Storica' cabinets

Cavour never thought that there was a contradiction between state intervention in the economy and participation in the international free trade regime which Britain, with the passing help of the French Second Empire, imposed on Europe. Britain's free trade position was explained by its capacity to export investment goods which were indispensable to the industrialization and modernization of other countries, and, at the same time, the loan capital necessary to pay for those goods, while it imported food and raw materials.

It has been argued that Cavour's acceptance of the free trade and international convertibility regime is patent evidence of his Machiavellian approach to politics. It is more reasonable to attribute it to his awareness of the lack of alternative options available to a small open economy like that of Piedmont. Later on, the same reasoning was extended to united Italy, a political and economic actor endowed with a large population and a strategic geographical position, the result of a haphazard and improvised union of small states with few mutual economic relations, with a large country like the Kingdom of the Two Sicilies. The latter was very backward from the economic and administrative viewpoints, and moreover had not been included in early unification plans.

In the first two post-unitary decades the Italian leadership, including those of its members who had earlier been imbued with the spirit of laissez-faire, adopted interventionist economic policies. This may also be explained by the need to act fast to prevent southern sedition from degenerating into secession, with the risk of losing everything as fast as it had been gained. It was therefore an interventionism dictated by emergency, which made even the most reluctant members of the Italian ruling class accept measures and policies directly aimed at avoiding the early demise of the new country.

To impose on those who did not acknowledge the institutions of the new state the principle of continuity with the old Piedmontese monarchy meant running the risk of a 'fiscal strike', and that in fact occurred in the new provinces of the Kingdom, especially in the southern ones, which had been used to a state which gave little to, but also required little from, its subjects. Administrative continuity with old Piedmont was also motivated by the need to rapidly find the financial resources needed to quell the revolt of the South by military force. Without a rapid return of public order in the territories of the former southern Kingdom there would be no hope of obtaining the legitimacy required by international financial markets in order to grant the new Kingdom the loan capital necessary to balance a budget rich in expenditures but poor in revenues. That much the Italian ruling class understood very well, especially because it was reminded of it daily by the international press and European diplomats. The Italian governing élites thus found themselves trapped in a vicious circle. The new state's currency had to be tied to a regime of international convertibility, which was a precondition for the inflow of international capital. Very often that euphemism hid the reality of Italian capital, which had been parked abroad and required convertibility as a guarantee to come back into the country under the form of public debt purchases made through the convenient intermediation of powerful foreign financial houses. The money thus obtained from Rothschild and his allies, served to arm, equip, and maintain the expeditionary force sent to the South to quell the pro-Bourbon revolt. Roads and railways had to be built as fast as possible, for both strategic and law and order reasons, and the state could not wait for private capital to do it without the persuasive intervention of large public subsidies. Roads were therefore built directly by the state and railway companies obtained straightforward revenue-safeguarding guarantees. Some members of the élite even managed to convince themselves that there was nothing exceptional in such a situation. For the most part, however, interventionism represented a second best with respect to British doctrine and experience. Only after the success of another unification process, that of Germany, had transformed a myriad of insignificant little territories into the fastest growing economy in Europe, could the Italian élites avail themselves of an alternative model comparable to that of Victorian England. The Prussian model, however, postulated the legitimacy and necessity, and even the centrality, of state action to promote and sponsor socio-economic modernization.

Thus, the governing élite of united Italy adopted dirigisme and an active role of the state in the economy under the pressure of events, rather than for theoretical reasons. At the same time, and with the same lack of theoretical enthusiasm, Italians agreed to respect the rules of free trade and currency convertibility. When reading the writings of some of the protagonists of post-unification Italy, we get the clear impression of the lack of a precise economic ideology and of the presence of an awareness that it was necessary to act within an imperious context, to which they had to adapt, if they wanted to keep national unity, the prize they had so long dreamed of and so recently and suddenly won. That was an absolute priority, which could not be traded for any short- or long-term economic target. Evidence of that is given by Italy's intervention in the Austro-Prussian War of 1866, which was seen as a way of moving the political border nearer to the natural one of the Eastern Alps. The war buried currency convertibility and with it the chance of getting foreign loans. The Italian government could not foresee that international financial markets would close to peripheral countries anyway, when the Overend and Gurney crisis broke out in London, and that they would remain shut for fifteen years. However, they knew that, by taking part in the war, they were, at least for some time, taking their country out of the ruling international economic regime. But they cast the die without hesitation, also because there were previous illustrious examples of countries declaring inconvertibility because of war (incidentally, Austria did the same). Perhaps they thought gold payments could be resumed shortly after the war ended (as had happened to Britain and France after the Napoleonic wars), and did not foresee that it would take Italy sixteen years to go back to convertibility.

The declaration of inconvertibility ushered in a very long and vigorous phase of active economic policy-making, which would last well after the conquest of Rome marked the end of domestic emergency and gave permanent legitimacy to the new state. It thus fell upon the men of the 'Destra Storica' to discover the virtues of a managed and devalued currency while the government was engaged in balancing the budget with a fierce fiscal squeeze. And it was the most fiscally abstemious among them, Quintino Sella, who was repeatedly Finance secretary between 1862 and 1873, who distinguished himself most markedly in this very modern policy, even if it would be frankly excessive to credit him with a macroeconomic awareness of what he was doing.

Monetary and banking malaise stimulated international arbitrage in Italian public bonds. Their prices in Paris tended to fall relative to those in Italy. Arbitrageurs, by buying bonds in Paris sold large amounts of lire and thus caused the lira exchange rate to fall. Italian exporters benefited from depreciation, while imports were discouraged and domestic industrial production was enhanced especially in the textile sector. Rising gross domestic product thus made the bitter fiscal medicine easier to swallow, and the public budget was finally balanced without sacrificing expenditures which were almost all indispensable to the functioning of a modern state.

In the mid-1870s, the fall of the Destra Storica can be seen, at least partly, as a result of the impact of the 'Prussian Model', since the government fell because of a parliamentary revolt against its plan to nationalize the railways, following the Prussian example. The sacred union of Sicilian and Tuscan MPs which hatched that revolt can be seen as fired by the noble spirit of laissez-faire, or by the less noble desire to preserve the comfortable private monopoly enjoyed by railway companies mostly owned by Franco-British capital.

The left in power: riding the international financial boom of the 1880s

With the advent of the left, state intervention in the economy took a step backwards. One could interpret the new government's railway policy as the realization of the difficulty of replacing a private monopoly by a public one. The return to currency convertibility of 1882 can be seen as a step in the same ideological direction, were it not for the fact that it took place on account of the revival of international financial markets, which started once more offering very large amounts of capital to peripheral countries. Italy's return to convertibility is just one example among many that occurred in those same years. International loans were used to build not only infrastructures but also industry, so that the burden would not fall on the taxpayers' shoulders, at least for the near future. As a result, the left did not have to pay the political price for such an adventurous policy. In its endeavours, the state was powerfully helped by the newly founded 'mixed banks', investment banks which gave loans to new industrial and public works ventures and sometimes took a share in their equity. They had originated in France during the Second Empire and spread to Italy, aided by the abundant foreign capital inflows fostered by currency convertibility.

The last quarter of the nineteenth century witnessed what looked like a realization of the so-called 'Wagner's Law' which theorized the inevitable expansion of public expenditure induced by the growth of the state's functions. According to the German economist Adolph Wagner, the ever-increasing complexity of modern state organization determines the incessant growth of the public budget which has to finance the consequent continuous growth in expenditures. Cavour had been a precursor in the practice of that 'law' and, after it was formally enunciated, there were few contemporary statesmen and economists both in Italy and elsewhere who refrained from accepting it.

The enthusiasm of the left for intervention in the economy and related fields of government caused the part of the Italian ruling class which had lost office to nurture ever-increasing worries about the possible transformation of the country into a one-party state. Silvio Spaventa, the doyen of the Destra Storica, gave vent to theories which distinguished the will of the state from that of parliament. The economists of the Italian marginalist school rallied around the review *Il giornale degli economisti* and were galvanized by the powerful minds of Vilfredo Pareto and Maffeo Pantaleoni into a spirited defence of free competition against private and public monopolies, and of the parsimonious use of public funds at a time when the government abounded in generous subsidies for all manner of economic activities.

The calls to prudence of opposition politicians and neoclassical economists were long ignored by a government which could avail itself of the abundant supply of international capital and use it to build up infrastructures and industrial capacity, following more often the dictates of strategic and foreign policy considerations than the needs of economic development. The solution which the left cabinets proposed for the railway question is emblematic of the new regime. In 1885 the railtrack was nationalized, while the rolling stock was bought and operated by three separate private companies. It was a temporary concession, which was to last twenty years. It was expected that any further development of the rail network would have to be carried out directly by the state. Spaventa had repeatedly warned of the perils of this kind of solution. In fact, the benefits that had been expected did not materialize. At the end of the twenty years, in 1905, the government would again nationalize the whole railway network, including the rolling stock, paying off the private companies with 500 million lire (by comparison, total public expenditure that year came to 1500 million lire). The companies invested the largest part of the 500 million that they received from the state in the newly born electrical industry, while at the same time the re-nationalized railway companies completely renovated the rail network and especially the rolling stock, purchasing 60 per cent of the wagons and engines from Italian producers. The operation thus gave a double push to economic growth, enhancing two vital industrial branches, heavy engineering and electricity.

The emergency policies of the 1890s and the rise of public technocracy

When the next international financial crisis hit the Italian economy, at the start of the 1890s, all the forms of state intervention initiated by the left cabinets showed a meagre balance. The domestic financial crisis, ignited by the international one, floored even the large banks which French capital had introduced. They had to be rescued by the main bank of issue, the Banca Nazionale nel Regno d' Italia, which was in turn rescued by the government. In the next decades bank rescues were to prove one of the most durable forms of state intervention. Until the passage of the new Bank Act in 1936, which strictly separated commercial and investment banking, bank rescues were recognized as one of the distinctive features of the new Italian Kingdom's style of economic policy-making.

In a country (such as Italy was in its formative decades and has remained until quite recently) where private savings were not very large compared to GNP and were mainly channelled towards post office savings banks, public debt bonds, and savings banks, commercial banks that wanted to finance industrial ventures had to find investment capital abroad. Often only short-term loans could be found on the international market, and the result was great instability, as the purpose of the borrowers was to invest in industrial ventures, which promised to repay investors only after several years. With liquid finance used for structurally illiquid purposes, banks and industrial firms were continuously subject to the vagaries of the international financial market. Hence the cyclical recourse to bank rescues by governments of the most diverse political ilk and economic ideology. There were no Italian financial crises which were not caused by, or at least did not coincide with, international financial ones.

Another problem derived (and still does) from the fact that capital-exporting countries tend to lend funds abroad when domestic demand for funds is slack, i.e. when the domestic cycle is in a downturn. Capital exports thus generate demand for centre-country industrial exports. When the products come out of factories in the peripheral countries built with capital and investment goods imported from the centre areas, they have to beat the competition of products made in centre areas. As a result, industrial protectionism and bank rescues go hand in hand, and aim at salvaging the value of the capital invested in the peripheral countries, where it is very scarce.

Latching on to the great world expansion cycle, 1896–1907

After the great financial and industrial crisis of the early 1890s removed the Left from power, a great world cycle of growth, investment, and economic and financial integration began, which lasted everywhere until the 1907 international financial crisis, and carried on in the centre countries until 1914. The banks and industrial plants which the Italian government had salvaged in the mid-1890s prospered, perhaps benefiting also from the tariff protection introduced in the late 1880s. The external constraints under which the Italian economy had smarted since the very beginning of the new Kingdom became less harsh in the ten years of the so-called first Italian miracle. Because of the great international agricultural crisis, millions of Italian peasants migrated to the New World, and began to send home a great flow of hard-currency remittances which, together with the receipts from the nascent Italian tourist industry, could be used to pay for greatly increased imports. Import-substituting heavy industry sprung up and flowered, as well as export-led light industry (mainly textiles). Like the later growth spurt of the late 1950s and 1960s, the first was located in the north-west of the country, in the so-called industrial triangle comprising the cities of Milan, Turin, and Genoa. By 1914, that part of Italy was highly industrialized and had started producing and exporting technology-intensive products like naval vessels, automobiles, and even some chemicals, in addition to the mainstay exports, which were still light industrial products like silk and cotton.

We must not forget, however, what a price had been paid to get these results: Sidney Sonnino's fierce budget balancing policies had been so hard on the lower strata of Italian society that they had induced open revolt and barricades in Milan in 1898, repressed by bloody military intervention, for which the assassination of King Umberto in 1900 was seen as revenge. Social upheaval caused by stern economic policies would later calm down, as Giovanni Giolitti skilfully exploited the benefits coming to Italy from a booming international economy and decreasing interest rates to introduce social policies fashioned once again after the Prussian example. The spread on Italian state bonds drastically decreased and allowed Giolitti to launch a very impressive debt conversion operation in 1906. The Italian lira even went from a discount to a premium vis-à-vis gold.

The outbreak of another international financial crisis in 1907 was, however, sufficient to bring the first Italian miracle to a grinding halt. The Stock Exchange collapsed, and banks and the large firms financed by them encountered severe problems, so that a new rescue operation had to be launched by the government. The large investment banks, such as the Banca Commerciale, that had been the protagonists of the first industrial miracle, had been German-managed. They had replaced the French banks brought down in the financial crisis of the early 1890s. In 1907, however, the Bank of Italy, the Italian central bank built on the ruins of the Banca Nazionale in 1893, had become strong and authoritative enough to rescue the banking and financial system by slightly more orthodox methods than those used hitherto. There was, as a result, no financial and industrial bankruptcy, but growth rates flattened out for the rest of the period, until they were restarted by the outbreak of the First World War.

The state and economic growth in Liberal Italy: an assessment

The first fifty years of national economic history show, therefore, a direct link between the growth of the state and that of the economy. As they did not want to just sit and wait until private economic forces brought infrastructures and industrial development to the new country, the Italian power élites brought in the state directly to build the infrastructure and even the industrial structure, and very often ended up asking the state to operate them. In order to do so, the state had to train entrepreneurs and managers, as well as workers, who were not to be found in a pre-industrial country like Italy. Most of them, as a result, came from other careers and professions, and had to be induced to get involved in the new ventures by very substantial perks, like direct subsidies, cheap capital supply, tariff protection, or long and very advantageous monopoly concessions.

The industrial élite that came into being through unrelenting state efforts was as a result biased towards giving high priority to technical and engineering problem-solving and disregarding financial viability, as it faced what can be considered soft budget constraints. The cultural and technical level of the entrepreneurial class of the new Italy was probably higher than that of its equivalent in the more developed European countries.[2]

---

[2] S. Lanaro, *Nazione e lavoro: saggio sulla cultura borghese in Italia, 1870–1925* (Venice, 1979).

Italian industry and the new technocrats in the First World War

This emphasis on technical prowess and the focus on technical feasibility rather than on economic viability put the new Italian entrepreneurial class, both private and public, in an excellent position to face the mobilization effort necessary when the First World War broke out. Emigrants' remittances dried up, as well as the receipts from tourism, but the dreaded 'external constraint' on growth could be overcome with the help of the international loans which first the British and then the Americans were ready to grant their Italian ally. Thus, Italian entrepreneurs and managers could freely engage in a gigantic experiment in the widening and deepening of productive capacity, replacing a large mass of sophisticated industrial products which had been imported from Germany until the outbreak of the war with domestic production. Germany had become by far Italy's most important trade partner during the two last decades of the nineteenth century.

Of the three industrial miracles which have marked the development of the modern Italian economy, the one which occurred in the course of the First World War is certainly the most remarkable. It was a really interesting case of symbiosis between public interest and private initiative, and high-level bureaucrats soon rose to positions of great eminence in the planning of the war economy. For five years, total war mobilization, orchestrated by these high-ranking 'mandarins', succeeded in sending millions of troops to the war theatres, and in keeping them there reasonably well fed and clad, and sufficiently well armed. They also managed to allow private large-scale industry to expand its operations almost tenfold, as plant capacity grew apace, while goods and services were distributed to the non-fighting population. It could be said that in Italy the electrical engineering and chemical industries were born with the war. Shipyards and the engineering industry grew so much that their structure was altered completely. By managing the economy, the Italian public technocrats acquired a self-confidence and leadership abilities they had never possessed before. But the war also allowed equally able private entrepreneurs and managers to come to the fore. In the intervening forty years those men would, by their cooperation and frequent quarrels, shape the destiny of the Italian economy and society.

The Italian economy in the transition from Liberalism to Fascism

At the end of the war politicians, little aware of the new *Zeitgeist* which pervaded the country, tried to regain the position at the helm of public affairs which they had enjoyed before the outbreak of war. They found, however, their path blocked by the new class of public and private entrepreneurs and managers created by the war, who had no intention of dismantling the new system of technocratic management of the economy which had been introduced to face war mobilization. Conflict broke out between public and private managers about who was going to steer the economy, and traditional politicians were not able to mediate between the two factions. Only a little later Benito Mussolini would succeed in the task, in the name of nationalism. In order to rise to power, the shrewd chieftain of the Fascists did not hesitate to play the role of the apostle of free enterprise, advocating the immediate dismantling of all forms of wartime planning of economic activities. He thus touched the heart of the small-scale entrepreneurs who produced traditional labour-intensive industrial goods; but he would soon afterwards abandon them in favour of the large-scale industrial entrepreneurs who produced capital-intensive products and the great public managers.

If we take the whole span of the Fascist experience, it is unquestionable that, save for the four initial years of laissez-faire boom, marked by inflation and devaluation, which made the fiscal retrenchment carried out at the same time by the Fascist government acceptable to the part of the population directly engaged in production, we can detect a strong continuity between the Fascist years and the experience of wartime economic dirigisme. Of the whole industrial structure that had come into being because of the war, only the big textile industry suffered severely, after its great post-war production and export records came to an abrupt end in 1926. This was a result of the drastic revaluation of the lira ordered by Mussolini and organized by Alberto Beneduce and Giuseppe Volpi, the two chief economic experts who replaced Alberto De Stefani, the laissez-faire economics professor who had been Minister of Finance from 1922 to 1925, at the helm of the Italian economy. The textile industry would come out of mothballs in 1936, to clothe the soldiers mobilized for the Duce's wars, and again after 1945 to take advantage of the early post-war demand for textiles, replacing German and French producers, whose plants had been destroyed by war, while British textile producers could not cope with the whole of world demand alone.

The rest of Italian industry, and in particular its capital-intensive components, found it convenient to carry on expansion through import substitution and protection throughout the whole Fascist period, starting up whole new technically innovative sectors. Economic nationalism, which had prevailed in the first fifty years of the new Italy's history, thus continued to be enthusiastically practised for the whole inter-war period, and received a further impulse after the serious industrial and financial repercussions of the world economic crisis of the 1930s in Italy.

Industrial and banking policy in Fascist Italy

In the 1920s, Alberto Beneduce, who was the real protagonist of Fascist economic policy-making, had already started introducing his alternative mode of industrial financing, which was based on government guaranteed bonds sold directly to the public. They were issued by special credit institutions he had invented, which were publicly owned but managed like private concerns. They financed new capital-intensive industrial investment in sectors with slow returns, like electricity and public works, which, however, enjoyed monopoly pricing and thus drastically reduced lender risk.

The new special credit institutions devised by Beneduce, however, could not solve single-handedly all the huge problems accumulated by the large Italian commercial banks in the decades of fast growth, followed by the revaluation of 1926–7, and by the abrupt world crisis of the early 1930s. They financed large-scale industry and gathered funds on the international short-term interbank deposit market, which flourished in the 1920s and died a sudden death as a result of the 1931 international financial crisis. The commercial banks had, however, begun to suffer in the second half of the 1920s, as a direct result of the revaluation policy imposed by Mussolini, which spelt immediate trouble for Italian exporters. The explosive mix of domestic revaluation and international financial crisis brought industry and banks to their knees. Another giant bank rescue became mandatory.

The Fascist economic leadership and its supremo, Alberto Beneduce, did not, however, follow the time-honoured examples of earlier Italian bank rescues. This time, they managed to kill two birds with one stone. They introduced the new financial model hatched by Beneduce, whose pivot was a new banking law which cut the deep ties between commercial banks and industrial firms. Banks had owned industry and industry in turn owned banks. This was now stopped and banks were confined to short-term deposit collection and loans. At the same time, Beneduce was able to settle an old nationalist grudge against the formerly German-owned Banca Commerciale Italiana (BCI), whose industrial assets were confiscated when the BCI became insolvent and transferred to the newly invented Istituto per la Ricostruzione Industriale (IRI), a state-owned but profit-motivated institution which came to own a very substantial part of large-scale, capital-intensive industry. Ownership of the other big commercial bank which had to be rescued, Credito Italiano, was, like the BCI, transferred to IRI, but its industrial holdings were returned to its former private owners, who were capable of exerting great political pressure even on a dictatorial government.

By this sweeping institutional reform, whose impact would be felt by the Italian economy and society until the early 1990s, the public managers who had distinguished themselves running the wartime economic effort came back into power, this time directly running a very large chunk of Italian industry and most of the big commercial banks. It was their ambition to show that they could do a better job of it than their private equivalents had been able to, and in all honesty it must be recognized that until the early 1970s they succeeded in putting Italian capital-intensive industry on a more efficient footing, and in allowing it to take part in several innovative ventures, which effectively used the abilities of Italian researchers and workers.

In the early 1930s, the Italian economy was thus completely reshaped by large doses of institutional engineering planned in Rome. In addition to IRI, another special credit institution by the name of IMI (Istituto Mobiliare Italiano) was started to provide industry with long-term finance, and the other Beneduce financial creatures, ICIPU and CREDIOP, special banks invented in the 1920s to finance public works through state-guaranteed bond issues sold to the public and to savings banks, were allowed to grow.

The new Banking Law, passed in 1936, crowned the whole operation, at the end of which the balance of corporate governance and ownership in Italy shifted heavily in favour of the state. Public managers were thus free to plan industrial development at the micro-economic level, and for the whole Fascist period they did so with the final aim of replacing private industry in the most important sectors. After the Second World War, however, they were allowed to manage the new semi-public corporations and banks only on condition that they succeeded in reducing costs, thus increasing profits for the large privately owned corporations that Mussolini had saved from bankruptcy and given back to their original owners, the great industrial families, some of which have survived to the present day.

If we look back, we can see that, beginning in the 1880s, an autarkic model of industrial development was set in motion in Italy. Foreign imports were partly restrained because of tariff protection and subsidies, while, first emigrants' remittances and revenues from tourism, and later the Allies' wartime and post-war loans, financed the trade deficit. This attempt to build up an almost complete industrial matrix in Italy as quickly as possible was endowed with almost (by Italian standards) unlimited financial resources and was successful until the second half of the 1960s. Industrialization was therefore a continuous process which only momentarily stopped in the last three years of the Second World War.

To achieve a complete industrial matrix, the Italian state mobilized all its resources in addition to those belonging to private entrepreneurs, who were persuaded to invest heavily in new and innovative plants. This was ensured by the guarantee of certain returns and by the assurance that their costs would be borne by the public and all returns would be their own. After the creation of IRI and the special credit institutions, and the passage of the new Banking Act of 1936, the industrialization effort was also protected from the vagaries of the international financial cycle, which had negatively conditioned it in previous decades. As industrial investment was directly linked to private saving, by the issue of long-term bonds, for a few decades one might have thought that the Italian leadership had found the philosophers' stone, so stable and reassuring the new financial mechanism appeared to the beholder. It was even able to allow the state to build a modern steel industry and a national oil industry in the 1950s. But it also allowed private industry to build a very large automobile industry, a reasonably large chemical and pharmaceutical industry, a powerful tyre and rubber cable industry, and an office machines industry that managed to stay for several decades at the leading edge of technology. These were all state of the art plants, built thanks to the new method of financing. And for that reason, they were even able to win respectable export markets for themselves. With early tariff protection, one of the world's leading textile industries was built almost from scratch; after both world wars, it was able, for a while, to replace the major world exporters while they were knocked out of business and, what is more, develop a powerful artificial fibres' weaving and spinning industry.

Alberto Beneduce's great invention, his philosophers' stone, was the corseting of the financial market, transformed into a rigid financial system, from which private free intermediaries were excluded by directly linking private savings to industrial investment through the essential state guarantee for special corporate bonds. When, after 1934, free foreign exchange transactions and capital movements were severely controlled, the Beneduce system achieved perfection.

Public debt: an essential feature of economic policy in Liberal and Fascist Italy

In the experience of united Italy, very few governments had the luck of being able to plan their budgets without having to provide as an absolute priority the sums necessary to service the existing stock of public debt. Only the Republican governments of the first two decades following the Second World War were placed in that fortunate position by the virtual cancellation of the real value of the stock of public debt they had inherited from Fascist Italy, because of the drastic rise in the price level engendered by early post-war inflation.

With the exception of those twenty years, the governments of all other periods in the history of united Italy were obsessed with the problem of having to grapple with an overbearing public debt burden. The Destra Storica, which governed Italy between 1860 and 1876 started by accepting responsibility for the stock of debt of the Piedmontese Kingdom of which the Kingdom of Italy was officially declared to be the continuation. And, in the course of the seventeen years they were in power, they managed to accumulate an even greater mass of public debt. Its total stock went from 3 billion lire in 1861 to 11 billion in 1876. As a percentage of GDP, it grew from 60 in 1861 to 96 in 1870. Three years of fiscal retrenchment saw it go down to 70 in 1873.

Fiscal retrenchment was, however, the source of such popular discontent that balancing the budget led to the Destra Storica being toppled from power in 1876. The governments of the Left which were voted into office in its place changed the course of economic policy and returned to fiscal profligacy. In 1880, the public debt was already back at 87 per cent of GDP. In 1887 the alarming level of 120 per cent was reached. The boom which world economic expansion induced in Italy in the following years saw the debt/GDP ratio go down to a much more manageable 80 per cent in 1913.

We must, however, be very prudent in giving an economic meaning to the figures we have just quoted. If we look at pure public debt accumulation, we notice that the Left cabinets only increased public debt from 11 to 14 billion lire. The Destra Storica had, by comparison, quadrupled the absolute level of public debt in the years they were in office. The Left had, however, the bad luck of being in office in the two decades of the famous first world economic depression (1876–96) which was, as will be recalled, especially a world price deflation, which continuously brought down the level of GDP measured at current prices. This was the cause of the drastic worsening of the debt/GDP ratios we have quoted.

A comparison with the years of the 'golden age' when Giovanni Giolitti was prime minister will make this even clearer. From 1896 to 1913, public debt grew from 14 to 17 billion lire. The Italian economy, however, experienced—as we already noted—a much more rapid rate of growth in those years. Hence the substantial decline in the debt/GDP ratio.

The Destra finance ministers, especially Sella, had managed to limit the impact of fiscal retrenchment somewhat by an expansive monetary policy. They had no hope of getting foreigners to lend Italy fresh funds, as the international financial market was dominated by French lenders for loans to European governments and virtually dried up as a result of Napoleon III's defeat at Sedan in 1870.

The Left's ascent to power coincided, on the contrary, with a reopening of world financial markets. The Italian government was again able to borrow. In order to do so, the lira had to be brought back to gold-convertibility, a status it had lost in 1866. This was achieved in 1882, and a decade of rising foreign indebtedness ensued. This strategy would yield positive results in the long run. However while the Left was in office, the high international value of the convertible lira made Italian exports expensive and imports cheap, at a time when the American Plains and the Argentine Pampas were being won to agriculture and modern railways, and ocean-going steam vessels brought their produce to Europe.

The agricultural slump in Europe in the 1880s was so drastic that most countries resorted to heavy tariff protection against imports. Italy simply followed the prevailing trend, somewhat belatedly, and could not prevent the high lira, coupled with the depression of world prices, from wreaking havoc with its agriculture and newly born industry. Falling nominal GDP made servicing the recently accumulated foreign debt very hard, and the next international financial crisis (in the early 1890s) saw lira convertibility as one of its victims. It brought in its wake, as we noted above, the destruction and subsequent salvage of the Italian banking system, including the Banca Nazionale.

It would be interesting to conduct a counterfactual thought experiment and imagine what international monetary policy the Destra Storica governments would have adopted, had they not been toppled in 1876. Would they have carried on with lira inconvertibility and an expansionary monetary policy? Or would they, like the Left governments, have seized the opportunity of the availability of foreign loans to bring the lira back to gold and further increase the public debt? If we have to judge from what the Destra did in this respect between 1861 and 1866, when international financial markets freely supplied loans to willing governments, we can say that, in all probability, the Destra would have followed the course the Left actually adopted. This implies that we believe that credit markets are really dominated by lenders, the borrowing governments being eager at all times to borrow as much as they can. Moreover, we can say that industrialization and infrastructure building were bipartisan priorities for the young Italian ruling élites and that so was a currency linked to gold, which was seen as an essential perquisite of all 'civilized' countries.

All Italian governments in the first three decades of national history were thus obsessed with the problem of servicing public debt. Italian government budgets show very large primary surpluses between 1870 and 1910, while the weight of interest payments declined from 40 per cent of GDP in 1870 to 25 per cent in 1910. If we remember that the weight of military expenditure, again considered as a top priority by the whole political élite, was also overwhelming in these years, we can understand how little leeway Italian governments had for other state activities.

In the 1920s there was another instance of public debt reduction. The level went from 120 per cent of GDP in 1921 to 61 per cent in 1927. How was this remarkable result achieved? Mainly by cutting public expenditure, is the reply. It was, however, the end of extraordinary war expenditure that made possible the reduction of public expenditure to 13 per cent of GDP, near to pre-war levels. The stock of public debt also fell. It decreased to 50 per cent of its highest level, if we calculate foreign debt at the nominal exchange rates current at the time of the Foreign Debt Agreement (end-1925). Debt servicing costs were 4 billion lire in 1925, out of a public expenditure total of 20 billion.

Domar's Law, according to which the sustainability of public debt mainly depends on GNP dynamics, was proved right also in the interwar years. In 1926 the short-term part of the debt (about 30% of the total) was forcibly converted into the so-called Prestito del Littorio, and nominal interest rates drastically declined in the 1930s. In spite of that, however, the weight of public debt had become unsustainable by 1934, because GDP foundered as a result of the world depression and it became impossible to find the funds necessary in the public budget to keep public debt within sustainable limits. It must be added that this occurred in spite of the virtual disappearance of inter-ally debt in

1925–6 and the provision of a 100 million dollar loan by the Morgan Bank in 1927.

Once again, what made public debt unsustainable were the mutually exclusive policies adopted by finance ministers De Stefani and his followers. Borrowing a leaf from the Destra Storica's finance ministers' book, De Stefani adopted a policy mix involving monetary expansion leading to lira depreciation and fiscal restriction. After the Allies dictated, and Mussolini enthusiastically accepted, a return to lira convertibility at 1922 levels, monetary policy turned restrictive, and became very tough indeed when the wave of foreign loans subsided in 1928. A giant forced conversion of public debt had already been carried out in 1926. It had proved acceptable, because the short-term debt was mainly in the coffers of the banking system (especially in those of savings banks). Further conversions had by necessity to involve long-term debt, and that was mainly held by middle-class private savers. This made the success of conversions very precarious and problematic. In 1935 the new finance minister, Guido Jung, tried his hand at it. Results were not very good for the public coffers, in spite of the fact that the Fascist regime was at the height of its popularity with Italians. To shore up public accounts, the banking system had to be subjected to a regime of total regimentation, imposed by a new and very dirigiste Banking Law in 1936. Italian international accounts were, more or less in the same year, subjected to a regime of total inconvertibility, which would last twenty years, as far as trade was concerned, and much longer, as far as capital movements were concerned.

Italy in the international system, 1900–1922

Thomas Row

Between 1900 and 1922 Italy pursued the foreign policies of a great power without always possessing the means to pursue them successfully. The aim of those policies was to assert the Kingdom's position in the state system as a power whose interests and status could not easily be ignored by the other, greater powers. Ruling a relatively new state and a comparatively backward one, the Italian élite was particularly sensitive to their country's place in the world. Foreign policy was not only influenced by systemic events, but by domestic politics as well. In the Italian case these were particularly important, for the sinews that bound the state and the monarchy to the broad social masses were particularly weak. The central event of this period was the First World War. Liberal Italy entered the conflict in order to strengthen itself. The war, however, undermined the Liberal system and ultimately set the stage for its destruction.

Italy, the least of the great powers

The state system in the first quarter of the twentieth century was a system dominated by a handful of great powers. In each of the great powers, with perhaps the exception of the United States, traditional élites sought to maintain their grip on power while adapting to new political situations brought about by economic and social change in the nineteenth century. In all cases, nationalism and patriotism proved powerful cement for bonding the state with society. Since the 1880s, the great powers had all been engaged in expansionist drives to extend their spheres of influence to the rest of the world. The new imperialism reflected and intensified the jealousies and rivalries amongst the great powers. From the point of view of the ruling élites, questions of status and prestige, far from being marginal, were central in shaping great power foreign policy. Thus, the rulers of the great powers faced challenges on two different levels. On the level of the state system, they sought to maintain and increase their great power status. On the level of domestic politics, they could use the appeal of nationalism to bolster the legitimacy of their positions internally. Foreign policy decision-making, therefore, resulted from the interplay of domestic and systemic considerations. This was very much a Darwinian world in which rulers increasingly felt menaced by rival powers abroad and by social protest at home.

Italy was a great power, albeit 'the least of the great powers', and was a significant, if secondary player in the great power game. Italy was a newcomer to the state system, having been unified in 1860. Italy's unification did not pose the problems to the European balance of power that Germany's did. Italy's economic development lagged behind that of Germany. Italy's geopolitical position was not in the heart of Europe, but rather straddling the Mediterranean. The more powerful British and French navies caged in Italy. Thus, any potential Italian colonial expansion in the south would have to come either with the acquiescence or at the expense of these powers. The obvious target for Italian great power ambitions was the Habsburg monarchy, the country's traditional enemy. Here, Italy could look to reclaim the *terre irredente* and dream of marching further—to the Brenner and the Julian Alps. But Austria was a stubborn and formidable enemy. And, from 1882, Italy was bound with Austria in the Triple Alliance, a treaty concluded to end the country's diplomatic isolation. Until 1900 Italy lacked the means and the diplomatic support to pursue great power goals with any measure of success.

Italy's foreign policy was conditioned by the country's domestic situation. High politics were conducted by a small group of insiders: the monarchy, the army, the bureaucracy, and the small Liberal political class that dominated parliament and local administration. Attachment to the monarchy, the national ideal, and great power status were values prevalent amongst this élite. They penetrated to a certain extent the urban middle classes, but were rejected or unknown by a great many Italians. Italy remained a highly fragmented society with strong regional ties and traditions. Class and cultural divisions were fundamental. The minority of 'insiders' had to govern the majority of 'outsiders' to the Liberal political system. The most dangerous outsiders were the working classes, which grew in great strength between 1900 and 1914. Increasingly organized by the trade unions and the PSI, they challenged many of the basic foundations of Liberal rule. The other major group of outsiders was the peasantry. In the absence of any settlement of the Roman Question, the Catholics, too, were outside of the Liberal system and often hostile to it. Thus a narrow ruling elite of insiders sat upon the pyramid of contentious outsiders. The process of nation building or of nationalizing the masses was far from complete in pre-war Italy.

Under Italy's constitution, the Statuto Albertino of 1848, the king held extensive, if not exclusive, powers over treaties and declarations of war, and he commanded the army. More important, as the symbol of the state, his actions, no matter how inopportune, had to be defended by the Liberal ruling class at all costs. The status and prestige of the monarchy in the international arena were thus bound up with the status and prestige of the Kingdom as a whole.

Despite fundamental political weaknesses, between 1900 and 1914 Italy was able to prepare the material base necessary for upholding a realistic great power position. The key sector was that of the economy. The world economy of the *belle époque* presented a favourable external environment for growth. The Italian domestic economy rose to the challenge. Between 1896 and 1914 Italy experienced its first 'economic miracle' and the foundations of a modern industrial sector in steel, engineering, and armaments were laid down. The new industrial sector, centring on the industrial triangle of Milan, Turin, and Genoa, was the outcome of activist state policies. In some cases, such as that of the Terni steelworks, these policies were designed with national security in mind. The result was a significant, if fragile, base. Even so, Italy's productive capacity paled in comparison with that of Britain, France, or Germany.

In military terms, as well, the period 1900–14 saw a build-up of the nation's armed forces. Like the monarchy, the army was a pillar of the Risorgimento state. The relatively large peacetime army was modernized after the Franco-Prussian war. One of the chief purposes of the army, however, was to maintain domestic control—a policing function. Therefore the army was less well poised for offensive actions against other states. Despite large expenditures on the army, Italy still lagged behind the other powers. In 1914 Italy could count 25 permanent infantry divisions (250,000 men) compared with Austria-Hungary's 48 (475,000 men).[1]

In the pre-war period Italy also began to build a modern navy. With state support, the navy expanded hand in hand with the development of the arms and steel industries—so much so that it is possible to speak of a naval–industrial complex in these years. The new navy of 1914 was growing and, for the most part, modern. It was too small, however, to challenge Britain and France, though equal to the task of fighting Austria.

Italy then was a great power. If its overall military and economic might placed it below Britain, Germany, France, Russia, and to a certain extent, Austria, its position was certainly higher than that of other states in Europe. Italy moreover demonstrated a constant will to assert its status, even when lacking the resources to back its ambitions up. This will to great power status served to create a consensus within the narrow Liberal élite around the fragile nation state. To a certain extent, Italian ambitions stemmed from an inferiority complex. By asserting the country's place in the world, the state could compensate for a relative backwardness compared to the other powers. Italy's demonstrations of the will to power irritated the other powers but, it should be remembered were fundamentally of the same nature as those practised by all of them.

The Triple Alliance would be the cornerstone of Italian foreign policy until the outbreak of the First World War. However, it contained a fatal contradiction, for not only were Austria and Italy traditional enemies, but, increasingly, their real interests were on a collision course. Not only was Austrian Italy an obvious target for Italian expansion (there were significant Italian minorities in Istria and Dalmatia as well), but both powers had powerful ambitions in the Balkans. Until 1900 these contradictions could be papered over, in

---

[1] M. Isenghi and G. Rochat, *La grande guerra* (Milan, 2000), p. 48.

part because of a cultural reorientation of the Italian élite. But between 1900 and 1914 these contradictions moved to the fore. Increased Italian irredentism and renewed competition over eastern expansion put Italy and Austria on a collision course. The Triple Alliance was nevertheless renewed just shortly before the outbreak of war. In the final analysis, however, the conflict was not resolvable. After the outbreak of the war, Austria could not afford to make the concessions demanded of it by the Italians. Italy thus abandoned its ally. This has been seen as treason by the Austrians and dishonourable by others. It was in fact rational policy following the logic and practice of all the great powers.

1900–1914: international and domestic problems

Between 1900 and 1914 several developments contributed to the revival of a more assertive Italian foreign policy. First, Italy's remarkable economic performance in this period gave rise to a new national self-confidence. The large industrial groups in steel, engineering, shipbuilding, and arms began to look beyond the domestic market and saw foreign markets as increasingly appealing. In particular, they looked for potential spheres of influence in the developing world (the Balkans and elsewhere in the Ottoman Empire) as fruitful possibilities. Here, however, the Italians came up against the fierce competition of the entrenched and more advanced great powers. Under the banner of economic nationalism, many of the most important groups and the large investment banks with which they were allied came to advocate a form of what the late historian Richard Webster identified as industrial imperialism.[2] In contrast to the previous African imperialism, this new drive pointed towards the acquisition of investment opportunities and markets for Italy's new industries. A second development was a general popular nationalist revival, which in particular brought Italian irredentist claims against Austria to the fore. To the extent that a nascent industrial imperialism and a revived irredentism and popular nationalism became stronger,

[2] R. Webster, *Industrial Imperialism in Italy, 1908–1915* (Berkeley, 1975).

the potential for conflict with Austria widened, for the new national-ist claims could only be satisfied at the Habsburg monarchy's expense. The Bosnian annexation crisis of 1908 outraged much of Italian public opinion, for it appeared that Austria had made a pre-emptive strike to carve out a Balkans position without taking Italian interests into consideration.

We must now turn briefly to domestic politics, for it was the task of the government to mediate between domestic pressures bearing on international policy and those imposed by the state system itself. Between 1900 and 1914 Italian politics were dominated by the figure of Giovanni Giolitti.[3] Giolitti's long-term strategy was inherently lib-eral: his aim was to maintain the Liberal political system while grad-ually assimilating and co-opting those groups of 'outsiders' who were hostile to, and not part of, the system. In practice this meant opening at times to the Left and at times to the Catholics, while trying to pass a series of social reform measures. Giolitti's efforts faced great difficulties and ultimately would fail with the crisis of the Great War.

By 1910 a hard core political and cultural group was forming on the Right in opposition to Giolitti and his liberal strategy. This group, which would on the eve of the war take form as the Italian Nationalist Association linked intellectuals, industrialists, journalists, and con-servative Liberals. Although small in numbers, the Nationalists exerted a very large influence on public opinion and policy. In domestic politics, the Nationalists favoured a roll-back of Giolitti's liberal policies and a tough line on the working classes. In economic policies they would eventually adopt a platform of militant corporat-ism and economic nationalism. In foreign policy, they called for an imperial assertiveness. In the long run, their aim was a repudiation of Giolitti and his system. In the short term, their aim was Tripoli.

In 1911 Italy declared war on the Ottoman Empire and launched the conquest of Libya and the Dodecanese islands. This new imperial war undermined the integrity of the Ottoman Empire, contributed to the outbreak of the Balkans Wars, and must be considered to be one of the most destabilizing events in the run-up to the First World War. Why did Giolitti act? The answer is in part to be found in consider-ations of foreign policy. The government felt that after France's gains in the Second Moroccan crisis Italy had to act, or it would be

---

[3] See the chapter by Paul Corner in this volume.

permanently shut out from North Africa. Equally, if not more important, however, were considerations of domestic policy. A conquest of Libya would be a bone to throw to the Nationalists. In this way Giolitti gambled that he could appease the new right and perhaps co-opt them as well into his liberal project.

The Libyan War was a disaster on all fronts. Militarily, the war was expensive and more difficult than had been expected. The Italians were eventually to control the coastal areas, but the hinterlands remained outside of their control. (These would be 'pacified' by inhumane means in the 1930s by Mussolini.) The destabilizing systemic consequences have already been mentioned. At home, Giolitti's war failed twofold. On the one hand, the right-wing nationalists were by no means appeased by the Libyan war. On the other hand, protest over the war led to the triumph of the maximalist socialists over the moderates in the PSI. Giolitti now found himself weakened, with an implacably hostile Right and Left.

In the spring of 1914, just a few short months before the outbreak of war, Giolitti resigned. This was intended to be one of his periodic retirements from direct rule (after all, he still commanded a majority in parliament). The new prime minister, a conservative southern lawyer, Antonio Salandra, was deeply suspicious of the Liberal drift under Giolitti. He hoped to establish a more serious conservative restoration and to roll back the Giolittian programmes. As fate would have it, it would be the conservative Liberal Salandra, rather than the reformist Liberal Giolitti who would be faced with managing the diplomatic crisis following the assassination in Sarajevo. Nor is it too much of an exaggeration to say that Salandra saw in war a vehicle to block *Giolittismo* and to restore order and discipline to the country.

Then, just a few days before the Sarajevo assassination a violent series of workers' protests swept across the Marches and the Romagna. This 'Red Week' was characterized by strikes, violent protests, and severe repression. While the left was galvanized, the right was alarmed.

Thus, as the world plunged into the catastrophe of world war, Italy was divided by class conflict. The Liberal reformer, Giolitti, was in country retirement. The reins of foreign policy decision-making were in the hands of three men: the prime minister, Salandra, who sought a conservative restoration, the king, Victor Emanuel III, who sought to aggrandize his kingdom, and the foreign minister, Antonino di San

Giuliano, dying of cancer and resting at a seaside resort. In the July crisis, Italy's fate rested in the hands of these three men.

The decision to intervene

When the World War broke out in August 1914, the principal pillar of Italian foreign policy remained the Triple Alliance linking Italy with Germany and Austria. On 2 August, the Italian government formally adopted a policy of neutrality. This decision was based upon Article VII of the Treaty of the Triple Alliance that provided for prior consultation and compensation in the event of an Austrian expansion in the Balkans. Thus, Italy's first response was to stay out; the *casus foederis* did not exist. For Italy this decision was important: it bought the country time to see how the great struggle would develop. It provided the government with the freedom of manoeuvre to prepare a strategy in line with state *realpolitik*. Needless to say, the Austro-Hungarians were outraged by Italy's 'treason'. A medal was even struck portraying an Italian Judas facing a Christ-like Austria. More concretely, Italy's neutrality enabled the French to transfer troops from the Alps and Africa to the Marne, thus helping to consolidate the French position there against Germany.

From the point of view of high politics, neutrality was and could only be a short-term policy. In order to remain a great power, Italy would eventually have to take a stand. Italy was already vulnerable to Anglo-French naval power in the Mediterranean. In the case of an Entente victory, the country could expect no favour. On the other hand, if the Central powers won, Italy would find itself in the position of a despised betrayer of its former allies. To come out of the war with nothing in hand would menace the prestige of the Savoy dynasty and the hegemony of the Liberal system. Thus, the stakes were high, and for the handful of men who determined Italy's entrance into the war—the prime minister, Salandra, the new foreign minister, Sydney Sonnino, and the king—the task at hand was to drive for the best bargain possible from the two contending blocks.

In essence, Italy's leaders faced two options. Either the country could enter the war on the side of the Entente powers, or, it could maintain a benevolent neutrality that de facto favoured the Central

Powers. The question was: how much could Italy get in return for throwing its weight in one direction or the other? Negotiations, or bargaining, took place from the autumn of 1914 till the spring of 1915. These dealings closely followed the ebb and flow of events on the battlefields elsewhere in Europe. In the end, Italy was to side with the Entente powers. The Entente could offer Italy territorial expansion at the expense of Austria-Hungary. The Habsburg monarchy, for its part, simply could not afford to make such sacrifices to the despised Italians. Italy's foreign policy has often been portrayed as somehow more cynical and less moral than that of the other powers. It should be remembered, however, that all the great powers entered the war for reasons of state interest. Italy was no exception. Italy entered the war for Trent and Trieste and for the glory of the Italian Kingdom. Universalistic ideological rationales for the war would come, with the messages of Wilson and Lenin, only in 1917.

The decision to enter the war was also taken within the context of a difficult, polarized domestic political situation. It is not an exaggeration to argue that for the new conservative government and the new right, intervention in the war was a means to subordinate class conflict to the demands of the nation state and to re-establish a Liberal hegemony, that, many believed, had been undermined by Giolitti.

The vast majority of the Italian people were either indifferent or hostile to the idea of entering the war. Nevertheless, in the months preceding Italy's entry into the war, a fierce debate erupted over the question of intervention vs. neutrality. This debate, though the work of a minority, drew in much of Italy's politically active and educated élite. The fierceness of the debate, and the struggles to influence the *piazza* left a lasting bitterness that characterized the war years and their aftermath.

Giolitti and the majority of moderate Liberals favoured neutrality. They had considerable doubts about the country's ability to wage a long war and hoped that *parecchio* (quite a lot) might be gained from negotiations with Austria-Hungary. Giolitti, however, was out of power and unable to directly mobilize his parliamentary minions. Moreover, his '*parecchio*' remark made him the target of a savage campaign by the rightist and pro-war press. Out of power and vilified, Giolitti soon found himself in a position where he was unable to influence events.

Most Roman Catholics, too, favoured neutrality. The new Pope

Benedict XV (elected 3 September 1914) looked with dismay at the prospect of war amongst Catholic states. Later, he would denounce the war as an *inutile strage* (a useless massacre). It must be remembered that in 1914 the Roman Question had not yet been settled (priests for example were drafted into the regular army) and the Vatican was concerned with the effects of war on its relations with the Italian state. Nevertheless, most Catholics ended up by reconciling faith and nation and supported the war.

On the left, the principal pacifist and neutralist movement was that represented by the Italian Socialist Party (PSI). Unique amongst the European socialist parties, the PSI maintained its opposition to the war. This it did despite the collapse of the Second International after the assassination of Jean Jaurès. The PSI's maximalist stance cut it off from other left-wing movements—radical, democratic, syndicalist— which had come to favour war on the side of the democracies. The PSI was to pay a political price for its stance, for although it adopted the slogan, *nè aderire nè sabotar* (neither adhere nor sabotage), it would be seen by many as an 'anti-patriotic' movement.

For the Italian left, the greatest betrayal and greatest heresy from the party's stance was that of Benito Mussolini. Through the summer of 1914 Mussolini was a declared pacifist, a leader of the party's maxi- malist faction and editor of the party's paper *Avanti!*. As the autumn got underway, however, he began to experience a conversion, which ultimately led him fully into the camp of intervention and war. On 24 November 1914 he was expelled from the Socialist Party, having in the meantime founded a new paper, *Il Popolo d'Italia*. Henceforth, Mussolini would be the principal leader of the revolutionary social- ists who embraced nationalism, and thirsted for war, and through it, revolution. The immediate origins of Fascism are to be traced here.

The Giolittian moderate Liberals, the Catholics, and the Socialists were powerful groupings in favour of some sort of neutrality. Yet they were out-shouted, outperformed, and pushed off centre stage (in the *piazzas*) by the variegated groups who favoured intervention. Democrats, Freemasons, and Radicals quickly jumped aboard the bandwagon in favour of war aside Republican France. They were soon joined by the Reformist Socialists[4] and left Liberals. For the democratic interventionists, the war was to be for idealism,

---

[4] The group which had seceded from the PSI in 1912.

democracy, and internationalism—a continuation, in sum, of the struggles of Mazzini and Garibaldi.

Another variegated set of interventionist groups was of an altogether different stamp. For the Nationalists (many of whom had previously been sympathetic to the Central Powers) intervention in the war was an essential expression of Italy's great power status. For the avant-garde Futurists, war was a good in its own right: as F. T. Marinetti put it, 'Marciare non marcire' (March not rot). The idea of war appealed to both democratic and nationalist irredentists alike. In addition to Mussolini, other defectors on the left included anarcho-syndicalists who formed a new Unione Italiana del Lavoro (UIL). This 'mood of 1914' was shared by countless students, intellectuals, and dreamers, all of whom were searching for some new meaning at the beginning of the war.

Throughout the spring of 1915 Italy struggled towards intervention. In the press and in the *piazzas* the interventionist and neutralist forces fought each other and fought for the soul of public opinion. On 5 May—at Quarto where Garibaldi had launched his expedition of the thousand—the poet Gabriele D'Annunzio delivered one of the most passionate and violent discourses in favour of the war. Soon the *piazzas* across the country were in turmoil.

Meanwhile and despite this turmoil, the key decisions about the war were being made in high places. On 26 April Italy signed the Treaty of London. This bound the country to enter the war on the side of the Entente against Austria-Hungary. Upon victory, Italy was to receive the Trent and the Tyrol to the Brenner pass, Trieste, Istria, Gorizia, and much of Dalmatia. This was a classic treaty of the old diplomacy that would substantially augment Italian crown lands at the expense of the Hapsburgs. A last attempt by Giolitti (who still had a parliamentary majority) to stall the precipitation of war, failed. The monarchy, Salandra, and Sonnino were too exposed to be compromised. On 21 May Parliament voted the government war powers and on 24 May Italy was at war.

Italy's decision to enter the First World War marked a rupture in the country's liberal evolution. The decision was made against the backdrop of the great crisis of the international system and the weakening of Giolitti's reformist domestic programme. The key diplomatic choices had been made on the traditional basis of *raison d'état* by Salandra, Sonnino, and the King. But their choices were also conditioned by domestic politics, by the desire to re-establish the political hegemony of the Liberal political class against the perceived threat of the left and the advance of a Catholic movement. The great reformist minister Giolitti was isolated, and, to all intents and purposes, the parliament had been left out of the decision-making process. Despite the thunder of the interventionists, a majority of Italians had no desire to enter the world conflict. Italy went to face the supreme test of war, then, not united, but confused and divided.

The ordeal of war

Italy went to war relatively unprepared to do so.[5] Many of its best troops were still engaged in Libya. The high command had changed only recently, when the former commander, General Pollio died suddenly in July 1914. Italy's general strategy, while never fully trustful towards Austria, had nevertheless been bound to the Triple Alliance and the possibility of an Italian intervention against France was the basis of the principal war plan. More important, the army was short on arms and munitions, particularly machine guns and heavy artillery. Mobilization in the Po Valley was a disorganized affair and the Austrians had plenty of time to retreat to defensive positions along their borders. These were inauspicious conditions for those who foresaw a rapid march on Vienna.

The Italian Front in the First World War was a long and difficult one. It has often been compared to an inverted 'S'—the top loop of which represents the Trentine salient, a 'dagger' pointing at the heart of the central Po Valley. What is most striking about this front is the fact that it is virtually entirely an Alpine one. Here, from the Swiss border all the way to the eastern frontier, Italian and Imperial troops would face off under the most astounding mountainous conditions. This was a unique terrain for warfare, where rapid advances and swift movements of armies were extremely difficult. Only in the far east were conditions different and more favourable to battle. At this point the river Isonzo marked the end of the great Friulian plain. To the east rose the Carso, a rocky plateau occupied by the Austrians. Here,

---

[5] See P. Pieri, *L'Italia nella prima guerra mondiale* (Turin, 1965).

across the Isonzo and into the Carso was Italy's most promising point of attack. Trieste lay just a few kilometres beyond the front.

The man in charge of Italy's war effort was General Luigi Cadorna. While the sovereign held overall command, it was Cadorna as *capo di stato maggiore* who commanded in practice. Cadorna would become one of the most contentious figures in the history of the war. He was a general of the old school; his father had participated in the liberation of Rome in 1870. Austere, rigid, taciturn, and set in his ways he shared some of the virtues and many of the vices of other commanders elsewhere during the war. Three aspects of Cadorna's generalship stand out: first, his dislike of politicians and the government which led him to run for the most part an independent war, without much civilian interference; secondly, his unwillingness to cultivate relations of trust with his subordinates. Officers were routinely sacked on a high scale. Finally, as for the troops, little effort was made to look after their well-being. Indeed, Cadorna had a deep mistrust of the reliability of the Italians. He saw subversion, tragically, everywhere. The result was a demoralized, overly rigid army that might crack under extraordinary pressures.

Cadorna's strategic and tactical choices were few in number and were dictated by his training and temperament. Italy had declared war on Austria-Hungary and therefore Italy must take the offensive. The most advantageous ground for an offensive was across the Isonzo towards Trieste. With any luck, Ljubljana could be reached in a few weeks and Vienna shortly thereafter. Cadorna was not unaware of the new conditions in warfare that favoured defensive firepower. Despite reports from the Western Front, he continued to hold that with a proper offensive spirit and artillery preparation, men could triumph against fire. This was the essence of his own infantry manual that was the guidebook for soldiers in 1915.

In 1915 the Italian army moved to attack. In the first year of battle many young Italians were moved by an enthusiasm seen in the rest of Europe in August 1914. 'I am proud,' wrote one soldier, 'to give my part to Our Country, so that she may affirm through the sacrifice of her sons her greatness in the face of the whole world.'[6] Many of these noble sentiments were crushed during the brutal campaigns of 1915. Cadorna launched four offensives against the Austrian positions

---

[6] A. Omodeo, *Momenti della vita di guerra* (Turin, 1968), p. 16.

along the Isonzo in that year. 62,000 Italians were killed and 170,000 wounded, without any appreciable change in the situation.

Italy's entrance into the First World War had not proved to be the decisive event that many had hoped. To be sure, the Italian Front drew off Austrian forces that might have been employed in the Balkans and the East, thus weakening the dual monarchy's efforts there. On the other hand, the Austrians enjoyed a strong defensive position that could be maintained at a relatively low cost. In 1915 Italy had been unable to force a definitive strike against its enemy. The Italian Front had settled into a sideshow, while greater battles were waged elsewhere.

Italy's war was something of a sideshow also on the diplomatic front. Only over time and with great difficulty would Italy be able to forge the close political and economic ties necessary to create a grand coalition. Much of this had to do with personalities and the fact that a narrow directorate conducted Italy's war. Crucially, the foreign minister Sidney Sonnino took a narrow and nationalist approach to all issues. He stood by the Treaty of London and was unwilling to budge from it. Italian ambitions in the Balkans angered the Serbs and the Allies and rendered a common front in the Balkans all but impossible. Both Salandra and Sonnino were reluctant to meet with their allied counterparts, so that no sort of mutual exchange was developed. For the Italian leadership, the country was conducting what amounted to a parallel war: Italy did not even declare war on Germany until August 1916! This Italian stubbornness would soon change in the face of economic necessity. But it had already poisoned relations with the Allies and this would seriously affect Italy's diplomacy at the peace conference.

The second year of the war saw profound changes in Cadorna's relations with the government, within the government itself and between Italy and its allies. The dispute between Cadorna and the government centred on the question of sending an Italian expedition to Albania. While the General was most concerned with concentrating his resources on the Isonzo front, Salandra and Sonnino persisted in pursuing their geopolitical objectives of staking out an Italian position in the Balkans. The resultant stand-off led to a compromise, whereby Italy did, in fact, intervene in Albania, but Cadorna's authority was reaffirmed. In a dispute between civil and military authorities, Cadorna had largely carried the day.

The crucial military event of 1916 was the *Strafexpedition*—the great 'punitive expedition' launched by the Austrians in the Trentine salient. The plan was to push through the mountains and plateaus to reach the Po Valley. Henceforth, the route to Verona and Bologna would be open to conquest. This was the first major Austrian offensive and it shocked the Italian command and public. In the following weeks the Italian army regrouped and counterattacked. The enemy's thrust was contained.

Although the possibility of a major defeat had been averted, discontent bubbled to the surface within the state and the army. The first casualty was the prime minister, Antonio Salandra. Criticized by the High Command and by a wide spectrum of political forces, he was replaced by the 78-year-old Paolo Boselli who was to preside over a wide-ranging 'national government', including elements of the democratic left. The new combination was soon blessed with the capture of Gorizia in the summer of 1916. It was a victory of no great importance, but for a country which had seen so few, it soon became magnified into a major triumph.

As the war continued, Italy's relations with its allies continued to develop. These relations might be viewed on three levels. First, there were the military connections between the high commands. These had improved since the beginning of the war. An interesting possibility occurred in early 1917. At a conference in Rome both Lloyd George and Cadorna proposed a major offensive on the Italian Front. This would take the pressure off the West and might lead to a breakthrough. Although rejected by the French and British generals, it remains an interesting counterfactual. Henceforth, the Italian Front would remain a major, but only secondary, field of operations.

On the diplomatic front, relations remained strained. Sonnino's secretiveness and obstinacy made easy rapport difficult. Sonnino was particularly alarmed at Franco-Russian designs for the future partition of the Ottoman Empire. As always, Italian diplomacy held out an eager hand for a share in any future Near Eastern spoils.

It was, however, on the economic front that inter-allied relations were most important. Italy had come to depend for food, energy, and capital on its allies Britain, France, and after 1917, the United States. The war had completely upset Italy's traditional pattern of trade and payments. Former export markets had disappeared. Sources of imports, too, had declined. Naval conflict and submarine warfare had wrecked shipping and transport. Perhaps the biggest problem was that of financing the war. Here, Italy ran up a large public debt, both domestic and foreign. The point to be stressed here is that regardless of the state of political relations with the Allies, Italy, by war's end found itself in a complex, binding, and not entirely autonomous web of economic relations with them.

At the end of 1916 the First World War was a stalemate. At Verdun, despite enormous casualties, the French had held. On the Somme, Great Britain had sacrificed a generation. In the East, the Brusilov offensive had met with some success, before grinding to a halt. Poor Romania had joined the fight, only to be crushed. Italy had held off the *Strafexpedition* and had taken Gorizia. To support Romania, Italy had fought the seventh, eighth, and ninth battles of the Isonzo, losing 58,000 dead and 140,000 wounded. As 1917 approached, the country faced enormous economic, social, and political problems. There had been two years of war with scant results. Could the centre hold?

The year of Caporetto

1917 was to be a decisive year in the war. On the home front, the stresses and strains of waging total war began to tear away at the fabric of the country's economy and society. This inevitably had repercussions for the restricted political class that was in charge of the war effort. Abroad, American intervention and Wilsonianism, and the Bolshevik Revolution and Leninism changed the ideological character of the war. Then, in October 1917, Italy suffered its greatest military defeat, with the collapse of its entire eastern front at the battle of Caporetto.

Before 1917, the government had been hesitant to pursue an extreme policy of austerity. While a system of industrial mobilization had been set up, not enough had been done to control consumption and prices. Shifting production from 'butter' to 'guns' inevitably caused great disruptions in agriculture and industry, and in the balance between them. By 1917 discontent within the country had begun to surface. The most serious events occurred in Turin in August, when bread riots soon turned into demonstrations for peace and revolution, and the army was forced to step in. Popular discontent never congealed into a significant effective national political

movement against the war, but it did frighten Italy's wartime leadership, which came to view internal subversion as a major threat.

The entry of the United States into the war and Wilson's message
of the 14 points had an important, if relatively short term, impact on
Italian public opinion. Above all, America's entry meant that a rich
and powerful new ally had entered the fight. Not only would the
United States help tip the balance against the Central Powers, but also
Italy could now seek out financial and material resources that it des-
perately needed. Given the strong connections established by millions
of emigrants, 'America' and Wilson were at first viewed as saviours.
Unfortunately, a large gap existed between the Italian and the American leadership. Italy had not entered the war to make the world safe for
democracy. It had entered it for the Treaty of London. When, as indeed
happened at the Peace Conference, Wilsonian notions of national
self-determination clashed with Italy's territorial aims, no easy reso-
lution was possible. Ultimately, Wilsonianism would find support
mainly among the small current of democratic interventionists.

The Russian revolutions of 1917 were to have a greater and more
lasting impact in Italy. The collapse of the Eastern Front and
Russia's impending withdrawal from the war, of course, raised the
spectre of a one-front war in which the Central Powers could concentrate their forces against the Western powers, including Italy.
This was the most important immediate concern. At the same time,
the revolutionary message and Lenin's formulations of it had an
extraordinary impact on Italy's hard-pressed and discontented
people. Would not revolution lead to the end of the war and a
better future? Rhetorically, the appeal of the Russian Revolution
had a widespread impact, especially among workers. In practice,
however, there is little evidence that it had any significant concrete
consequences within the army. Nevertheless, Cadorna and the
military command were convinced that red subversion was at the
heart of all their problems.

Thus, as Wilsonianism and Leninism opened up a new ideological
phase in the war, a gap was created between Italy's political class and
the new creeds.[7] Wilsonianism was to prove incompatible with Italian
territorial ambitions and war aims. Leninism menaced the very
authority of the Liberal state. The rejection of both Wilsonian

---

[7] See R. Vivarelli, *Storia delle origini del fascismo*, Vol. I (Bologna, 1991).

liberalism and Leninism eventually would open the political space for a third way, based on nationalism and the war experience. This third solution, created by the former socialist Mussolini, was Fascism.

It was against this background of domestic difficulties and the changing ideological nature of the war that Italy suffered its greatest military defeat at the battle of Caporetto. So great was the trauma that the word 'Caporetto' has entered the Italian cultural vocabulary as a symbol of national crisis. The battle consisted of a great offensive manoeuvre on the part of the Austrians and the Germans.[8] The German contribution to victory was decisive, for by this time the Austrians had been considerably weakened. The offensive was carefully planned and three elements were essential. First, the Austro-Germans effectively organized a surprise attack; secondly, they used a short, but intense, bombardment of explosives and gas to wreck Italian command and control; and thirdly, they adopted the new tactics of infiltration. The result was a penetration of the Italian lines, which soon led to their collapse.

Even though the Austro-Germans had conducted a skilful attack, the Italian command must bear the responsibility for the magnitude of the defeat. Cadorna simply did not prepare his forces for a defensive battle, nor did the commanders in key sectors of the front (Capello and Badoglio). The historian Giorgio Rochat attributes this to a 'fossilization' of the offensive mentality. The Italian positions were placed so rigidly on the offensive that when a new attack came, they were brittle, and cracked. And the crack was severe indeed. The Italian retreat turned into a rout, and the army fell back first to the Tagliamento, but was then forced back further to the river Piave where the line was stabilized on 9 November. The far north-east of Italy lay in enemy hands.

Cadorna, disgracefully, blamed the cowardice and defeatism of his own troops for the defeat. This calumny has led to the widespread disparagement of the Italian soldiers in the First World War. A definitive judgement is difficult to reach. On the one hand, there were a relatively high number of desertions in the Italian army. Against this, however, must be placed the severe discipline of the army. There was a fundamental lack of trust between the command and the troops.

---

[8] This account is based on the authoritative work of Giorgio Rochat, see Isnenghi and Rochat, *La Grande guerra*, pp. 367–85.

This lack of trust reflected the general gap between the state and society in the country as a whole. Until Caporetto little was done to propagandize the troops or to care for their moral and material welfare. It is in fact surprising that the soldiers fought so well, given the way they were treated. The Italian army never experienced the outright mutinies that the French army did.

Perhaps the most tragic illustration of the attitudes of the war leadership towards the troops concerns the treatment of prisoners of war.[9] Naturally, the command wanted to discourage desertion, but in the Italian case official military and state policy took a brutal form. In contrast to the other powers, the Italian state blocked supplies from going to the prisoners. As a result, it is estimated that 100,000 men died. Almost one in six of Italy's total war casualties was thus a victim of his own country's actions.

Caporetto was a turning point. After it, the country was fighting for its survival. While a great military defeat, it must be remembered that it did not lead to the total collapse of the army or to the breakdown of the state. The Risorgimento state held. Italy was not to be the Russia of 1917 or the Austria-Hungary of 1918.

Victory and a mutilated peace

In the aftermath of defeat, the Italian war leadership regrouped and reformed to provide a stronger control over the war effort. The more diplomatic and flexible Armando Diaz replaced Cadorna as commander-in-chief. A new government was formed under Vittorio Emanuele Orlando, with the energetic Francesco Nitti at the Treasury. Sidney Sonnino remained as Foreign Minister. The new government moved quickly to bolster war production, improve relations with the Allies, and sought to keep the hard-pressed economy afloat. At the same time, a hard line was taken against any form of potential internal dissent. A sizeable Allied force was sent to strengthen the Italian positions.

In 1918 across the Western Front and in Italy the decisive final

---

[9] This story was ignored until the research of Giovanna Procacci. See G. Procacci, *Soldati e prigionieri italiani nella grande guerra* (Rome, 1993).

battles of the war were fought. There was considerable allied infighting over the disposition of troops between France, where the Germans were on the offensive, and Italy, where the Austrians saw a chance for a final knockout blow. In September, however, the French and British began to roll back the Germans on the Western Front. The Italian government was resolved that it too must act lest the war end while enemy troops were still on Italian soil. Thus, the army launched the last great offensive, the battle of Vittorio Veneto, which drove back the army of an empire already in full dissolution. On 4 November the Austrians signed an armistice at the Villa Giusti near Padua. Italy's war was over.

Italy was a victorious power, but what exactly had Italy 'won'? The country had intervened in the conflict without any clear consensus over war aims. So too, it ended the war without any clear notion of victory. The costs were clear: 650,000 casualties, years of hardship, inflation, a distorted economy. The majority of 'outsiders' who had been either indifferent or opposed to intervention had, in the end, been brought into the war effort. Now they had expectations, both political and economic, for a new system. In 1919 the first mass Catholic political party, the Partito Popolare Italiano(PPI) would be formed. On the Left, the PSI and the trade unions demonstrated a new militancy. They, too, would advance claims for sacrifices made during the war.

For the old Liberal élite, the problem was to put the genie of popular demands back into the bottle. In an immediate sense, however, the principal task was to achieve the aims set out in the Treaty of London. This document, which had been made public by the Bolsheviks, became something of a fetish to the government and to Sonnino in particular. The treaty came to embody the nationalist aspirations of many Italians. 'This is what we fought and died for.' As the costs of the war had risen, so had the stakes. What had begun as a war for Trent and Trieste, now became a post-war struggle for the Brenner and Fiume (which was not included in the treaty's provisions). By war's end nationalism had become a powerful force within Italian public opinion, and this proved to be a powerful constraint on the Italian government's diplomatic manoeuvrability.

Italian diplomacy faced two major problems. First, with the disintegration of the Habsburg monarchy and the establishment of a Yugoslav state, Italian ambitions in the Balkans faced a serious obstacle. Secondly, Italy's 'old diplomacy' claims at the Paris Peace Conference were very much out of step with Wilsonianism and the notion of national self-determination. In fact, the Italians were asking for the German-speaking South Tyrol and Slav-speaking Dalmatia (under the terms of the Treaty of London) as well as Fiume (under the principle of national self-determination). The conflict with Wilson broke into the open and led to Italy's temporary withdrawal from the conference. The government had been humiliated and was diplomatically isolated. Italy's role in the final peace settlement was to be marginal.

In fact, the settlement was quite favourable to Italy. It received Trent, Trieste, the Brenner, and even some territories not stipulated in the Treaty of London. She was given a permanent seat in the League of Nations and a participation in German reparations. Nevertheless, the nationalists and much of public opinion were outraged by what was now viewed as a 'mutilated' victory.

This generalized nationalist angst, which spread among the middle classes beset by inflation, among returning soldiers, among disaffected intellectuals, and among the many who had hoped that the ordeal of war would produce a 'new' Italy, had a powerful impact on Italian political life. Ultimately, it would form one of the ideological underpinnings of Fascism. To a certain extent, in character though not in aim, it was similar to the post-war discontent within the Left and among the Catholic masses. The post-war Liberal governments would find it difficult to manage and contain all of these.

The currents of nationalist discontent all came together over the incident of Fiume. The Adriatic city by the summer of 1919 had become a ticking bomb. Claimed by the Italian nationalists, but denied to Italy by the powers, it was a symbolic as well as a real target for action. In September 1919 the poet Gabriele D'Annunzio, accompanied by battalions of *arditi* (shock troops), deserters, romantics, and adventurers marched on Fiume and seized the city. His move galvanized nationalist and public opinion. The powers and the Yugoslavs were outraged. The Italian government was paralysed. Although it would take several years to resolve the issue, the weaknesses of Italy's domestic and external position had been made clear.

Perhaps the figure who learned the most from D'Annunzio's Fiume escapade was Benito Mussolini. He was able to see the powerful spell that nationalism could cast over the disaffected. So, too, he could empathize with the post-war disorientation of the returning soldiers. As a former socialist and populist he could relate to those whose expectations were unfulfilled after the war. Mussolini the Fascist was a product of the Great War. The cult of the war, the cult of the fallen, and of sacrifice would become one of the hallmarks of his movement. Perhaps more than the left, the Catholics, or the Liberals, Fascism was able to provide a meaning for the sacrifices the country had experienced during the war. The heroic and mystical death of youth was more powerful than the Treaty of London.

Four years after the end of the First World War, in 1922, Mussolini came to power. In the preceding years Italy had returned to its status as the least of the great powers, scrambling hither and yon for influence in Yugoslavia or in Central Europe—but with little influence in the councils of the great. The new prime minister's rise was accompanied by the death of Liberal Italy. The Liberal regime had entered the war to strengthen itself and Italy's position in the state system. It had accomplished neither. With Mussolini's rise, Italy had managed to snatch defeat from the jaws of victory. The new regime would try again, and more defiantly, to assert Italy's status as a great power.

Fascism: ideology, foreign policy, and war

MacGregor Knox

> Macbeth's self-justifications were feeble—and his conscience
> devoured him. Yes, even Iago was a little lamb too. The imagin-
> ation and the spiritual strength of Shakespeare's evildoers
> stopped short at a dozen corpses. Because they had no *ideology*.
>
> (Aleksandr I. Solzhenitsyn, *The Gulag Archipelago*)

Fascism emerged from a great war and perished a quarter-century
later in that war's far greater second act—which it sought fervently to
bring about. Its trajectory from war in 1915–18 to ruin in 1940–5 was
no accident. And the force that propelled it along that path was above
all the force of ideas.

Mythic origins: war and national integration

Those ideas were with one major exception in no sense peculiar to
Fascism as a movement and as a regime; what Fascism above all
supplied was the necessary obliviousness to the immense risks
inseparable from their full implementation. The underlying con-
ceptions derived from the loathing and contempt with which many

pre-1914 Italian intellectuals regarded the parliamentary state born through territorial unification in the 1860s. The Risorgimento, they had ceaselessly lamented, had been the work of a tiny minority, achieved by diplomatic trickery and French and Prussian victories: 'the [Italian] people was absent'. The military humiliations of the Piedmontese-Italian armed forces in 1848–9 and 1866 against the Austrians and in 1896 against the Ethiopians seemingly symbolized the founders' failure to instil a national spirit capable of fusing into a combative unity Italy's workers and middle classes, its town-dwellers and peasants, and its cities and regions separated by mutually incomprehensible dialects. From the frenetic prophets of the Italian Nationalist Association (1910–23) on the Right to the founding saint and foremost anti-Fascist martyr of the Italian Communist Party, Antonio Gramsci, on the Left, general agreement reigned. In Gramsci's famous words, the Risorgimento's creation was a 'bastard'; united Italy had failed as a modern state.

The remedies proposed differed. But the majority view among the post-1861 state's many critics, particularly in the light of the intense competition for empire among the advanced industrialized powers evident from the 1880s onward, was that Italy must find its domestic unity and achieve true great power status through war and conquest. In the much-quoted 1889 formula of the amateur historian Alfredo Oriani, an eccentric but influential recluse from the Romagna, 'The future of Italy lies entirely in a war which, while giving it its natural boundaries, will cement internally, through the anguish of mortal perils, the unity of the national spirit.' Yet any such enterprise would foreseeably fall foul of the 'elemental and endemic rebelliousness of the popular classes' (in Gramsci's eloquent and all-too-accurate words) that redemptive war was supposed to assuage. As in domestic politics, where that same rebelliousness caught the Liberals between their laudable aspiration to widen the state's restricted franchise and narrow political base, and their fear both of inchoate revolt and of the rising Catholic and Socialist mass political forces, national integration through war appeared to require a measure of coercion.

Those who thirsted for the unity of the national spirit therefore in many cases also aspired to replace the allegedly feeble parliamentary regime—which had, in their view culpably, tolerated the rise of the Socialist Party—with a new authoritarian state that would impose internal unity in the cause of external expansion. That '*Stato nuovo*' was above all the Nationalists' pet project, but its influence extended far beyond their ranks. The 'make-up examination' (as a prominent young historian of Nationalist leanings described it) of Italy's conquest of Libya in 1911–12 made the point clearly. Widespread patriotic enthusiasm for the violent acquisition of a North African colony did not prevent strikes and riotous demonstrations against the war, and a revolutionary left turn by the Socialist Party under the leadership of its most fiery and talented demagogue, Benito Mussolini. Small wars were clearly not enough to 'make Italians'.

European crisis soon transmuted the pipe dreams of the intellectuals into blood-drenched deeds. Italy courteously declined to intervene at the side of its German and Austro-Hungarian allies in August 1914: British and French command of the nation's seaborne coal, iron, and grain supplies, the public's hostility to Austria, Austro-German highhandedness in launching war without Italian concurrence, and the obvious uncertainty of the outcome all imposed caution. But by September–October Imperial Germany's bid for swift victory had demonstrably failed, and Italian élite opinion turned to thoughts of an Italian war for Italian objectives. Mussolini tried and failed to carry the Socialist Party toward war in its own interest and in that of national unity. Then he joined the motley front of interventionists that by late autumn 1914 ranged from nationalist Syndicalists and liberal-democratic intellectuals on the left through the Liberals around Italy's greatest newspaper, the *Corriere della Sera* of Milan, to the Futurists and other ornaments of the literary-political avant-garde, and thence to the Nationalists on the right.

Mussolini's 1914–15 appeals to his new constituency contained many of the fateful notions that drove his later career as a Fascist. Neutrality was pusillanimous, 'eunuchoid', 'worthy of people beneath history'. War must destroy 'the ignoble legend that Italians do not fight, it must wipe out the shame of Lissa and Custoza [the great defeats of 1866], it must show the world that Italy can fight a war, a great war; I say again: *a great war*'. Only such a war could fulfil the mission that Oriani had assigned Italy: 'the unalterable enemy, Austria; *mare nostro*, the Adriatic'. Either war, 'or let us finish with this *commedia* of [claiming to be] a great power'.

These appeals were not notably original; passion, simplicity, and repetition, not originality, are the secrets of propaganda. Mussolini's objective—to drown in blood a widely felt sense of national inferiority—was all too familiar to his audience. But Mussolini added a twist that defined his domestic-political goals both as interventionist and as Fascist. Whereas the Liberal Establishment entered war in fear of a domestic revolution should it fail to seize the historic objectives of Trent and Trieste from Austria (a notion both Nationalists and Mussolini sought eagerly to encourage), Mussolini proclaimed the *unity* of war and revolution: 'today it is war; tomorrow it will be revolution'; the day Italian bayonets crossed the Ringstrasse in Vienna, 'the Vatican's death knell [would] sound'. The Right-Liberal government's plan to fight a 'state war' in the age of the masses Mussolini presciently dismissed as a delusion; once mobilized for war, the masses might well escape from tutelage.

And so it proved. The Right-Liberals' entry into war in the 'radiant May' of 1915, contrary to their intentions, partook of the age of mass politics. Mobs of students and *interventisti*, whipped up by Mussolini and above all by the fanatical national poet-prophet, Gabriele D'Annunzio, bayed for war and hunted neutralist deputies through the streets of Rome. That unpardonable violence in the national cause opened the active or latent civil war that raged until Mussolini's own execution by Communist partisans 'in the name of the Italian people' on 28 April 1945.

War destroyed Liberal Italy. Military failure against Austria-Hungary's thinly but stubbornly held defences in the Alps and among the arid limestone hills west of Trieste consumed its governments, while Mussolini, before and after serving at the front, gleefully attacked their lack of zeal and ruthlessness. Its character as a civil war between *interventisti* on the one hand, and Liberal neutralists and Socialists on the other, persisted and intensified. Widespread resentment of this 'war of the landlords' by the peasants who supplied most of the infantry and thus the majority of Italy's 650,000 war dead further poisoned the atmosphere. Even the breakthrough at Caporetto by a German expeditionary force in October–November 1917 and the precipitate retreat of the Italian armies to a line immediately east of Venice failed to produce more than a momentary flush of national unity, although the army rallied. For Caporetto coincided with Lenin's revolution in Russia, which triggered and then sustained three years of revolutionary paroxysms among Italy's Socialists.

The *interventisti*, Mussolini foremost among them, responded with intensified demands for merciless endless war against 'enemies without and saboteurs within'. Caporetto became the symbol of Socialist treason—although innate deficiencies of the army officer corps and German tactical and operational skill were the root causes of disaster. Mussolini and others railed against the 'evil brood of *caporettisti*' who had 'stabbed the nation in the back'. As in Germany, where a far more powerful stab-in-the-back legend with an anti-Semitic leitmotif gained an unparalleled grip on the national imagination, those who had willed the war perpetuated it with loving care after 1918.

From myth to reality, 1919–1940: programmatic and ideological bases

The Fascist movement founded by Mussolini and a colourful assembly of left-wing *interventisti*, demobilized junior officers and veterans of the shock troops (*arditi*), Futurist warrior-aesthetes, and nationalist students in March 1919 espoused the 'defence of victory' against both the wartime 'internal enemy' and Italy's French and British allies. Yet while the Socialists—and the Slovenes and Germans of the newly annexed border areas—were all too easily cowed by the paramilitary violence of the Fascist movement's blackshirted action squads, the British and French were and remained beyond Italy's— and Mussolini's—reach. They swiftly 'mutilated' Italy's victory (in D'Annunzio's typically lurid phrase) by blocking effortlessly the realization of the grandiose war aims that had included domination of both shores of the Adriatic and the long-sought hegemony over East Africa.

Italian weakness nevertheless did not prevent Mussolini from evolving between 1919 and 1926–7 an integrated programme premissed on the use of force both internally and externally. At home, neither Fascism's intensifying violence against the Socialists throughout north Italy from 1920 onward, nor its elevation to government in October 1922, nor even its assumption of dictatorial power and abolition of the opposition in 1925–6, were enough. Mussolini's power remained conditional on the backing of King Victor Emmanuel III and of the army—and what king and generals had given they might also take away. As Mussolini admitted some months before his proclamation of open dictatorship on 3 January 1925, the 1922 'March on Rome' had merely been a 'victorious insurrection', not a revolution: 'the revolution comes later'.

He outlined the domestic content of that revolution throughout the mid-1920s in a series of speeches, some of them secret, to the party faithful. Fascism's 'ferocious totalitarian will' would impose the national integration for which the intellectuals had yearned: 'tomorrow Italian and Fascist, more or less like Italian and Catholic, will be the same thing.' A new ruling class, spawned 'in the laboratory', would emerge. A 'warrior education' would rear Italy's youth to brutish xenophobia and a 'sense of virility, of power, of conquest'. State-encouraged demographic expansion, land reclamation, and economic self-sufficiency would fit Italy with the sinews of conquest. And at the core of Mussolini's programme, but concealed from all but trusted associates—and the German ambassador, who reported Mussolini's pro-German sentiments with relish in late 1924—was the essence of the revolution Mussolini had promised: a great victorious Mediterranean war against France that would give Mussolini all North Africa, and the prestige 'to have himself acclaimed emperor while easily pushing aside the unwarlike king'. That ambition was a logical extrapolation, in the light of experience, of Mussolini's 1914 notion that war could entail revolution. The Great War that Mussolini had preached had destroyed Liberal Italy and had made him Duce of Fascism and head of government. A victorious sequel would predictably make his power total.

A new great war could have only one ultimate target: Italy's wartime allies. From the spring of 1919 onward, despite occasional tactical protestations of conditional friendship with France and especially Britain, Mussolini fulminated intermittently against the world hegemony of the 'plutocratic and bourgeois' powers, and especially their domination of the Mediterranean, the 'sea that was Rome's'. He repeatedly denounced them as 'parasites' and proclaimed publicly the aim of helping to 'demolish' the British Empire, while secretly avowing that same aim to Indian revolutionaries to whom Italy promised support.

From the Nationalists and from the Italian navy, which inevitably sought to justify an increased share of the national budget, Mussolini acquired the rudiments of a geopolitical theory. Italy—an image with roots in the pre-1914 musings of the intellectuals—was a prisoner in the Mediterranean. An inner ring of French and British bases at Toulon, Bizerte in Tunisia, and Malta encircled the peninsula. Worse still, Italy's dependence on foreign coal, oil, iron, grain, and fertilizer threatened economic strangulation at London's pleasure by distant blockade enforced at the British-controlled choke points of Gibraltar and Suez. That threat Mussolini's navy minister, Grand Admiral Paolo Thaon di Revel, emphasized repeatedly in parliament with all the weight of authority acquired as his service's war leader. In spring 1925 Mussolini caused consternation at the foreign ministry with private threats to break—through a new war—the 'chain that permits England to encircle, to imprison Italy in the Mediterranean'. By the following year he had elevated that animosity into a general law, which he imparted to a group of senior officers: 'A nation that has no free access to the sea cannot be considered a free nation; a nation that has no free access to the oceans cannot be considered a great power; Italy must become a great power.'

Mussolini's fusion of the great power aspirations of Italy's élites with Nationalist and navy geopolitics had a long subsequent career as the central concept underlying Fascist foreign policy. Mussolini mentioned it in cabinet in 1929 when pressing for a larger navy: Italy must achieve Mediterranean mastery 'or founder'. It reappeared immediately before and during the Ethiopian war, and in a secret speech of February 1939 to the Grand Council of Fascism that solemnly proclaimed a 'march to the Ocean' against Italy's British and French jailers. And it was the centrepiece of Mussolini's secret war directive of March 1940 and of the public speech of 10 June 1940 that launched Italy against the Western powers.

A corollary to Mussolini's vision of geopolitical salvation was the alliance structure required to bring it about. He had recognized at least from spring 1922—as he put it then—that 'the axis of European history passe[d] through Berlin'. That was no momentary individual insight. Italy's previous German connection—the Triple Alliance from 1882 to 1914—had served its claim to great power status and to consideration in the sharing out of colonial spoils. At least some in Italy's governing élite had regretted the alliance's collapse; the stern *generalissimo* of 1914–17, Luigi Cadorna, had initially inclined toward a lightning war alongside the Central Powers that would—he retrospectively lamented in 1918—have yielded Nice, Corsica, Tunisia, and Mediterranean predominance. United Italy's perennial foreign policy requirement, given its vast ambitions, was an ally far mightier than itself capable of breaking the resistance of France and Britain to Italian aims.

Mussolini explicitly acknowledged that requirement by word and deed in the 1920s. He sought unsuccessfully to woo republican Germany's canny and durable foreign minister, Gustav Stresemann, and in 1924 sent a high Italian commander of the Great War, General Luigi Capello, on an unofficial mission to Berlin to make contact with the nationalist Right and army. But as the dictator privately lamented to his war minister, General Pietro Gàzzera, in mid-1929, 'Germany is disarmed—we cannot negotiate for possible cooperation against France (Capello in 1924).' Despite Italy's grudging adherence to the Locarno security pact in late 1925, hope nevertheless remained alive; Mussolini foresaw throughout the late 1920s and early 1930s a great European crisis arising from the already-scheduled end of key post-war restrictions on Germany such as France's occupation of the Rhineland and Saar. Some months after Adolf Hitler's National Socialist Party had dramatically increased its parliamentary showing from 12 to 107 seats in the German election of September 1930, Mussolini predicted to Gàzzera the 'accession to power of the German Right' by 1934–6. That event—which implied German rearmament and made a German war of revenge on France likely—would restore Germany's potential as an Italian ally.

Mussolini at no time confided more than parts of his programme even to trusted subordinates. He preferred to allow them to assume, as have some imprudent historians, that the dictator indeed possessed the sure 'animal instinct' and merciless realism that he and his propagandists relentlessly claimed. But those who served him most closely came sooner or later to the conclusion summed up most eloquently by Dino Grandi, the Fascist chieftain from Bologna who acted as Mussolini's under-secretary and then minister for foreign affairs from 1925 until 1932.

Grandi, despite an initial interest in war against France and an abiding infatuation—widely shared in the foreign ministry—with an Italian attack on Ethiopia, likewise thought himself a realist. He later tampered with the texts of his own speeches in order to claim Mussolini as an adherent of his own pet theory of Italian foreign policy, that Italy should exploit for its aggrandizement a position of 'decisive weight' between the Western powers and Germany.[1] He was also well-enough attuned to international realities and to Italy's weakness to despair—at least to his diary—from 1930 onward at Mussolini's posture as 'the Pope of anti-democracy' in command of an 'anti-democratic crusade throughout the entire world'. Mussolini's 'ador[ation] of *the Idea*', which Grandi identified with dictatorship, was coupled with an '*unreal* conception of diplomacy. [Mussolini] calls this conception revolutionary, but the truth is that it is *unreal* [*irreale*]'. And Grandi, like his feckless successor as foreign minister from 1936 to 1943, Galeazzo Ciano, came to recognize that Mussolini's unrealism was fundamental, irremediable, and programmatic:

I have asked myself [Grandi wrote despondently after his abrupt relegation to the London embassy in July 1932] why the Boss is so taken with Hitler. [Mussolini] has searched breathlessly for the last ten years or so, wherever they might be found, for 'allies' for a revolutionary foreign policy destined to create a 'new order' in Europe, a new order of which He considers himself the supreme Pontiff not only in the spiritual but also in the material sense. . . . An international action founded exclusively on the Party, on the Regime, on a revolutionary ideology.[2]

Yet the core of that ideology was and remained remarkably nebulous. Mussolini and his movement's propagandists and intellectuals had asserted with increasing conviction since 1919–20 that parliamentarism and socialism alike were putrescent nineteenth-century superstitions, and that religion—both before and after Mussolini's Faustian pact with the Roman Catholic Church in 1929—was significant primarily as a means of expanding and reinforcing state power. Yet these ideas lacked a pivotal mechanism or organizing concept, despite the foundation in 1930 of a school of 'Fascist mysticism' (*mistica fascista*) and the appearance of a much-publicized Mussolini encyclopaedia article of 1932 on the ideology of Fascism co-authored with the philosopher Giovanni Gentile. The article inevitably asserted the centrality of war to human existence, but beyond an invocation of empire as the regime's ultimate goal, it contained only platitudes.

At the centre of the ideological fare the regime offered for public

---

[1] On Grandi's forgeries and their implications for the interpretation of Fascist foreign policy, see MacGregor Knox, 'I testi "aggiustati" dei discorsi segreti di Grandi', *Passato e Presente*, No. 13 (1987), and reply to Paolo Nello, ibid., No. 16 (1988).

[2] Grandi quotations: entries of 12 Sept. 1930, 6 Jan. 1931, 20 Mar. 1932, Grandi diary, 1929–32 (microfilm), rolls 15, 17, 22, Georgetown University Library, Washington, DC.

consumption was above all Mussolini's own cult of personality ('the Duce is always right'), reverence for the Fascist 'new state' ('everything in the state, nothing outside the state, nothing against the state'), and the revolutionary myths and slogans of youthful nationalist heroism ('live dangerously'; 'better a day as a lion than a hundred years as a sheep') of the *arditi* and of the paramilitary *squadre* of 1919–22. These three disparate ingredients coexisted uneasily; indeed each one was notably antagonistic to the others.

The 'cult of the Duce' waxed increasingly powerful after 1922–5; as Max Weber taught, charisma is made manifest and consolidated by *success*. Mussolini's charisma, like that of his eventual ally, Adolf Hitler, was always far more powerful than the ascendancy of the single party, which in both Italy and Germany enjoyed a deserved reputation for corruption, incompetence, and abuse of power. The king, the Vatican, the Italian Establishment, and the Italian middle classes supported or tolerated Mussolini because he had ostensibly prevented revolution, not because he aspired to make it. Their *mussolinismo*, although sometimes highly emotional, was thoroughly conditional. Ageing blackshirted thugs and the new levies from the Fascist youth organizations might burn to conquer and die for the Duce, but as the regime entered its second decade many found his failure to deliver revolution and foreign adventure disorienting. Mussolini (as one mournful *squadrista* poet and artist put it in 1928), might yet 'sound an unscheduled reveille' and launch his loyal followers 'across the frontiers'. But clearly the moment had not yet come.

The 'myth of the State'—a phrase that belongs between quotation marks because the Fascists themselves employed it as an all-purpose incantation—was equally double-edged. Unwise commentators have written with reverence of Mussolini's purported 'sense of the State', but without fully appreciating the extent to which Mussolini intended his assertion from 1922 onward of the state's supremacy over the party as an assertion of his *own* supremacy over his unruly rank and file. His success in imposing his authority was indeed a fundamental source of conservative support for his cult, and the myth of the state that he thereby appropriated for his own purposes enjoyed a wide pre-existing following. It also held a concealed but mortal danger: the Italian state had existed before Fascism, and might prove separable from it.

Finally, the early Fascist tradition of romantic nationalist violence was anything but congenial to a public scorched by the fires of 1915–18 and of post-war political violence. The regime sought to overcome the quietism of the middle classes and of the long-suffering peasantry with the propaganda of national greatness. But even the indoctrination of the young, in which Mussolini initially placed considerable faith, was not enough. Only glorious deeds and revolutionary careers for his followers—which would in turn threaten the conservative political base acquired through Fascism's purported restoration of order in Italy—could give the dictator the fanatical adherents needed to shatter the old order for good. Conversely, foreign policy risks— and even the slightest hint of failure—might alarm the timorous and embolden the regime's opponents, undermining the prestige Mussolini needed to maintain his grip on power.

Fascism thus faced its self-assigned foreign policy mission from a position of weakness, a weakness compounded by the absence, in its ideological foundations, of anything resembling the powerful ideological mechanisms that gave Marxism-Leninism and National Socialism their fanatical élites and masses. The Soviet and Nazi myths of the salvation of the human species through proletarian or racist revolution had no Fascist counterpart. The best Mussolini could offer was a blackshirted version of the visions of nineteenth-century prophets such as Vincenzo Gioberti and Giuseppe Mazzini: the creation of a 'new civilization' centred on Rome that would enjoy primacy in Europe and the Mediterranean basin. That vision lacked the credible world-revolutionary dimensions of the projects of Mussolini's principal ideological rivals, Hitler and Stalin. It also, even more damagingly, lacked the pseudo-scientific links between the regime's goals and the historical process found in Marxism and National Socialism. Stalin's followers killed millions at his command in the name of 'the [Marxist] classics, created out of knowledge of reality'.[3] Hitler could ask the impossible of the German people because he—and enough of them—fervently believed that their alleged racial superiority had made them lords of the earth. In that arena, Fascism was almost as outmatched as in the hard world of economic and military power that Mussolini aspired to overturn.

---

[3] 'Mit den Methoden der Klassiker, welche geschöpft sind / Aus der Kenntnis der Wirklichkeit' (Bertolt Brecht, 'Lob der Partei', in Die Massnahme (1930), Gesammelte Werke, Vol. II (Frankfurt am Main, 1967), p. 657).

From war to war: geography, economics, military power

Mussolini's 'decade of good behaviour'—as it is commonly misnamed—began in 1922–3 with public protestations that the new Italy, although proven in war, loved peace. Relative quiescence—briefly interrupted by the Corfu crisis in 1923—was not a matter of choice. Domestic consolidation occupied most of Mussolini's attention even before his personal gang of thugs murdered Giacomo Matteotti, the government's most prominent Socialist critic, in June 1924. The ensuing parliamentary and press uproar led to a further and more drastic foreign policy hiatus of well over a year. Until the abolition of the opposition by savage beatings and by legislation in 1925–6, Mussolini was not sufficiently supreme at home to devote himself wholeheartedly to external expansion. Even thereafter, and despite his sapping of the monarchy's powers by measures such as the 1928 law giving the Grand Council of Fascism a role in determining the royal succession, he faced both the king's constitutional monopoly of declarations of war and the tendency of the officer corps to look to the ever-hesitant monarch for a lead.

Nor was Italy's post-1922 financial, economic, and strategic situation propitious. The 'least of the great powers' emerged from the Great War heavily in debt to the United States, Britain, and France, whose loans had supplied 13.2 per cent of the immense cost of the nation's 1915–18 effort. Italy relied heavily upon German reparations, particularly coal, to mitigate its persistent balance of payments deficit. Not until 1925–6 did Mussolini achieve—at the price of pretending respect for the post-war order and accepting a role in the Locarno treaty structure—debt rescheduling and financing agreements with the United States that allowed the stabilization of the sagging lira. Italy depended for the foreseeable future on foreign financial support that was in turn contingent upon Mussolini renouncing war.

Fascist Italy was also gallingly reliant on foreign sources for virtually all its oil—the basis of modern warfare. And the railroads and factories of the peninsula, even after full exploitation of the hydroelectric power of the Alps, required a million tons per month of imported coal. Steel production—from plants that in general used imported scrap as their raw material—never exceeded two-fifths of French production during the inter-war period, and in 1938 amounted to about one-tenth of German steel production. In the aggregate, Italy had achieved by 1929 a mere 45 per cent of the total industrial potential of France, 27 per cent that of Great Britain, and 23 per cent that of Germany. A scant decade later, in 1938, Italy had gained slightly on France (62% of French potential) but had fallen further behind Britain (25%) and Germany (21%). That resource dependence and industrial weakness was potentially crippling to Fascist ambitions. By the late 1930s the economy theoretically required twenty-one to twenty-two million tons of imports annually, of which half was coal and one-third oil. And approximately three-fifths of that twenty-one million tons passed in peacetime through Gibraltar and Suez.

Britain's seemingly unbreakable stranglehold was galling to a power whose leaders had exulted in their total victory in 1918 over Italy's historic enemy, Austria-Hungary, and had welcomed less publicly the bleeding white of France, Italy's remaining continental rival. Mussolini's first important foreign policy initiative, the naval bombardment and occupation of the Greek island of Corfu in September 1923 after guerrillas had massacred an Italian army delegation delimiting the Greco-Albanian border, contributed mightily to focusing the dictator on Italy's geo-strategic subjection. The navy leadership, which had looked forward to bullying the Greeks with as much relish as had Mussolini, confessed shamefacedly during the resulting international crisis that it could protect neither Italy's coastal traffic, nor the great maritime cities, nor even its own bases. Mussolini's diplomats, above all the secretary-general of the foreign ministry, Salvatore Contarini, rescued the Duce and Italy from embarrassment by cobbling together with their equally emollient British and French counterparts a face-saving formula for Italian withdrawal from Corfu. And for the next half-decade Mussolini cultivated the favour of the Foreign Office, despite London's misgivings at the Duce's seemingly incorrigible antics in the Balkans.

In the medium term, and despite Italian weakness, Mussolini trusted to Italian rearmament as well as German help to fit Italy for Mediterranean conquest. Despite the travails of the lira and the enduring economic trauma of the Great War, military expenditure as a proportion of national income more than doubled from 1923–5 to

1931, from 2.6 per cent to 5.4 per cent. The army gradually rebuilt a core of serviceable divisions from the debris left by the demobilization of 1919–20. The navy's 400,000 tons of combat units (1926) grew steadily to 550,000 tons in 1933 and 700,000 tons in 1939–40. And by the late 1920s Italy's air force was at least on paper a world leader. The regime also created in the 1920s an elaborate bureaucratic apparatus for the 'organization of the nation for war': a National Research Council for military and autarchic research; an interministerial Supreme Defence Commission under Mussolini's chairmanship to coordinate military-economic preparations; and a Committee for Civil Mobilization with regional and local branches to oversee firms producing armaments and strategic goods. Mussolini himself, as well as serving as minister of each of the armed forces from 1925 to 1929 and from 1933 to 1943, acquired in 1925 a 'chief of general staff', General (Marshal from 1926) Pietro Badoglio. Badoglio's vulnerability to criticism—his army corps had been the first to crack at Caporetto—may have appeared welcome reinsurance against potential military encroachments on the dictator's power. And in 1927, as Mussolini consolidated his own dictatorial position, he also reduced the marshal's originally extensive powers, which had included command of the army, to those of a sort of consultant for strategic planning and coordination of the armed forces.

The resulting highly centralized and seemingly purposeful structure was almost completely ineffectual. Mussolini himself lacked the time, the military understanding, and until the mid-1930s the political power to dictate to his generals and admirals the force structures and interservice coordination and planning needed to fight effectively in support of his bid for Mediterranean hegemony. Yet centralization outside his own person would threaten both his grip on power and his dictatorial prestige: he could not delegate the task of military preparation to others. And he appears to have lacked any sense of how decrepit and intellectually backward both the Italian army—the senior and predominant service—and Italian industry were and remained.[4] The regime thus embarked upon its career of

---

[4] See particularly (General) Mario Montanari, *L'esercito italiano alla vigilia della seconda guerra mondiale* (Rome, 1982), esp. p. 251 ('atavistic intellectual narrowness') and Antonio Sema, 'La cultura dell'esercito', in *Cultura e società negli anni del fascismo* (Milan, 1987), pp. 91–116. On industry, see the survey, based on the work of Lucio Ceva, Andrea Curami, and others, in MacGregor Knox, *Hitler's Italian Allies* (Cambridge, 2000), particularly pp. 42–6.

external violence from a position of weakness that derived both from its historical inheritance and from its own inadequacies. It nevertheless pursued the two paths to empire inherited from Liberal Italy persistently and concurrently: the Mediterranean and Africa on the one hand, and the Balkans on the other.

The quest for war, 1922–1934

Imperial self-assertion required first of all that Italy seize full control of the colonies it already possessed. The last Liberal governments had already inaugurated the reconquest of Libya, annexed in 1911–12 but never subdued. Mussolini intensified the process, subjugating most of Tripolitania by 1925–8 with armoured cars and aircraft, then sending out Badoglio to supervise the conquest of the guerrilla-infested mountains of Cyrenaica. The marshal carried out to the full his threat, made in his initial proclamation to the Arab population, to 'make war with methods and weapons so radical and powerful that they will be long remembered. . . . I shall destroy all, both men and things.' In the summer of 1930 Badoglio and his chief subordinate, the later Marshal Rodolfo Graziani, deported the entire nomadic population of Cyrenaica—up to 100,000 men, women, and children—to desert concentration camps, depriving the guerrillas of recruits, food, and intelligence about Italian troop movements. Perhaps 50,000 Libyans died from hunger, disease, maltreatment, and battle, along with up to 90 per cent of the sheep, goats, camels, and horses that were their livelihood. By 1931–2 the revolt was over, and Libya became an indispensable recruitment ground for native troops for use elsewhere. Somalia, Italy's desert colony on the Horn of Africa, had received similar treatment in 1923–8 under the command of the frenetic and brutal former leader of the *fascio* of Turin, Cesare Maria De Vecchi.

With France barring the way across north-west Africa, only Ethiopia—and the prospect both of avenging Liberal Italy's humiliation and of outflanking Britain's choke hold at Suez—remained. Italy had aspired in 1915–18 to acquire French and British Somaliland from its allies and thus encircle and throttle the one remaining independent African state. Britain and France had inevitably demurred. Mussolini nevertheless foresaw as early as the summer of 1925 the need 'to prepare . . . militarily and diplomatically in order to profit from a future disintegration of the Ethiopian empire'. But he recognized that Italy could not 'achieve a total violent solution unless there [was] chaos in Europe'.

That happy result was however elusive. In 1925–6 Mussolini deluded himself that Britain's conflict with Turkey over the oil of Mosul would cause London to welcome an Italian seaborne attack on Anatolia. But the Turks were prepared to fight, and London preferred to settle its disputes diplomatically without Italian help. Albania, a recognized Italian sphere since 1921, was more promising, and by 1926–7 Mussolini and his diplomats had fastened on its government a network of treaties that assured Italy's grip on the entrance to the Adriatic. That success in turn helped bring to incandescence Italy's always difficult relations with its post-1918 eastern neighbour, Yugoslavia.

The last Liberal governments and Contarini between them had succeeded at least in delimiting the much-disputed mutual border. But there prospects for Italo-Yugoslav amity had ended; Fascist Italy saw small powers only as satellites or victims. The quest for Adriatic hegemony had helped launch Italy into war in 1915. Nationalists and Fascists alike had aspired to rule Dalmatia. And the early Fascist movement had distinguished itself through bloody deeds against the Slovene inhabitants of the eastern borderlands acquired in 1918. The Fascist regime continued that campaign after 1922, inevitably provoking outrage in Belgrade.

The point of no return arrived in 1926–7, as Mussolini's increasing control over Albania and pressure on the Slovenes within Italy led Yugoslavia to order defensive military preparations and to seek assistance from France. The Duce, in full enjoyment of his new freedom from parliamentary opposition, reacted fiercely. In early 1927 he began supporting Macedonian terrorists operating against Yugoslavia and contracted secret agreements with Yugoslavia's hostile eastern neighbour, revisionist Hungary. That July he demanded of Badoglio and the service chiefs the 'systematic preparation' of a war against Yugoslavia involving an '*offensive* war plan' and a 'sudden aggressive attack'. War might come soon or late, 'but it will certainly come', a prediction Badoglio qualified by setting a planning date of 1932. Mussolini in turn intensified his efforts to encircle Yugoslavia, seeking to enlist both Greece and Turkey, his former designated victims, and Austria, which by 1927 Italy was seeking to dominate through lavish support of the paramilitary rightist *Heimwehr* movement.

Yugoslav and French countermeasures—the Franco-Yugoslav pact of November 1927 and French support for modernization of the Yugoslav army—soon made war appear daunting to Italian planners. The treaty seemingly promised a devastating French attack on Italy if Mussolini struck eastward, and Yugoslav rearmament appeared to cancel out the advantage in mobilization speed upon which Italian staffs had counted to ensure a breakthrough. Mussolini toyed with notions of a sudden attack on southern France (army contingency planners, in a moment of apparent lunacy, had in 1926 envisaged a lightning Italian drive along the French Riviera to Marseille). But subversion appeared less risky and more promising. In October 1929 Mussolini met personally with a leader of the newly formed Croat terrorist movement, and promised his support. Italian and Hungarian money, arms, and bases made possible a series of Croat raids on Yugoslavia and assassination attempts against its king over the following five years.

Yet terrorist pinpricks were no remedy for the strategic paralysis that French-Yugoslav cooperation imposed on Italy. Mussolini fell back on the long-standing hope that German resurgence would make possible what he had matter-of-factly described to Gàzzera in mid-1930 as 'the war with France and Yugoslavia'. He also sought in spring 1930 to rouse domestic opinion with thunderous speeches proclaiming Italy's warrior vocation: 'words are beautiful things, but rifles, machine guns, ships, aircraft, and cannon are still more beautiful.' The moneyed public reacted with shock; government bonds fell, endangering Italy's already precarious financial situation as the Great Depression deepened. Grandi, to whom Mussolini had delegated the foreign ministry in late 1929, consequently received a welcome chance to give Italian policy a pacifist façade aimed at undermining the position of France, Europe's most heavily armed state.

That façade did not last. The events of 1932 appeared to confirm Mussolini's long-standing expectation of German revival. At the Duce's orders, the Italian press loudly supported Adolf Hitler in the electoral campaigns that brought Nazism to the threshold of power. That summer and autumn, Mussolini abruptly dismissed Grandi for 'going to bed with England and France' and rendering Italy 'pregnant with disarmament', ordered his minister of war to 'study' the seizure of Corsica, and rejoiced in Japanese aggression in Manchuria. And in January 1933, prematurely convinced that the French were so hypnotized by the German threat that they would tolerate anything, he pressed Gàzzera to organize an attack on Croatia in cooperation with the terrorists.

That demand met with a resistance that demonstrated graphically the limits of Mussolini's power: Gàzzera insisted that war with France would lead to 'a lesson that would last us for a century'. He also appealed to the king, who predictably concurred. Mussolini thenceforth could find his longed-for war only in Africa—a lesson driven home by Yugoslav troop movements and rumours of French interest in a preventive attack on Italy before Hitler's Germany, as it had become on 30 January 1933, was ready for war. Mussolini responded in March 1933 with another round of bogus pacifism: a proposal for a consultative pact of the four Western European great powers. Ironically in view of Mussolini's concurrent description of such pacts as a 'formula to put [the democracies] to sleep', the Four-Power Pact or *Patto Mussolini* enjoys to this day a bizarre reputation as a genuine expression of the dictator's aims, of his alleged passion for assuming the role of mediator between the Western powers and Germany.[5] It certainly fulfilled its immediate purpose: diplomatic wrangling over its terms distracted the powers while the Italo-Yugoslav crisis slowly cooled.

In the event, and through no fault of his own, Mussolini found the new Germany a disquieting partner. Hitler's most powerful henchman, Hermann Göring, descended on Rome in April 1933 and disclosed to the Duce that National Socialism intended to seize power in Vienna as it had in Berlin. Mussolini had implied to his Hungarian allies in 1927 and to Grandi in March 1933 that he was willing to sacrifice Italy's Austrian buffer-state to secure the German alliance— not statements he had reason to make unless he meant them. But Göring's frontal assault, and still more the Nazi Putsch in Vienna of

---

[5] But see MacGregor Knox, *Common Destiny: Dictatorship, Foreign Policy, and War in Fascist Italy and Nazi Germany* (Cambridge, 2000), pp. 131–2, 135–6, and id., 'The Fascist Regime, its Foreign Policy and its Wars: An "anti-anti-Fascist" Orthodoxy?', *Contemporary European History*, 4: 3 (1995), pp. 353–4, 359–61.

July 1934 and the resulting murder of Mussolini's client, Chancellor Engelbert Dollfuss, forced the Duce to resist. He could not surrender the Austrian bastion to peremptory demands or to violence, or tolerate overt threats to the Brenner frontier, which practically all educated Italians regarded as the greatest of the strategic prizes for which Italy had paid an immense price in the Great War.

The result was a period of Italo-German hostility with paradoxical results: Mussolini's demonstrative deployment of troops at the Brenner after Dollfuss's death persuaded Paris that the dictator might prove a precious ally against Germany—a foolish conviction that opened the road to Italian aggression elsewhere. Even the final Croat terrorist spectacular, the murder at Marseille in October 1934 of King Alexander and the French foreign minister, Louis Barthou, furthered rather than destroyed the prospects for Italo-French agreement. Barthou's successor, the naive-unscrupulous Pierre Laval, sought skilfully to defuse Yugoslav and international outrage over the Marseille murders, in which Italian and Hungarian complicity was all too evident. Then Laval leapt nimbly over his predecessor's corpse to visit Rome and clinch an agreement with Mussolini in person in January 1935. France, it appeared, had recruited the Duce as a defender of the European status quo from the Brenner to the Rhine, and Italy had given up many of the treaty rights and protections France had accorded the largest Italian population in Africa, the southern emigrants who had settled over the previous half-century in Tunisia. But perhaps the publicly announced Rome Agreements were not the entire story.

'Founder of the Empire', 1935–1936

Appearances were indeed deceptive. Laval had already distinguished himself in Italian eyes in 1931 by seemingly offering to Grandi French backing for aggression in East Africa. Mussolini had reacted violently: Laval's remarks were a French trick to distract Italy from more rewarding prey in Europe. The Duce had nevertheless authorized planning for an attack from late 1932 onward, along with port and road improvements in Eritrea, the Red Sea colony that—as in the ill-fated Adowa campaign of 1896—was the predestined base for the main Italian expeditionary force. By autumn–winter 1934–5 Mussolini was ready: even King Alexander's murder had failed to trigger Yugoslavia's disintegration, the one scenario that might have persuaded king and generals to allow the Duce to risk conquest in Europe.

Instead, Mussolini demanded and Laval conceded the famous 'free hand' in Ethiopia. Laval, although concerned to preserve what a later age would describe as plausible deniability, assured Mussolini that 'he underst[ood] very well the Italian concept'. The French foreign minister could indeed scarcely have harboured illusions. In December 1934 a convenient fire-fight at the oasis of Wal-Wal, on the Ethiopian–Somali border, had given Mussolini's propaganda apparatus the necessary chance to pillory the alleged barbarism of Italy's chosen victim. Only violence could thenceforth ensure the 'Italian penetration in Ethiopia'—in Laval's own words—to which he had so readily consented.

A week before Laval's arrival—if the date on the document is to be believed—Mussolini had spelled out Italy's objectives in a memorandum for his immediate subordinates: '*the destruction of the Ethiopian armed forces and the total conquest of Ethiopia*; the Empire cannot be made in any other way.' Italy would strike in October 1935, and Mussolini promised the generals that he would spare neither blood nor expense: Italian forces would enjoy crushing superiority in vehicles, aircraft, artillery, and mustard gas against an enemy armed only with rifles. With French acquiescence and with widespread élite backing for 'avenging Adowa'—from the colonial and foreign ministries, to the navy, the air force, the ex-Nationalists, the Fascist Party, the initially reluctant army hierarchy, and the ever-hesitant Badoglio—Mussolini had no fear of the royal veto that had blocked him on Italy's eastern border.

In the weeks that followed Laval's contented departure from Rome, a Fascist war of national effort took shape. From February onward army and blackshirt militia units mobilized and embarked for the long journey through the Suez Canal to Eritrea and Somalia. By the end of the campaign the following year, Italy had deployed a well-equipped and lavishly supplied force of half a million men: 330,000 Italian troops, 87,000 East African and Libyan native troops, and 100,000 Italian labourers. The aim of this immense effort was not merely to crush Ethiopia quickly, before diplomatic pressure or complications in Europe forced Italy to relent. Mussolini aimed at a major war; only a great war could fuse the Italian people and his regime, and give him at last the personal prestige he would need to supplant the monarchy. And on the horizon, as Mussolini repeatedly stressed to close subordinates, was the ultimate prospect of encircling and conquering Egypt to free Italy from the 'servitude of the Suez canal'.

As Italian forces deployed, the British Foreign Office slowly awoke and cautiously sought to restrain Mussolini. But German rearmament—now well on its way to becoming the motor of world politics—caused Britain to handle the Duce gingerly. Mussolini was delighted to pose as the leader of a British-French-Italian anti-German 'front' that met at the lake resort at Stresa, near Milan, in April 1935. But his famous proviso—that the three powers, as they declared publicly, sought to preserve the peace *of Europe*—concealed a universe of duplicity which the statesmen of Britain and France unwisely declined to explore.

As summer drew on, British alarm grew. Anthony Eden, then at the beginning of his political career, visited Rome in June 1935 and sought to fob Mussolini off with scraps of territory while presenting Ethiopia with an outlet to the sea—an outcome Italy could not accept short of defeat in war. That ill-judged offer predictably met a proud dictatorial rebuff. Britain, caught between its public commitment to peace through the League of Nations—of which Ethiopia was a member—and the fatuous hope that Italy might yet prove a militarily valuable and politically dependable ally against Germany, unerringly chose the worst possible course. It deployed to the Mediterranean naval reinforcements capable of crushing Italy's fleet, then plaintively assured Mussolini that it sought above all else to avoid war. The naval deployment terrified both Badoglio (who judged that war with Britain would 'reduce us to a Balkan level') and the king. But Mussolini held firm in the supreme and justified confidence that London lacked the will to destroy him. On 3 October 1935, with 220,000 troops deployed on the far side of Britain's choke point at Suez, Italy attacked Ethiopia.

Mussolini's forces, after an initial leap forward of 15 kilometres, paused in November–December to resupply and reinforce; the army had to build roads as it moved. A courageous Ethiopian counter offensive briefly threatened the main Italian line of supply, then petered out under a hail of fire from Italian artillery, aircraft, and machine guns. By February 1936, with Badoglio as new theatre commander—a post to which he had laid claim by abandoning his initial hostility to the enterprise—and the army's forward supply dumps filled, Italy was ready. In three months of methodical advances preceded by powerful artillery concentrations, amid air strikes that included lavish use of mustard gas aerosol bombs on Ethiopian water supplies and communications, Badoglio defeated and dispersed the Ethiopian armies. As forces led by Graziani struck swiftly northward from Somalia, Badoglio launched a motorized column of army and Fascist militia troops toward the Ethiopian capital, Addis Ababa. The Italians secured the city on 5 May, as the emperor of Ethiopia fled into exile. Mussolini hailed before an immense and delirious crowd 'the reappearance, after fifteen centuries, of Empire above the fateful hills of Rome'.

Victory had its price. Britain shrank from using its overwhelming naval power and its effortless control at Suez of Italy's East African supply line. But London did dare to champion League of Nations sanctions against Italy, and dragged an embarrassed Laval to oppose the Italian aggression that France had helped unleash. Laval and his British counterpart, Sir Samuel Hoare, nevertheless had a last try in December 1935 at bribing Mussolini with parts of Ethiopia that he had already seized. The plan leaked to the press, Hoare resigned amid public outcry, and a secretly relieved Mussolini proclaimed Italy's resolve to fight on. Sanctions raised the already astronomical cost of Italy's war, and cut vital imports drastically. Yet the Western powers had no stomach for imposing an oil embargo, the one non-military step that promised eventual results. And Germany, with whose leader Mussolini had been clandestinely improving ties since May–June 1935, stepped in: from November 1935 to the end of 1936 it provided roughly two-thirds of Italy's all-important imports of coal.

Mussolini for his part proclaimed ever more insistently his long-standing contempt for the democracies; as Italian forces attacked in October he mocked to the German ambassador the 'age-enfeebled' forces of conservatism that sought to restrain new and dynamic nations such as Italy and Germany. And on 6 January 1936 he took a momentous step toward Germany. In a gesture that made sense only as a bid for the long-sought German alliance against the Western powers, the Duce urged Hitler, through the German ambassador, to make Austria 'in practical terms a satellite of Germany'. Later that month Mussolini assured a Hitler envoy that a 'community of destiny' joined the two dictatorial powers. When Hitler gave confidential notice in February 1936 that Germany intended to violate the Locarno security treaty—a step that would predictably overturn the strategic balance in Western Europe—Mussolini conveyed his approval. And Italy, as Mussolini had undertaken in January, gave its blessing to the Austro-German treaty of June 1936 that brought Austria within Berlin's growing sphere of influence.

Mussolini's diplomatic staff watched the abandonment of Austria and the approach of the German alliance with growing dread. But as 'founder of the Empire' Mussolini could now aspire to a degree of reverence that largely silenced discordant voices. He soon insulated himself further against unwanted advice by discarding his diplomatic advisers for a new foreign minister: his son-in-law, the young Galeazzo Ciano, a diplomat and propagandist by training with Fascist credentials freshly acquired through bombing Ethiopians. Mussolini nevertheless retained firm control over the main lines of foreign policy.

That policy did not waver, despite Britain's embarrassed abandonment of League sanctions and repeated conciliatory gestures. France, which acquired in June 1936 a Popular Front government supported by the Communists and led by a Socialist of Jewish descent, Léon Blum, attracted the particular vituperation of Mussolini and of the Fascist regime's tightly controlled press. Then, in July 1936, Spanish army plotters rose in bloody revolt against the Popular Front government of the Spanish republic. The emerging supreme leader of the plotters, General Francisco Franco, appealed immediately for Italian arms, and for aid in solving his immediate problem, that of ferrying his striking force of foreign legion and Moorish troops from Spanish Morocco to southern Spain. Italian air force intervention followed after brief hesitation. It was almost inconceivable, to use the language of a later era, that someone might give a war and Fascist Italy not attend. Fascist war against the Spanish republic was an ideological blow against France and a thrust toward domination of the western Mediterranean. It was also a further step forward in what Mussolini described to Ciano as Fascism's 'permanent revolution': 'When Spain is done, I'll think of something else: character must be instilled in the Italian people through combat.'

Ground forces that grew by early 1937 to roughly 50,000 men

followed the commitment of Italian air and naval units. Hitler likewise contributed an air transport and striking force, but German intervention was carefully calibrated to create the maximum distraction for France with minimum outlay for Germany, while encouraging an Italian overcommitment that weakened Italy's residual ability to maintain Austrian independence. Mussolini nevertheless continued on the path of ever-closer ties with Berlin inaugurated in January 1936. In October Ciano journeyed to Hitler's Bavarian mountain retreat—from which the Führer was pleased to show his guests spectacular views of his Austrian homeland—and secured agreements on mutual cooperation against the Western powers. And on 1 November 1936 Mussolini hailed in a speech in Milan the 'axis' between Rome and Berlin that now united the two dictatorships.

'An alliance to change the map of the world', 1937–1940

The Axis relationship, even before the military alliance signed in May 1939, was from the beginning the firmest bond with a foreign power that Fascist Italy ever formed. In October 1937, Ciano summed it up pithily with an echo of Mussolini's earlier words to the Germans: 'The *alliance* [emphasis added] between the two nations is above all based on the identity between their political regimes, which determines a common destiny.' That destiny led Mussolini to an enthusiastic visit to Germany in September 1937; he returned convinced he had found the ally he required for the 'inevitable' war against Britain and France. In November–December 1937 Italy joined the Berlin–Tokyo Anti-Comintern Pact, in reality directed against Britain rather than Soviet Russia, and at last left the League of Nations. Mussolini and Ciano revelled in Italy's membership in the 'most formidable military-political combine that has ever existed'.

Ciano nevertheless angled cynically in 1937 and early 1938 for an agreement with Britain that would recognize Italy's conquest of Ethiopia and growing power in the Mediterranean—and also further humiliate the French, whose alleged decadence Mussolini repeatedly and publicly mocked. But the twin fruits of that policy, the comically misnamed Anglo-Italian 'Gentlemen's Agreement' of January 1937 and the Easter agreement of 1938, were subordinate to Mussolini's pursuit of war alongside Hitler in Spain.

The central events of 1938 indeed confirmed and strengthened Mussolini's commitment to a 'common destiny' with National Socialist Germany. Hitler surprised his quasi-ally—not for the last time—with his lightning annexation of Austria in March 1938. But Mussolini's ready acquiescence to an outcome that was implicit in his abandonment of Vienna in 1936 earned Hitler's assurances of undying gratitude ('tell the Duce I will never forget this . . . never, never, never') and a solemn declaration that the Brenner frontier would remain inviolable 'for all time'. The creation of a 'Greater Germany' on Italy's northern border, even if compensated by German backing against France and Britain, was nevertheless a blow to Mussolini's domestic prestige that narrowed his foreign policy freedom—for a time. When Hitler visited Rome that May, Mussolini and Ciano politely evaded a German bid for a formal military alliance: Italian opinion was not ripe. That excuse was anything but bogus.

But Mussolini nevertheless immediately took two further swift and momentous steps on the path to war and ruin at Germany's side. He mounted an insistent racist campaign that culminated, in October–November 1938, in the passage of legislation similar to the Nuremberg Laws of 1935 by which Hitler and his party had divided the German population into 'Germans' and 'Jews'. Fascism's racist vocation dated from its origins, but had largely vented itself in Africa and against the Slavs of the borderlands. Now it came home with a vengeance: Fascist Italy and Nazi Germany stood united in persecution of their Jewish minorities. Worse still—in terms of maintaining national cohesion in the coming conflict—the regime turned on the Italian middle classes as well. The 'revolting craven bourgeoisie', with its rapidly increasing alarm at the regime's radicalization and its alleged admiration for English, French, and American ideas, fashions, and music, became the antithesis of Fascism and the regime's designated internal enemy.

And in the world of relations between states, Mussolini offered his enthusiastic public support to Germany's demands on Czechoslovakia in August–September 1938. The Western powers were too craven to fight—and if they should dare, Mussolini was confident of Axis victory: 'force of arms, irresistible force of the spirit'. Then Britain's prime minister, Neville Chamberlain, beseeched Rome to intercede so that war could be postponed long enough to allow Britain and France to present Hitler with the German-inhabited portions of Czechoslovakia that he ostensibly sought. Mussolini was evidently nonplussed but felt unable—as Ciano described the scene in his diary—to take on the heavy responsibility of refusing. If war came, the very national integration that Fascism sought would depend on the illusion that the Axis was blameless. Mussolini therefore presided as 'senior dictator'—not as a mediator, but as Hitler's Axis partner—at the conference held at Munich on 29–30 September 1938 at which Germany, Italy, Britain, and France dismembered Czechoslovakia. Jubilant crowds along the railway from the Brenner south to Rome cheered the returning Duce not as 'founder of the Empire' but as saviour of peace. His life's work of creating a warrior nation was evidently far from complete.

In the aftermath of Munich, Mussolini began negotiations for a tripartite Rome-Berlin-Tokyo war alliance, telling Hitler's foreign minister, Joachim von Ribbentrop, that 'we must not make a purely defensive alliance; . . . no one is thinking of attacking the totalitarian states. We want instead . . . an alliance to change the map of the world.' While pressing the attack domestically against Jews and 'craven bourgeoisie', he also picked a public quarrel with France. The French had crumbled at Munich, and might perhaps yield to Italian demands as well; their hostility was in any case necessary to make the German alliance palatable to Italian opinion. At the end of November, the Fascist legislature rang with orchestrated cries of 'Tunis, Corsica, Nice, Savoy'; that evening, in a secret speech to the Grand Council, Mussolini announced 'the immediate goals of Fascist dynamism': Albania, Tunis, Nice, Corsica, and possibly the Italian-speaking regions of Switzerland. A plaintive visit to Rome in January 1939 by Chamberlain and his foreign secretary, Lord Halifax, suggested to Mussolini that he need not fear Britain; these men were 'the tired sons of a long series of rich generations; and they will lose their Empire.' Less than a month later, Mussolini solemnly informed the Grand Council that Italy must secure its geopolitical independence by defeating Britain and France through a 'march to the ocean'.

Hitler's next surprise unnerved the Duce briefly: on 15 March 1939 Greater Germany tore up the Munich agreement and seized Prague—Germany's first conquest of an area not ethnically German. But

Mussolini recovered swiftly; he had committed his own prestige and the future of the regime to the German alliance, and could not retreat now. His reply was the almost bloodless seizure of Albania—many of whose leaders Ciano's agents had sapiently bribed—on Good Friday, 7 April 1939. The German war alliance, which Tokyo's foot-dragging and ultimate withdrawal had long delayed, swiftly followed. On 22 May 1939 Fascist Italy and National Socialist Germany solemnly signed the 'Pact of Steel'. As Mussolini had requested, the treaty had an offensive hair-trigger. Instead of the customary requirement that one of the parties be victim of 'unprovoked aggression' before the other was obligated to fight, the Axis pact became operative if either power became 'involved in warlike complications'. In an embarrassed postscript to Berlin, the Duce spelled out—along with fantastic plans for carving up the Balkans—a point the Italians had made to Ribbentrop during the negotiations: Italy desired to postpone the 'inevitable' war with the West until 1943, by which time Italy's armed forces would have fully rearmed.

Hitler replied that 'he was generally in full agreement' with the Italian position. He had however already set 1 September 1939 as the planning date for operations against Poland, and the day after Ribbentrop signed the Pact of Steel, the Führer informed his generals that he intended to attack 'at the first suitable opportunity'. As an intensifying propaganda barrage against Poland suggested that Germany, as in 1938, sought new conquests, Ciano journeyed north— not for the last time—to enquire diffidently what Hitler intended. On 11–13 August 1939 at Salzburg Hitler and Ribbentrop made clear that the German 'will to battle [was] implacable'.

The astonishing discovery that the Germans had 'tricked us and lied to us' shocked Ciano out of his support for Mussolini's radicalism; henceforth he sought intermittently to steer the Duce toward neutrality. But Mussolini resisted, despite the prospect that in a general war Italy would face alone the full weight of British and French naval power. The Allies—especially after the surprise announcement of Hitler's quasi-alliance with Stalin on 23 August 1939—might yet quail at war. Italy could then 'take [its] share of the booty in Croatia and Dalmatia'. In the end, only the lamentable unpreparedness and backwardness of the armed forces, the king's veto, and signs that Britain would fight restrained the Duce. A shamefaced request to Berlin for the eighteen million tons of strategic raw materials ostensibly needed before Italy could fight excused Mussolini's decision to announce Italy's 'non-belligerence'. Hitler graciously released the Duce from his obligations, as Germany attacked Poland on 1 September and the Western powers hesitantly declared war.

The Pact of Steel nevertheless remained in effect, for Mussolini burned with humiliation at Italy's failure to join Hitler's war. Through the long winter of 1939–40 the Duce meditated on a Mediterranean war 'parallel to that of Germany', and sought to delay any German attack in the West until Italy could strike. Hitler aimed to invade France without delay, but was still interested enough in well-timed Italian help—as a strategic distraction for the Western powers—to court Mussolini assiduously. In March 1940 he offered to provide Italy by rail, circumventing the British blockade, the full national annual requirement of twelve million tons of coal. That promise, Germany's lightning occupation of Norway and Denmark in April 1940, and above all Germany's swift and terrifying advance across France in May made an Italian war possible at last. By late May, as German armoured forces reached the Channel, the educated classes and the Establishment briefly entertained visions of a Mediterranean empire cheaply bought; perhaps the Duce was indeed always right.[6] The king resigned himself. Grandi the realist announced to Ciano his sudden conversion to war.

Badoglio and the generals and admirals had repeatedly confessed their impotence in the face of Anglo-French superiority, despite demands by Mussolini from March onward for at least an air-sea offensive 'all along the line'. But Hitler's triumph allowed the Duce to present his military leaders with a situation that met even Badoglio's exacting test for war: 'that a powerful German action . . . should have truly prostrated the enemy forces to such an extent that every audacity would be justified.' As the French army crumbled and the Royal Navy and RAF extricated Britain's battered army from Dunkirk, Mussolini chose the date of Italy's intervention. On 10 June Ciano delivered to the British and French ambassadors a solemn declaration of war, and Mussolini proclaimed from the balcony of Palazzo Venezia that Fascist Italy went to war to 'secure its maritime

---

[6] See the archive-based analyses of public opinion in MacGregor Knox, *Mussolini Unleashed, 1939–1941* (Cambridge, 1982), pp. 110–12, and Simona Colarizi, *L'opinione degli italiani sotto il regime 1929–43* (Bari, 1991), pp. 336–9.

frontiers' and achieve geopolitical freedom. The announcement, Ciano noted, did not 'arouse excessive enthusiasm' in the Roman crowd.

Fascist Italy's last war, 1940–1943

Mussolini's decision for war has seemingly held no mystery for contemporaries and historians. He 'declared war, in order not to fight it', in the words of Badoglio's chief assistant. The marshal himself, in his far from truthful memoirs, claimed that Mussolini had told him that he needed 'a few thousand dead' to entitle him to a seat at the forthcoming peace conference. But Badoglio had still pleaded for a month's further delay as late as 1 June; assurances of total military inactivity were Mussolini's only means of securing the agreement to war of his military chiefs and of the still-hesitant monarch.

Within five days, as the Germans took Paris, Mussolini had nevertheless ordered Badoglio point-blank to attack France across the Alps; Badoglio in essence refused. On 20 June, after meeting Hitler at Munich to agree on a joint position in the face of France's request for an armistice, the Duce confronted Badoglio, Graziani (now chief of staff of the army), and the chief of the air force, and over Badoglio's continuing hesitations ordered an immediate large-scale attack aimed at conquering southern France. That demand that his military subordinates actually fight was not Mussolini's last; the resulting massacre of Italian infantry by France's outnumbered defenders, whose main line of resistance the Duce's forces largely failed to reach, did not perturb the dictator in the slightest.

Simultaneously, the Duce had authorized Italy's theatre commander in Libya to operate in Egyptian territory, despite Badoglio's fears of a French attack from Tunisia on Italy's main Libyan base at Tripoli. After the French signed armistices with the Axis powers on 23–24 June, even Badoglio recognized that Italy was free to drive on Alexandria and Cairo. And Ciano and his assistants drew up an ambitious war aims catalogue: Nice, Corsica, Tunisia, and French Somaliland; Malta, Cyprus, British Somaliland, Aden at the mouth of the Red Sea and two strategic islands nearby; Egypt and the Suez canal; Syria, Lebanon, and Palestine; Iraq and its oil; and half of Switzerland.

In the event, the only prize that Mussolini secured—even temporarily—with his own unaided forces in the entire course of the war was a dusty and strategically useless corner of East Africa, British Somaliland. But rivalry with Hitler, fear of an Anglo-German compromise peace that would deprive Italy of its chosen booty, and what Ciano interpreted as his 'entire life's unrealized dream, glory on the battlefield' nevertheless drove Mussolini onward throughout the summer and autumn of 1940. The Duce's thirst for military glory was in reality far more than that. He sought, as he had since the 1920s, to acquire on the battlefield the prestige needed for the genuine Fascist revolution: the elimination of the monarchy, a drastic reduction of the influence of the Church, the remodelling of 'the Italians', and the fusion of Italian people and Fascist regime. That was why the regime—perversely in terms of the propaganda effect—loudly claimed this greatest of united Italy's wars as *la guerra fascista*. Monopoly over the prestige of victory was the first prerequisite for domestic revolution.

Victory seemed within Mussolini's grasp by September–October 1940. The Duce took comfort in Hitler's failure to invade Britain, remarking to Badoglio that a swift end to the war would be 'catastrophic'. His own ponderous offensive into Egypt, launched after much hesitation and delay by Marshal Graziani, paused for resupply in mid-September after penetrating a mere 80 kilometres. The admirals, after a brief and unfortunate encounter with the British fleet off southern Italy in July, announced that the navy would confine itself to supplying Libya. But Mussolini discovered—piqued by Hitler's occupation in early October 1940 of the Rumanian oilfields without, as usual, any warning to his ally—a new theatre where his military subordinates could not refuse to fight. Partly at Ciano's instigation, he determined to attack Greece ('an account payable since 1923'). Badoglio and the army appear to have had few qualms; the Greeks had no great reputation as fighters, and Ciano and his associates appear to have deluded themselves and others with the notion that bribery, as with Albania in 1939, would open the road to Athens.

Italy thenceforth fought simultaneously in the Mediterranean, Libya, and the Balkans. Disaster was immediate in all three theatres. Within a week of Italy's attack on 28 October 1940, the Greeks counter-attacked with skill and ferocity, eventually driving the Italian

army far back into Albania, while logistical c
primitive Albanian ports and the Italian theatre
in reinforcements piecemeal. Royal Navy carrier airc
Italian fleet at anchor in the shallow harbour of Taranto
of 11–12 November and temporarily sank three battleships. A
9 December 1940 until early February 1941, small but brillian
British mechanized forces destroyed Graziani's army in Egypt
eastern Libya, taking 130,000 prisoners. In the following months Brit
ish forces advancing from the Sudan likewise overran Italy's East
African empire.

These stinging defeats did not merely end Mussolini's war 'parallel
to that of Germany'—although Italy indeed had to plead for German
air support and ground troops for the Mediterranean and Africa. The
scale of defeat, its variety and simultaneity, and the fact that it
occurred at the hands of enemies—the putatively decadent British
and above all the unwisely despised Greeks—whom Fascism had
mocked for twenty years, meant the ideological death of the regime.
German power could still for a time maintain Mussolini as a vassal.
Victor Emanuel III had a healthy fear of ending in a cage at one of
Hitler's camps, and the public was too stunned by defeat to protest.
In summer 1942 the successes of the German Afrika Korps and
Luftwaffe even promised Mussolini a triumphal entry into Cairo. But
German tanks on the streets of Cairo could not have saved the Fascist
revolution; it had died in winter 1940–1 in the Albanian mountains
and the Egyptian and Libyan deserts.

The strategic direction of Italy's war largely passed to the Germans
once their forces reached the Mediterranean and Africa and overran
Yugoslavia, Greece, and Crete in January–May 1941. Yet even thereafter Mussolini and his generals managed to plunge Italy into further
and even greater disasters. The Duce remained obsessed with proving
Italy in the 'comparative examination' of war in any theatre in
which his ally was engaged. He committed by 1942 almost one-third
of the Italian army as auxiliaries to the Germans in savage Balkan
counter-insurgency campaigns. And he insisted—even against
Hitler's express wish—on sending Italian forces to join Germany's
racist war of annihilation against Soviet Russia. By autumn 1942
an Italian army of 229,000 men guarded the northern flank of the
German drive on Stalingrad; by the time the battered remnants
returned to Italy in spring 1943, almost 60 per cent of the original

...aos reigned in the
...command threw
...raft struck the
...n the night
...nd from
...ly led
...and

itated by frostbite, or missing in

Mussolini's strategic inspirations.
ly unable to comprehend that
s, were the decisive weapon of
te 1942 no one in the regime's
perceived Italy's true strategic
assistants had so little under-
er that they apparently never
claration of war on the United
r 1941. In November 1942, as
the German-Italian forces in Egypt at El
Alamein, the avalanche descended: the United States and Britain
invaded the French colonies of north-west Africa.

The Axis in response sought to hold Tunisia with fresh troops and
the remnants of the German-Italian army that had fled Egypt. The
result rivalled Stalingrad as a strategic defeat, if not in extent of carn-
age. A quarter of a million Axis veterans, committed across a sea and
airspace that the Axis navies and air forces could not command, surrendered with their equipment to the British and Americans in May
1943. Ever-intensifying American air bombardment of Italian ports,
railways, airfields, and cities followed; on 10 July 1943 Anglo-American
forces invaded Sicily. As US heavy bombers shattered Rome's rail
yards and housing areas on 19 July, Mussolini met Hitler in north Italy
to seek an exit from the war. But the Duce failed to summon up the
nerve to interrupt Hitler's customary torrential monologue.

As king and generals consequently prepared feebly and belatedly to
separate the Italian state from the Fascist regime by removing the
Duce, Grandi and Ciano engineered the fatal vote against their leader
at the Grand Council of Fascism of 24–25 July 1943. Mussolini's
deposition and arrest immediately followed; his regime was by now
so unloved that no one—with the exception of the chief of the official
press wire service, who committed suicide—died for it. In bringing
ruin and humiliation upon Italy, it had seemingly betrayed the very
Italian nationalism from which it derived and which it claimed to
monopolize. Even its much-appreciated role as guardian of the social
order was no longer credible; it had failed to drown in blood the great
strikes that spread from Turin across north Italy in March 1943.

The king and generals, whose tradition of military malpractice had contributed almost as much to national catastrophe as the dictator's megalomania, inevitably bungled utterly Italy's exit from the Axis. While secretly negotiating with Americans and British for an armistice, they invited or tolerated the deployment to Italy of large, well-armed, and vengeful German forces. When the armistice came in September 1943, the king and high command cravenly fled Rome for British protection, deliberately leaving the armed forces leaderless and condemning 600,000 Italian soldiers to Hitler's camps. But that outcome in no way obscured what Ciano ironically described as the ultimate proof of Mussolini's genius: 'the depth of the abyss into which he ha[d] plunged Italy'. The savage Fascist remnant that fought on across north Italy in 1943–5 for the Duce's puppet 'Italian Social Republic' returned to its original essence as a passionate minority. *Guerra fascista* in alliance with Hitler had destroyed Italian nationalism as a mass ideological force.[7]

Conclusion: 'one man alone'?

As Italy's armies crumbled in December 1940, Winston Churchill sought to separate the Italian people from dictator and regime in a famous broadcast speech:

One man, and one man alone . . . against the Crown and Royal Family of Italy, against the Pope and all the authority of the Vatican and of the Roman Catholic Church, against the wishes of the Italian people, who had no lust for this war, [had] arrayed the trustees and inheritors of ancient Rome upon the side of the ferocious pagan barbarians.

Churchill's brilliant rhetoric was better political warfare than it was history. Responsibilities were more widely distributed. The Duce's ideological lunacy had deep roots. He had taken the politics of Oriani, of the Nationalists, and of the pre-1914 avant-garde and had made them into the credo of a paramilitary mass movement. Along with the geopolitical notions largely borrowed from the Italian navy, that credo had then inspired a foreign policy that had sought—

---

[7] See the much-denounced reflections of Ernesto Galli della Loggia, *La morte della patria* (Rome–Bari, 1996), and the sober account of events in Elena Agarossi, *A Nation Collapses* (Cambridge, 1999).

beneath the mask ably held up to foreign audiences by Italy's diplomatic professionals—to remake the Italian state and people through war.

That aim had enjoyed wide acceptance because Mussolini had promised success in a long-thwarted enterprise—the creation of true national integration and the elevation of Italy to great power status—in which most educated Italians believed. Their belief had made aggression against Ethiopia the most popular of all the many wars of united Italy, and had given Mussolini the prestige to pursue his 'permanent revolution' in Spain and to clinch the long-sought German alliance. Hitler had in turn through his conquest of France in 1940 briefly liberated Mussolini to be himself with the support—or at least the willing suspension of disbelief—of Italy's élites. The abyss that opened thereafter consumed both the nationalist traditions descended from the Risorgimento and Italy's very independence as a state, as Hitler's far more grandiose enterprise consumed the nationalism and independence of Germany and of all Europe.

Fascism in power: the totalitarian experiment

Emilio Gentile

Why totalitarian?

Historians have variously described Italy's Fascist regime as an authoritarian nationalist regime, as a personal 'monocracy', a 'tendentially totalitarian State', 'an imperfect totalitarian state', and as an 'incomplete totalitarian state'. Others have simply described Fascism as *Mussolinismo*, arguing that Mussolini created a personal dictatorship based on an alliance with the traditional institutions of the Italian monarchist state that left the fundamental structures of the old regime virtually unchanged. To support this, they claim that Mussolini carried out the 'political liquidation' of the Fascist Party, which he then turned into a vast bureaucracy whose function was simply to orchestrate parades, organize consensus, create jobs and positions.

Until quite recently these interpretations of the nature of the Fascist regime were endorsed by a majority of historians, but studies published since the 1970s have forced us to reassess many of the most fundamental features of the regime and the role of the Fascist Party. These recent studies have made available important new information and new understanding on aspects of the regime that range from the role of ideology to institutional organization, and from mass politics to foreign policy, which indicate that Italian Fascism is best under-stood and interpreted as 'Italy's road to totalitarianism'.[1]

Since the term 'totalitarianism' has given rise to endless contro-versy, we must start by defining the meaning that will be attached to it in this chapter. The terms 'totalitarian', 'totalitarianism', 'total dictatorship', and 'party-state' were first invented in the years between 1923 and 1925 by the intellectual and political opponents of Fascism. They used these terms to pinpoint what made the Fascist dictatorship different from traditional dictatorial governments. The most novel feature of what many anti-Fascists were already calling a new 'experiment in government' was seen to be the determin-ation to concentrate a total monopoly of political power in the hands of a single political party which was committed to imposing its ideology as a form of secular religion. In April 1923 the anti-Fascist historian Luigi Salvatorelli wrote that Fascism aimed at achieving 'a total party dictatorship': 'it aims at the dictatorship of the party and the establishment of a "single party", which means the suppression of all other political parties, or in other words the end of political life as it has been understood in Europe over the last century'.[2]

In October of the same year the liberal anti-Fascist Giovanni Amendola, who was probably the inventor of the term 'totalitarian', insisted that the fundamental feature of the Fascist movement was a ' "totalitarian spirit" which means that in future no day would dawn without being greeted with the Roman-style Fascist salute' and which had unleashed in Italy 'a particular form of "war of religion" in the attempt to impose its ideology as a form of faith to be obligatory for all Italians'.[3]

A few months earlier a Catholic anti-Fascist had written of Mus-solini's claims to be 'the only interpreter and repository of the new religion of the fatherland':

'we are faced by a new dogmatic religion equipped with its own sacraments and its own infallible leader. Anyone who fails to love the fatherland in the ways desired by Benito Mussolini and in conformity

---

[1] For bibliographical references, please refer to the Further reading section.

[2] 'Secondo tempo', in *La Stampa*, 25 Apr. 1923.

[3] [G. Amendola], 'Un anno dopo', in *Il Mondo*, 2 Nov. 1923, in id., *La democrazia italiana contro il fascismo, 1922–1924* (Milan–Naples, 1960), p. 193.

with the rites that he has established is a heretic to be consigned to the purifying fire of the muskets of the national militia.'[4]

Early in 1925 and before Mussolini's speech of 3 January that set out the totalitarian programme that opened the way to the one-party state, the Marxist Lelio Basso had written:

The Fascist state no longer limits itself to defending the established order by means of a legal system devised for that purpose. . . . It now claims to represent the entire people and therefore excludes the possibility that there could be any political movement opposed to it or different from it, and should such a movement meekly show itself, it will immediately attempt to destroy it totally. When we have reached the point when the institutions that in theory embody the three powers of the state (the monarchy, the parliament and the magistracy, as well as the armed forces which translate their will into action) become the instruments of a single party that claims to be the interpreter of a unanimous will and of an undivided totalitarianism that shuts out the possibility of any further progress, we can confidently claim that the crisis of the state will have reached its climax and that the only alternatives remaining will be that either the crisis is resolved or that the state collapses.[5]

The term 'totalitarian' and its derivatives began to be used by the Fascists themselves after 1925, who adopted it as a badge of identity that defined their own conception of politics and of the state. This was based on the idea that all power should be concentrated in the hands of the party and its leader, and that the *fascistizzazione* of Italian society would be achieved through the expansion of the power exercised by the Fascist Party. This would extend to every aspect of social life to bring about what Mussolini referred to as 'the reformation of the character of the Italians' that was needed to make the Italians a race of conquerors and rulers.

In the following years, the anti-Fascists took up the concept of the totalitarian state and regime to describe all new one-party regimes. Luigi Sturzo, the founder of the Catholic Popular Party (PPI) who had been forced into exile in 1924, wrote in 1926, for example, that Fascism was advancing along the path 'towards "totalitarianism and absolutism"'.

During his imprisonment in the early 1930s Antonio Gramsci

---

[4] N. Papafava, 'Il fascismo e la costituzione', in *Rivoluzione Liberale*, 23 Aug. 1923.
[5] Prometeo Filodemo [L. Basso], 'L'antistato', in *Rivoluzione Liberale*, 2 Jan. 1925.

would also formulate a concise definition of the concept of 'totalitarian politics':

It is always the case that an individual belongs to more than one particular association and is often a member of associations that are in conflict with one another. The tendency of a totalitarian political system is to ensure (i) that the members of a given political party find within this single party the satisfactions that they had previously derived from a range of different organizations, thereby breaking the ties that previously connected these individuals to external cultural organizations; (ii) to destroy all other forms of organization or to incorporate them into a system which is controlled exclusively by a single party.[6]

After the Second World War, however, the term 'totalitarianism' and its derivatives lost their original meanings and became part of the armoury of Cold War propaganda and invective, and as a result were discredited as models for political or historical analysis. But the abuse and misuse of the terms in that period is no reason for banning them forever, and so long as they are understood in the terms in which they were originally defined by the opponents of the Italian Fascists they remain essential for understanding the nature of Fascism in Italy.

Totalitarianism and the nature of Fascist politics

The development of the Fascist regime in Italy is best studied, therefore, in terms of the concept of 'totalitarianism' as it was defined by those who first devised the term and with the meanings illustrated in the quotations cited above. This offers a valid explanation not only of the nature, but also of the dynamics of Fascism in power. Here 'totalitarianism' has the meaning of an experiment in political power undertaken by a revolutionary party with an integralist understanding of politics. The objective was to establish monopolist control over all forms of political power. Once that had been achieved by legal and illegal means, the aim was to destroy or radically transform the existing political system in order to create a new state organized around a single political party, flanked by the apparatus of a police state, and by the systematic use of terror to prevent or repress all forms of opposition and dissent.

---

[6] A. Gramsci, *Quaderni del carcere*, Vol. II, ed. V. Gerratana (Turin, 1975), p. 800.

The origins, nature, and dynamic of the Italian experiment in totalitarianism cannot be understood, however, without taking account of the specific nature of the political party from which it originated. The central objective of the totalitarian party, beyond the acquisition of a monopoly of political power, is to conquer and change society, in other words to subordinate, integrate, and regiment those governed on the basis of an ideology that asserts the *primacy of politics* in every aspect of human life. Totalitarian politics are based on the idea that the meanings and purpose of human life are expressed in myths and values that constitute a secular religion whose aim is to make the individual and the masses one. It therefore aims to bring about an *anthropological revolution* that will create a new type of human being, totally dedicated to achieving the political aims of the totalitarian party.

The concept of totalitarianism that we shall use in this chapter is not intended to imply, however, any underlying similarity between different totalitarian regimes. Defining totalitarianism as an experiment in political domination serves above all to emphasize that this was a *continuing process*, and hence it cannot meaningfully be judged to have been 'complete' or 'perfect'. No historical example of a totalitarian regime can be considered to have been 'complete' or 'perfect', because these are categories that exist only as abstract ideal-type models of the totalitarian state. History, by contrast, provides us with no examples of totalitarian experiments that were not subject to limitations, obstacles and resistance.

Nor was the Fascist totalitarian experiment limited simply to internal politics. Indeed, Fascist foreign policy was driven by the same objectives and its aim was to create an empire. The ultimate failure of Fascism was inseparable, therefore, from the ambitions for totalitarian power which drove the regime continuously to seek to acquire ever greater internal power and at the same time committed it to the pursuit of aggrandisement and territorial conquests overseas.

Mussolini and Fascism

The Fascist totalitarian experiment was closely associated with Mussolini, but was never simply Mussolini's personal creation. It has to be remembered that while Mussolini had been the original founder of the Fascist movement in 1919, he was not the main cause of its expansion or success after 1920. Fascism became a mass movement after 1920 as a result of what was termed *squadrismo*, the creation of paramilitary squads, each with their own charismatic local leader, organized at a provincial and local level. As a result, Mussolini had found himself faced by a major rebellion in the summer of 1921 when the provincial leaders of Fascism opposed his decision to enter into a 'pact of pacification' with the Socialists. Even after he came to power, Mussolini had to bow to the integralist Fascists who were demanding a much faster seizure of power by the Fascist Party and the immediate transformation of the liberal regime into a new state that would be controlled by the Fascist Party. Until as late as 1926 Mussolini was still not recognized as the unchallenged leader by many of the leaders of 'provincial Fascism'.[7]

In 1919 the Fascist movement had been born as an 'anti-party' that looked to recruit those who had no place in traditional political parties. Fascism was presented as a pragmatic, anti-dogmatic, anticlerical, and republican political movement that advocated radical institutional, economic, and social reform. The Fascists were contemptuous of parliamentary government and liberalism; they supported the activist politics of minority groups and were prepared to use violence and the politics of the street both in support of Italy's territorial demands at the Peace Conference and to combat the socialists.

Between 1919 and 1920 Fascism was of little significance, however. Its expansion began only after the collapse of the workers' occupation of the factories in the autumn of 1920, at which point the Fascists placed themselves at the head of the bourgeois reaction. It was at this point that Fascist squads, now armed and organized on a paramilitary basis, began a series of violent offensives that in the space of only a few months shattered the workers' organizations in the Po Valley and in central Italy, where they had previously been strongest and most numerous. This *squadrismo* was the real beginning of Fascism as a mass movement.

After 1920 the expansion of the Fascist movement was extremely rapid. Membership rose from 20,165 in December 1920 to 187,588 in May 1921 when the Fascists took part in the parliamentary elections

---

[7] See E. Gentile, 'Mussolini's Charisma', *Modern Italy*, Nov. 1998, 219–35.

and returned thirty-five deputies. But this mass party was already something quite different from the original Milanese fascism, and was essentially a composite of many different 'provincial fascisms' whose principal strength came from the Po Valley and Tuscany. By contrast, the Fascists had made little impact in the industrial regions and were virtually non-existent in the south, except for Apulia.

Strengthened by this rapid expansion, the Fascists fought the election campaign of 1921 on the slate of the 'National Coalition' headed by the Prime Minister Giovanni Giolitti. The aged statesman believed he could put an end to *squadrismo* by bringing the Fascists into the parliamentary system, but the plan failed. The Fascists obtained thirty-five seats, but Mussolini used this electoral success to force the collapse of Giolitti's government while the squads kept up their violent attacks on the socialists, communists, republicans, and the anti-Fascists in the Catholic PPI. A new government headed by Ivanoe Bonomi (June 1921–February 1922) tried to end the political violence by sponsoring an agreement between the Fascists, the Socialists, and the leaders of the principal trade union, the General Confederation of Workers (CGL) to abjure violence which was signed on 3 August 1921. This was the 'pacification pact' that the majority of the leaders of provincial *squadrismo*, including Pietro Marsich, Dino Grandi, Italo Balbo, and Roberto Farinacci, rejected outright, openly challenging Mussolini's right to act as leader of the Fascist movement. The crisis was one of the most critical points in the history of Fascism, and ended in a compromise reached at the congress held in Rome in November 1921. Mussolini's role as leader or 'duce' was recognized, but in return the movement was transformed into a political party, the Partito Nazionale Fascista (PNF), and the leaders of the squads forced Mussolini to abandon the pacification pact and acknowledge that *squadrismo* was the essence of the new party.

As a social movement, the main support for Fascism came from both the traditional and newer urban and provincial middle classes. The middling groups in Italian society had expanded notably in the early decades of the twentieth century. Between 1901 and 1921 they had risen from 51.2 to 53.3 per cent of the active population, in contrast to the wealthier bourgeoisie that had remained at 1.7 per cent while the working class had dropped from 47.1 to 45.0 per cent. The expansion of the lower middle classes had been most marked in the North (10%), in comparison with 7.1 per cent in Central Italy and only 2.0 per cent in the South. The largest contribution to this expansion had come from new landowners, who had risen from 18.3 per cent in 1911 to 32.4 per cent in 1921. The expansion in the peasant middle classes was concentrated primarily in Lombardy (increasing from 18.29% to 26.54%), in Emilia (from 13.33% to 20.26%), and in the Veneto (from 22.59% to 29.53%), that is to say precisely in the regions where Fascism had first developed as a mass movement. The vast majority of the organizers of the *Fasci* and leaders of *squadrismo* were from the lower middle classes. In 1922 of 127 national and provincial political officers, 77 per cent had lower middle class backgrounds as opposed to only 4 per cent from bourgeois families, while only one federal secretary was a worker. In terms of occupations, there were lawyers (35%), journalists (22%), teachers (6%), employees (5%), engineers (4.7%), army officers (4.7%), insurance agents (3%), and farmers (3%). Of some thousand Fascist leaders who ran local organizations, 80 per cent came from lower middle class backgrounds, 10.5 per cent from the bourgeoisie, and only 5 per cent were proletarians: the occupational groups most strongly represented were public employees (12%), students (9.5%), lawyers (9%), landowners (7.62%), artisans (7%), teachers (7%), farmers (6.7%), accountants (6%), manual workers (5%), and engineers (3.65%).

Youth was also a distinctive feature of the new movement. Of the thirty-five deputies elected in 1921, four were younger than 29 (which meant that they were below the legal age to be elected), and fourteen were aged between 30 and 40. Of the 101 federal secretaries in office before the 'March on Rome', half were under 32 years of age. Overall, the average age of the leaders of the Fascist federations was 31.8. The average age of the members of the National Directorate of the PNF, when it was founded, was 32.9, in contrast to an average of 45.2 for the Socialist Party, 37.7 for the Popular Party, and 36.7 for the Communist Party.

The 'militia-party' and the seizure of power

The youth of the new party gave the violence of the Fascist squads and the hostility towards liberal democracy the appearance of a generational revolt and almost of a struggle between two different and incompatible 'anthropological types'. The Fascists hated their adversaries on the left, the socialists and the communists, whom they considered as human beings with quasi-animal features that made them uniquely bloodthirsty and destructive. But they also despised the liberal bourgeoisie, whom they portrayed as timid and superannuated politicians with no sense of idealism or grandeur, because they had degenerated and been corrupted by the politics of compromise and clientelism.

The majority of the militants of the PNF had served in the Great War, which for many of them had been a genuine initiation into politics. As a result Fascism had come into being as a militia-party, not because the Fascist Party had an armed paramilitary force from the start but because Fascism made the *militarization of politics* its key identifying feature. Fascism institutionalized the militarization of politics through its organizational structures, through its ideology, values, and patterns of behaviour, and through the methods of political combat it used. Fascist culture rejected rationalism, exalted mythical thought, and set up as the highest form of political consciousness a secular religion rooted in a cult that combined worship of the fatherland with the community sense of camaraderie, the ethic of combat and the principles of hierarchy. The nationalist and anti-democratic ideology of the militia-party was expressed through myths, rituals, symbols, and a 'lifestyle' in which the militarization and the *sacralization of politics* were combined in ways that were both original and effective.

This continued to be the essential distinguishing feature of Fascism after the establishment of the regime. The Fascists claimed a 'privileged difference' that set them apart from all other political parties, and they saw themselves as a *new aristocracy* that had been forged in the wartime experience of the trenches and during the civil war against the 'internal enemy' that had followed. The Fascist mission was to regenerate politics and create a new state founded on the dogma of the nation and on the privileged role of the Fascist Party, which was the only party capable of expressing the will of the nation. For that reason, the Fascist Party alone had the right to govern Italy and lead it to the conquest of new greatness. While they condemned bourgeois society as materialist and individualist, the Fascists nonetheless defended private property and praised the leadership qualities of the productive bourgeoisie. While they advocated the need for inter-class co-operation (*corporativism*), they accepted that the sub-ordination of the working class to the bourgeoisie was the best way to maximize production (*productivism*) and hence to provide the material resources needed to make Italy a great power and to support imperial expansion. With regard to the liberal state, the Fascists also asserted their privileged diversity which, they claimed, placed them above the law because they were the sole interpreters of the will of the nation. All this, in short, served to legitimate violence and the domin-ation which the Fascist Party had imposed over many regions of northern and central Italy, to the resounding cheers of the bourgeois nationalists and the consent, from motives either of sympathy or weakness, of the political and military authorities, who looked on the Fascists as defenders of the fatherland and of order.

By 1922 the PNF already had over 200,000 members, a private army, women's and youth associations, and trade unions with over half a million members. It was the most powerful and dynamic political party at a moment when all the other Italian political parties, and especially those of the left, were in crisis caused by internal divisions that made them more interested in fighting amongst themselves than in uniting against the Fascists. But they were also subject to unrelent-ing violence from the Fascist squads. Throughout most of northern and central Italy the PNF had by now established unchallenged control and was beginning to operate like a state within a state. To flout their strength and to challenge the liberal state, the *squadristi* staged care-fully orchestrated occupations of whole towns, cities, and provinces to force the resignation of administrations run by their political opponents, or to obtain concessions from the government and even, as occurred in Bologna in 1922, to demand and obtain the removal of a government prefect deemed to be hostile to Fascism. The Fascist Party openly avowed its aversion to democracy and the liberal state. Dem-ocracy, Mussolini stated in August 1922 'has done its work. The century of democracy is over. Democratic ideologies have been liquidated.'[8]

In preparation for the seizure of power, the militia-party took responsibility both for defending the existing institutional, economic and social structures and for implementing a political revolution through which a new state would be constructed that neither in theory nor in practice would tolerate the coexistence of any other

---

[8] B. Mussolini, 'Fiera di "Demos"', in *Il Popolo d'Italia*, 19 Aug. 1922.

political parties. As far as outlook, organization, methods of political conflict, and ideology were concerned, the blueprint for the future Fascist totalitarian experiment had already been drawn up within the party. In July 1922 the anti-Fascist paper *La Stampa* noted that:

Fascism is a movement that strives with all its means to gain control over the state and the entire life of the nation in order to establish an absolute and unique dictatorship. The fundamental means for achieving this, in the programme and in the intentions of the leaders and their followers, is the complete suppression of all public and private constitutional liberties, which is to say the destruction of the Constitution and the entire liberal state that was the creation of the Italian Risorgimento. Once that dictatorship is established, for any institution to exist it must take no action nor utter any word except that of total dedication and obedience to Fascism. Only at that point will it be prepared to suspend the use of violence, for lack of targets, while always reserving the right to revive it at the first sign of any new resistance.[9]

The project for the March on Rome came about after the failure of an attempt by the Alliance of Labour to organize a 'legalitarian strike' in protest at Fascist violence early in August 1922. The PNF reacted by taking violent reprisals and destroying what remained of the workers' organizations. Once again the weakness of the liberal state was evident, as was the inability of the anti-Fascist parties to reach any agreement that might have given rise to a government capable of restoring the authority of the state. During the summer and autumn of 1922 and right up to the March on Rome, the Fascists continued to wage a violent offensive against their political opponents and against those representatives of the state who failed to support them, while the Liberal government proved completely unable to check the escalating violence of the *squadristi*. The PNF now developed new tactics for the revolutionary seizure of power that combined terrorist actions with political manoeuvres. Fascist insurrections in many cities in northern and central Italy led to the occupation of many government buildings, post offices, and railway stations and would certainly have collapsed had there been a direct confrontation with the army. But the Fascists succeeded because they were able to sow confusion within the highest political levels of the state, while Mussolini was at the same time negotiating his rise to power with the leaders of the Liberal regime and the world of business and finance.

[9] 'Il Governo e la Destra', in *La Stampa*, 18 July 1922.

For that reason, the March on Rome brought the highest returns at minimal risk. It wrecked attempts to form a new government led by Salandra or Giolitti, which the monarchy together with many industrialists and moderate Fascists would have supported, and resulted instead in a government headed by Mussolini, when the king refused to end the Fascist insurrection by proclaiming a state of emergency. On 31 October Mussolini formed his government, which included Liberals, the Popolari, Democrats, and Nationalists. With overwhelming majorities it obtained votes of confidence in both the Chamber of Deputies and in the Senate that conceded full powers to enable the new prime minister to implement fiscal and administrative reforms. But parliamentary approval could not hide the gravity of what had happened. For the first time in the history of European liberal democracy, government had been entrusted to the leader of a militia-party whose parliamentary representation was small, which openly repudiated liberal democracy, exalted the militarization of politics, and proclaimed its revolutionary determination to bring authoritarian changes to the state.

The timing of the consolidation of the Fascist seizure of power was determined by the expansion of Fascist power and the introduction of laws that effectively destroyed the parliamentary system. In the first phase, Mussolini established a political coalition with the parties willing to collaborate with him while at the same time working to disunite them, and he also brought the Nationalist Association into the PNF (February 1923). Legal means of repression were used against the anti-Fascist parties, but they continued to be the targets of the violence of the *squadristi*. The same combination of terrorism and government intervention was used by the Fascists to rapidly complete the seizure of control of local government. Immediately after the March on Rome Mussolini launched the Fascist takeover of the southern provinces. This was again achieved by using the powers of the state exercised in each province by the prefect, together with the creation of new *Fasci* in the South which recruited the local notables and the mass of new lower middle class and bourgeois militants eager for positions and power.

This caused a major crisis for the Fascist Party, however, as thousands of new adherents rushed to jump on the bandwagon, and the rapid expansion in membership split the party into rival camps of moderates and intransigents. In many provinces dissident and independent *Fasci* were formed that opposed the line of the party and the government, and appealed instead to the ideals of what was vaguely defined as 'original fascism'.

The central conflict was between the 'revisionism' of those who advocated the normalization and demilitarization of the PNF and the 'integralism' of the intransigent Fascists who insisted on the supremacy of the 'militia-party' and were determined to continue to use violence until the Fascist revolution had brought about the total conquest of power and had created a new state. After the March on Rome Mussolini had tried to deprive the PNF of its independence and subordinate it to his command. In December 1922 he established a new institution, the Fascist Grand Council, of which he was president, and which included the leaders of the party and the party representatives who held office in the government. The new body took over control of the party and also acted as a form of 'shadow government' in which the laws that would transform Italy's parliamentary democracy were first drafted, before being submitted to the cabinet and being approved by the parliament. The first of these laws established the MVSN (Voluntary Militia for National Security, 14 January 1923) which legalized the squads but placed them under the control of the head of the government.

Mussolini tried to keep an ambiguous stance between the politics of terrorism and normalization, therefore, alternatively backing then restraining the violence of the squads as circumstances required. But his principal objective was always to strengthen his own power through a compromise with the traditional élites. In order to acquire a larger and stronger parliamentary majority he introduced an electoral reform, known as the Acerbo Law, which had been drafted by the Fascist Grand Council and which assigned additional seats to the coalition that gained the highest number of electoral votes. The law was approved by the Chamber of Deputies in July 1923 and first came into effect in the elections of April 1924. These were held in a climate of extreme violence and intimidation, and returned an increased government majority that was now composed mainly of Fascists, who received many more votes than the representatives of the old Liberals who were still supporting the government.

The assassination on 10 June 1924, immediately after the elections, of the socialist deputy Giacomo Matteotti by a group of *squadristi* acting on orders from Mussolini's closest advisers provoked a huge outcry that seriously shook Mussolini's government. A majority of the anti-Fascist deputies decided to leave their seats in parliament until a new government capable of restoring order and ending Fascist violence could be formed. The government was now also losing support amongst those political parties that had originally supported the Fascists, and was also being opposed by the bourgeois press and by many industrialists. Demands were growing for the restoration of constitutional government and the rule of law, as well as an end to Fascist violence.

Mussolini was only able to avoid disaster because the anti-Fascist opposition proved incapable of taking political advantage of the situation, and above all because the monarchy and those who looked to it for political leadership were willing to continue supporting the government on the condition that it would implement a policy of normalization and bring Fascist illegality to an end. The Matteotti crisis had, however, given the integralist Fascists, and especially the leaders of the provincial squads (or *ras* as they were called by the anti-Fascists), the opportunity to regain the initiative. At the end of 1924 it was they who demanded that the Duce take the decisive steps toward setting up the forms of authoritarian government that would provide the basis for the dictatorship of the party.

Mussolini's speech to the Chamber of Deputies on 3 January 1925 was the authoritarian step that made possible the consolidation and strengthening of Fascist power. The Interior Ministry was placed under the former nationalist, Luigi Federzoni, who took charge of the repression of the anti-Fascist political parties, but was also useful to Mussolini for keeping the Fascist extremists in check. But in this new phase of consolidation and expansion of Fascist power Mussolini also needed the support of the *squadristi* and their bosses. In February 1925 Roberto Farinacci, the principal spokesman of integralist Fascism, was appointed secretary of the PNF. Within only a few months, he had restored the internal unity and discipline of the party and became the principal supporter of radical measures aimed at destroying the remains of political opposition and establishing a one-party regime. Farinacci had his own view of the totalitarian party which, he believed, should retain its autonomy from the government, so that he as secretary of the PNF, or 'head of the party', would be on the same political level as Mussolini, the 'head of the government'.

This was a division of power that the Duce found totally unaccept-

able and, once the authoritarian reorganization of the state had concentrated all executive power in Mussolini's hands and consolidated
his personal power, Mussolini sacked Farinacci and replaced him
with Augusto Turati. Turati was another leading integralist, but was
more prepared to work with the Duce in transforming the state into a
one-party regime. He held the position until October 1930 and played
a decisive role in the reorganization of the party, leading a massive
operation to purge the party of corruption and indiscipline, which
made it easier to install the PNF as the fundamental and essential
pillar of the new regime.

The foundations of the Fascist regime

The transformation of the Italian political system into a single party
state was achieved through a 'legal revolution', in which the Italian
parliament gave its full approval to a complex of authoritarian laws,
most of which were drafted by Alfredo Rocco, the architect of the
Fascist state. These effectively destroyed the liberal constitutional
regime that had taken shape in the sixty years after Italy's unification
in the mid-nineteenth century, yet left the façade of a constitutional
monarchy intact. The laws of 24 December 1925 and 31 January
1926 established the supremacy of the executive power and the subordination of all ministers of state, as well as the parliament, to the
authority of the head of the government who was responsible only to
the king.

Local administration was also reorganized along authoritarian
lines, and the law of 4 February 1926 replaced formerly elected
mayors with the new office of *podestà*, a position filled by royal
nomination, which became effectively a dependency of the provincial
prefects whose powers had also been greatly increased by the law of
3 April 1926. The law of 25 November 1926 brought the freedom
of association to an end, but even before the authoritarian coup of
3 January 1925, the anti-Fascist political parties had in practice been
hardly able to engage in any activity. Immediately after the March on
Rome over 70 per cent of the leading figures in the PCd'I had been
arrested, and Luigi Sturzo, the founder of the PPI, had been forced
into exile. Leading anti-Fascists like Giovanni Amendola and Piero

Gobetti suffered repeated and brutal beatings and both were to die in exile in 1926 from the injuries they had received.

At the end of 1926 the secretary of the PNF announced that since the deputies of the anti-Fascist opposition parties had all been removed from parliament, all parties other than the PNF were now illegal. The press was brought under tight Fascist control and the opposition papers were either suppressed or else changed ownership and came into line with Fascist directives. No form of criticism of the government or of the state or its representatives was permitted after the law of 25 November 1926 which also reintroduced the death penalty for crimes against the state and established a special Tribunal composed of officers of the Fascist Militia and the armed forces, with jurisdiction over all crimes against the state or the regime.

The trade unions were also brought under the authoritarian control of the state. The law of April 3 1926 on labour relations made strikes illegal and created a 'magistracy of labour' to resolve all disputes between labour and employers. Eleven trade unions received legal recognition, and these were all Fascist organizations. The Confederation of Fascist Trade Unions that had been set up in 1922 had become a powerful organization and was led by Edmondo Rossoni. Rossoni was committed to the ambitious plan of implementing an integralist form of syndicalism that would have brought all workers and employers under the control of his federation. But in 1928 Mussolini destroyed this project when he insisted that the federation should be broken up into smaller organizations. The abandonment of the programme of Fascist syndicalism was to the advantage of the employers, and for the workers was only partially compensated by the social and welfare policies of the regime, consisting in the establishment of collective contracts, of measures to reduce unemployment, and the organization of workers' free time through the activities of the Opera Nazionale Dopolavoro.

The regime hailed its law on the trade unions as the first step towards the realization of a new corporate order that would lead to what the Charter of Labour (21 April 1927) called the 'united organization of all forces of production'. A Ministry of Corporations was established in 1926 and the National Council of Corporations created in 1930 was designed to be the central constitutional body of the new state, although the corporations themselves did not come into being until 1934.

The law of 17 May 1928 completed the reorganization of political representation by creating a single national electoral College and assigning to the Fascist Grand Council the right to select candidates for the Chamber from the names put forward by the Fascist trade unions and other bodies. This meant that the 'electors' were presented with a single list of deputies which they had to either approve or reject en bloc. The law of 9 December 1928 made the Grand Council the supreme body of the regime, with powers to amend the constitution, to draw up and revise a list of persons to succeed Mussolini as head of the government (the list was never drawn up), and to intervene in the succession to the throne. Since this law infringed the prerogatives of the monarchy it provoked strong, but ineffective, protests from the king.

The regime met no serious opposition from established institutions or from traditional economic and social interests as it set about demolishing the liberal state. The monarchy, the armed forces, and the industrial and agrarian bourgeoisie accepted the demise of parliamentary government with little evident sign of regret, and seemed more impressed by the advantages that the new regime had brought them by restoring order and discipline in Italian society, and in particular over the workers. These groups complacently assumed that once the Fascists had acquired a monopoly over the exercise of power, their political ambitions would be fully satisfied.

The crowning moment of the consolidation of the Fascist regime came with the plebiscitary elections held on 24 March 1929, when the Italians were called to express their opinion of the list of new deputies selected by the Grand Council with a single vote of 'Yes' or 'No'. 8,661,820 votes were cast, 98.34 per cent of which were 'Yes', with some 8,209 spoiled votes, and a mere 135,773 'No'—less than 1.57 per cent, and mainly from the North which accounted for 84.7 per cent of the contrary voters. The victory was a foregone conclusion, given the new circumstances of the dictatorial regime, that had by now fully consolidated the structures by which it controlled society, and which had in addition the support of a large part of the bourgeoisie and middle classes. Furthermore, the elections were held little more than a month after the signing of the Lateran Pacts (on 11 February 1929), which had gained the Fascist regime recognition by the Church and hence the support of the majority of the clergy and the faithful. The next plebiscite for elections to the Chamber of Deputies was held in

1934, and produced results that brought the 'Yes' vote even closer to 100 per cent.

Approval by plebiscite in no way attenuated the nature of the police state that Fascism had assumed from the start and which it would never abandon. Police repression took the place of the violence of the squads and was used to destroy any form of dissent, anti-Fascist organization, or activity. When the opposition political parties were suppressed, many of the leading anti-Fascists were sentenced to long terms in jail. This was the fate of Antonio Gramsci, the former secretary of the PCd'I. Other anti-Fascist political leaders and intellectuals like the socialist Filippo Turati, the former Prime Minister Francesco Saverio Nitti, and the historian Gaetano Salvemini managed to flee abroad where together with thousands of other anti-Fascist exiles they took up their struggle against the regime. Their arms were mainly books, lectures, and newspaper articles in which they tried to alert Western public opinion, which was often indifferent if not outright sympathetic to Fascism, to the danger that Fascist totalitarianism posed not just for Italy but for democracy and peace in Europe as a whole. In Italy, however, militant anti-Fascism existed only in tiny clandestine groups. But although intellectual anti-Fascism was very rare and was almost inevitably silenced by the punishment of house arrest or prison, it found an eloquent voice in the philosopher Benedetto Croce. The regime did not try to silence Croce partly because of his international reputation, but also because he was probably not considered to be politically dangerous.

In 1927 an Anti-Fascist Concentration was founded in Paris by the Italian socialist and republican exiles, but down to 1934 the communists continued to follow Stalin's orders and remained both isolated from, and hostile to, the other Italian anti-Fascist parties. In the clandestine struggle against Fascism, however, the communists and the militants of the liberal socialist movement known as Justice and Liberty (Giustizia e Libertà), which operated in Italy through small groups of activists that disseminated anti-Fascist propaganda, were the most active and best organized. But the police always caught up with them and their clandestine operations had become impossible by the beginning of the 1930s because of the efficiency of the regime's apparatus of repression, which relied on both the traditional police and on new secret police units known as OVRA that operated both in

Italy and abroad amongst Italian anti-Fascist exiles. Between 1922 and 1943 the police opened 114,000 new files on 'subversives' (there had been only 40,000 in the previous period) and these included militant anti-Fascists, their families, and other potential opponents. Even though the Italian totalitarian experiment did not resort to the mass terror and killings used by other totalitarian regimes, the repression of any form of opposition or dissent and the constant threat of violence were permanent features of Fascism. Between 1928 and 1932 the Special Tribunal issued only nine death sentences for political crimes, five of which were for Slavs accused of terrorist actions, and none before 1941. But between 1928 and 1943, 5,319 individuals appeared before the Special Tribunal of whom 5,155 received a total of 27,735 years of prison sentences, including seven condemnations to life imprisonment. Between 1926 and 1943 some 15,000 Italians were in addition subject to *confino*, which meant that they lost their jobs and were obliged to live under house arrest somewhere far distant from their normal place of residence.

The party in the Fascist regime

Under the leadership first of Turati and then of Giovanni Giuriati, who served as national secretary from 1930 to 1931 and continued the purges and the work of reorganizing the party, the PNF was placed at the centre of the new political system where it was rigidly subject to control by the Duce who became its sole and unchallenged leader. Mussolini proclaimed that in the Fascist regime the party was subordinate to the state just as the PNF's representative in each province, the federal secretary, was subordinate to the senior representative of the state, the prefect. But this claim was continuously overturned in practice. The prefect was not the representative of an abstract state that existed over and above political parties. The subordination of the party to the state was a rhetorical fiction as the dual nature of Mussolini's power as head of the government and head of the Fascist Party made evident, and it was this double set of powers that makes it unrealistic and historically inaccurate to draw any firm distinction between the Duce and the party as if they were in reality different entities.

Behind the façade of the regime's monolithic unity there were constant conflicts between the party and traditional institutions, which Mussolini neither wanted nor was able to stop. The conflicts between the provincial *federali* and the prefects, for example, continued until the last days of the regime. An attempt was made to solve the problem by choosing political prefects, in other words, men from the party: but this often simply created new causes of conflict with the *federali*. By 1935 over half the prefects were no longer career administrators, and already in 1934 out of a total of 65 prefects, 31 had backgrounds in public administration against 34 who were political nominees, 10 of whom had been *squadristi* and 13 provincial secretaries of the PNF. Of the total number of 79 Fascist prefects appointed between 1922 and 25 July 1943, 37 were still in office in July 1943. The political prefects were especially prominent in the major regional administrative centres like Milan, Genoa, Turin, Naples, and Palermo. The subordination of the *federali* to the prefect was not laid down in any law, nor was it part of the constitution of the PNF, which placed the federal secretaries directly under the orders of the National Secretary.

The party acknowledged its subordination to the state, but with reference to the myth of the Fascist state and not to the monarchic state. Particularly under the leadership of Achille Starace (National Secretary, 1932–9), the party conducted a tenacious, gradual and unremitting campaign of internal subversion against the old monarchist state, and as a result acquired ever-wider powers within the new totalitarian state. In 1937 the secretary of the PNF acquired the powers and responsibilities of a minister of state, while in the new constitution of 1938 the PNF was officially declared to be the 'only party', and its functions were defined specifically as 'the defence and strengthening of the Fascist revolution and the political education of Italians'. In 1941 the new PNF secretary, Adelchi Serena (1940–1), took a further important new step towards the totalitarian transformation of the state by creating a special party office with responsibility for preparing legislative reforms that would 'strengthen the position of the party in the state'. These included the law of 29 November 1941 requiring that the party be consulted before nominations were made for any public or political office. In the same year, and in anticipation of the victorious conclusion of the war, the party prepared a radical plan that would transform the PNF into an élite organization, together with a project for the reform of the state whose constitution would acknowledge the primacy of the PNF as 'the motor of the state'. The proposal envisaged that the Ministries of the Interior and Popular Culture would be controlled by the PNF, that the dual powers of the provincial *federali* and prefects would be resolved by instead creating a single representative of the PNF in each province, and that the secretary of the PNF would be recognized in the constitution as the most senior Fascist *gerarca* after the Duce.

The PNF's strategy for expansion

The symbiosis of state and party was the central characteristic of the Fascist regime. The intervention of the PNF reflected the presence of a new ruling caste whose power derived from control over the party bureaucracy, which was constantly trying to take over the state bureaucracy, or, if this proved impossible, to undermine its authority. From Farinacci to Serena, every leader of the PNF sought to expand the power of the party not only at the expense of traditional state institutions, but of all other institutions of the regime and Italian society. This strategy of expansion was gradual and advanced at speeds that were determined by changing national and international circumstances, but it was constant, unremitting, and resulted in mounting successes that brought the party ever-wider control over both the state and Italian society.

In the case of traditional institutions that the party was unable to get rid of quickly, its tactic was either to bring them under Fascist control or suppress them. The strategies of expansion were constantly being adapted according to time and circumstance to avoid provoking unnecessary reactions or resistance. In the case of the Chamber of Deputies and Senate, for example, the PNF's strategy of expansion followed two quite different tactics that were determined by the different political character of the two institutions, the former being elective, whereas the second was filled by life-time nomination.

Following the reform of political representation and the elections of 1929, the *fascistizzazione* of the Chamber of Deputies was virtually complete. The PNF then proposed a new reform that would abolish the Chamber of Deputies and replace it in 1939 with a Chamber of

Fasci and Corporations in which all vestiges of the principles of parliamentary representation would totally disappear. The new Chamber was a direct offshoot of the PNF and of the corporations controlled by the PNF. The party secretary was also given the power to impose punishments on the deputies and senators, and the statutes of the new Chamber laid down that any deputy who was suspended or expelled from the party was prohibited from continuing his parliamentary duties.

In the case of the Senate, the PNF instead adopted a tactic of infiltration resulting in a gradual process of *fascistizzazione* through the nomination of new senators. Between the March on Rome and February 1943, 596 new senators were nominated (in comparison with 398 between 1901 and 1914). This influx of Fascist senators was reinforced by the activity within the Senate itself of the Association of Senators, all of whom were members of the PNF. As a result, by the end of the 1930s the *fascistizzazione* of the Senate had been virtually completed.

New and greater possibilities for expanding the power of the PNF were offered by the various state agencies that operated in sectors ranging from agriculture to social welfare, from culture to tourism, from industry to public works, and from trade to transport. Under the Fascist regime these bodies multiplied much faster than in the past. Between 1901 and 1921, 102 new government agencies had been created, in contrast to 353 between 1922 and 1943. The creation of what came to be called the 'parallel bureaucracy' by the Fascists began immediately after the March on Rome and continued at varying speeds well after the establishment of the regime. In some cases the Fascists retained the managers appointed by previous Liberal governments because of their technical skills, providing that they were prepared to accommodate to the new regime and show loyalty to the PNF by becoming members of the party. But the majority of state agencies were managed and controlled by men chosen by the Fascist Party. Even in the case of the state bureaucracy, which for reasons of practicality and convenience Mussolini wished to keep out of the control of the party, the PNF gained increasing influence through the Association of State Employees which the party controlled. PNF representatives were to be found everywhere: in the central administration of the state, in the provincial administration, from the Higher Council for Schools to the Higher Council for Public

Health, from the National Research Council to the Commission of Theatre and Cinema Censors, from the commissions that awarded literary prizes to those responsible for overseeing wholesale fish and grain markets, from committees responsible for tourism to those for fairs and exhibitions.

The influence, control, and interference of the Party gradually also extended to sectors that had previously been outside the party's control, notably the magistracy. Membership of the PNF became an essential prerequisite for career advancement for judges, while measures were adopted to subject magistrates to close Fascist surveillance, and after 1939 all judges were required to undergo political and ideological retraining programmes and to attend special courses designed by Fascists.

The PNF's strategy of expansion was not as immediately successful in every branch of the traditional State as many integralist Fascists desired. The armed forces, for example, retained their independence, even though they were increasingly subject to Mussolini who as head of the government was also Minister for the Army and Navy. But the military was not an obstacle to the expansion of the totalitarian state. In 1933 army officers were permitted to join the PNF and in 1936 the requirement of PNF membership for civil servants was extended to officers and non-commissioned officers in the Finance Guards and to army officers.

Between regimentation and consensus: the *fascistizzazione* of the Italians

To celebrate its first decade in power and to demonstrate its solidity and security, the regime in 1932 offered a general amnesty to political prisoners. Under Starace's leadership, new efforts were also being made to intensify the *fascistizzazione* of the Italians through the various forms of regimentation controlled by the party and by the organization of consensus that focused increasingly on the myth and the cult of the Duce. In addition to his institutional role as permanent head of state, Mussolini's charismatic role was accentuated through the development of the cult of the *littorio*. This was a secular Fascist political religion, with its own creeds, myths, rites, and symbols that came to play the fundamental role in integrating the Fascist state and the single mass political party. The Duce's frequent public rallies were the culminating point in the organization of consensus, and in these carefully prepared and choreographed settings the emotional meeting of the leader and the masses offered a dramatic and mystical symbol of the unity of the nation expressed by its highest interpreter.

The cult of the *littorio* took a central place in the organization of consensus and derived from the notion that the masses were an aggregate governed by mythical and irrational forces. This made them incapable of developing an independent political awareness derived from a sense of individual responsibility that would enable them to engage directly in the choice of their own rulers. Instead, a conformist mentality could be inculcated in the individual and the masses, as throughout their entire existence they would be subject to parallel processes of regimentation, indoctrination, and integration in accordance with the values and principles of the totalitarian party. This project was premissed on the notion of the primacy of the political, or in other words the total assimilation of the private to the public and with it the total subordination of all those values belonging to the private sphere (religion, culture, morality, love, and so forth) to the supreme political value which was embodied in the state alone, the supreme entity before which individuals and society were no more than the instruments through which the state achieved its objectives of greatness. Within this perspective of totalitarian Fascism, politics was an all-embracing experience that alone gave meaning and purpose to human existence. This could only be achieved within the specific context of the Fascist state and through the constant activity of the single state party, whose task it was to organize and educate the masses in order to transform Italians into a totalitarian community united by a single faith, disciplined in every aspect of their lives and totally subordinated to the will of the Fascist Party, which was committed to the achievement of power and expansion.

Seen in these terms, mass politics in Fascist Italy took the form of permanent totalitarian education. Different means with different objectives were used depending on the sections of the population that were addressed, but this operation of totalitarian education was conducted by every institution of the Fascist state, from elementary schools to the Opera Nazionale Dopolavoro that had been created to organize the leisure time of Italian workers. But the key role of 'The Great Pedagogue' of the masses belonged to the PNF. 'Political educa-tion' in Fascist Italy revolved around the Fascist understanding of the relationship between politics and the masses. To educate Italians pol-itically meant nurturing in each individual the mentality of the 'citizen-soldier' whose entire existence must conform to the simple dogma: 'believe, obey, and fight'.

In line with these principles, Fascism set out to indoctrinate the masses and especially the younger generations. The *'fascistizzazione'* of young Italians of both sexes between the ages of 6 and 18 was entrusted to the Opera Nazionale Balilla and then after 1937 to the Gioventù Italiana del Littorio (GIL) which brought all the Fascist youth movements together under the leadership of the PNF. Within the broader project of regimentation and the organization of con-sensus, the *fasci femminili* had a more specific role. Fascism ostenta-tiously worshipped male virility and was explicitly anti-feminist. All forms of political activity were reserved exclusively for males, while the role of woman was that of spouse, mother, and teacher, and hence always subordinate to that of the male. At the same time, Fascist politics also gave women new, albeit highly contradictory, functions both in the home and in the totalitarian state. As wife and mother, women were entrusted with the task of producing children for the fatherland and providing them with their first training and educa-tion, while as members of the party they were also militants commit-ted to creating the Fascist 'new man' and hence with responsibilities that went far beyond the family. This meant that as well as the trad-itional model of the woman as mistress of the household and guard-ian angel of the home, the party's mission also created the alternative model of the Fascist 'new woman', who, although confined exclusively to the spheres of welfare and education, was nonetheless actively engaged in party work. This resulted in the mobilization of women outside the traditional private sphere of the family, and gave militant Fascist women, and especially younger women, opportun-ities to take part in the great enterprise of the *fascistizzazione* of the masses.

The totalitarian party was the first attempt to impose a single form of organization on all Italians based on rigidly centralized principles that aimed at creating a single mass ideological identity. It is still difficult to measure the effectiveness of these attempts to organize consensus on those who for nearly twenty years were subject daily to the incessant hammering of pervasive and omnipresent propaganda. The party was a capillary organization that operated uniformly throughout Italy and involved all Italians in an experiment in political socialization that had no precedent in Italian history. But the impact and effectiveness of these policies on a population that had no opportunity to escape the tentacles of the party or to stand aloof from the regime—except at the risk of being ostracized from all forms of public life, and probably also the loss of a job—varied from city to city, province to province, region to region, and from one period to another. Reactions also differed according to generations, and the reactions of those who had known parliamentary government and competition between rival political parties and who had possibly been themselves victims of Fascist violence were different from those of the younger generations, who had grown up knowing only the totalitarian regime, and who had been educated in the noise and clamour of Fascist triumphalism. Resistance to the organization of consensus was greatest in those regions where there had previously been strong Catholic associations, or where there was still some memory of the now prohibited former political parties. In the more backward regions, and especially in the South, the party also found it very difficult to organize and mobilize the population except in the larger cities. But even anti-Fascist observers were agreed in the 1930s that the regime's initiatives in welfare and in the organization of leisure activities had enabled it, as one Communist observer noted in 1932, 'to succeed in influencing the greater part of the masses with its ideology'.[10] It was because of the regime's success in regimenting and organizing the masses that the leaders of the Communist Party decided in the second half of the 1930s to adopt the tactic of infiltrating Fascist organizations to try to reach 'our brothers in black shirts'.

More than in any other field, the party was especially intransigent and integralist when it came to education. This led to direct confrontation with Catholic Action, its most powerful rival, which in 1931 caused a major conflict with the Catholic Church when the regime asserted the party's exclusive role in the education of the young. During the 1930s the Party's role in education had been systematically strengthened with the expansion of the Fascist youth organizations.

---

[10] Istituto A. Gramsci, Archivio del partito comunista, 1138/1.

This too was ground on which the party did not hesitate to openly challenge the Catholic Church, and in 1938 it again asserted its right to monopolize the education of Italian youth in the values of its own ideology. While the regime looked on Catholicism as a useful tool in the bid to organize consensus, it also held Fascism to be the secular religion of the nation and of the state, that demanded the undivided devotion of all citizens.

The new oligarchy

By the end of the 1930s the tentacles of the party had come to reach every part of Italian society . As one Communist militant wrote in November 1938:

Fascism keeps the entire life of the Italian people under strict control, and the great mass of the petty bourgeoisie, workers, peasants and intellectuals can only live by submitting themselves to the controls imposed by Fascism. The organization of the state makes it impossible, except in the most exceptional circumstances, for anyone to live outside its parameters or outside the control exercised by the Fascist Party and its various organs. There is no alternative: whoever has to live in Italy has to adopt the Fascist label.[11]

One of the leaders of the liberal-socialist organization, Giustizia e Libertà, reached similar conclusions in the same year:

Fascism does not oppress and control simply by means of its police apparatus: it oppresses and controls by means of its trade unions, through its schools, through its footholds in industry and the banks, through the vast bureaucracy that it has created, directs and maintains, through the press and the radio. The whole country is swallowed up by this apparatus: any manifestations of protest or lack of loyalty are reported immediately to the centre and are then suppressed through the use of those forms of aggression against which the discontent was originally directed.[12]

Membership of the Fascist Party had become an indispensable prerequisite for anyone seeking to enter any form of public or local government service, in local or para-state agencies. A circular issued

[11] 'Qual è la vera situazione presente', 16 Nov. 1938, cited in S. Colarizi, *L'Italia antifascista dal 1922 al 1940*, Vol. II (Rome–Bari, 1976).

[12] Report of Alberto Cianca, 13 June 1938, in Colarizi, *L'Italia antifascista*, p. 386.

by the Interior Ministry in 1937 declared that the PNF membership card had the same status as an identity card, while the Party's constitution of 1938 declared that anyone 'who ceases to be a member of the Partito Nazionale Fascista is to be relieved of all positions and responsibilities he may perform'.

The leaders of the party and its principal organizations now formed a new oligarchy of privileged citizens. In the GIL alone there were 33,958 officers and 250,000 male and female youth leaders. The totalitarian party also gradually transformed the traditional local élites, who were replaced with new men who saw themselves as part of the new Fascist aristocracy, and enjoyed the prestige and authority, and to a lesser extent the power, which derived from the totalitarian party.

Control of the party, and hence of the regime, remained almost entirely in the hands of the political class from which Fascism had originated. Of the members of the Fascist Grand Council in office between 1923 and 1943, nearly 70 per cent had been members of the original *fasci di combattimento* between 1919 and 1922, hence from before the March on Rome, and of these about 40 per cent had been *squadristi*. They came predominantly from Emilia-Romagna (18.0%), Tuscany (11.3%), Lombardy (9.8%), and the Veneto (9.0%). 81.4 per cent of the National Directorate had been party members before the March on Rome and 59.2 per cent had been *squadristi*, while 65 per cent were army veterans. Of the federal secretaries, those who had joined the party before the March on Rome amounted to 74.5 per cent, and 44 per cent had been *squadristi*, while the regional breakdown showed the same pattern as for the Fascist Grand Council and the National Directorate.

Within this oligarchy of 'Fascists of the first hour' the only form of renewal was by the recruitment of new senior figures from the youth organizations, although in practice very few younger people joined the Fascist aristocracy. The number of Fascist federal secretaries coming from the new generation that had entered the party after 1926 in what was called the ritual of the 'Fascist call-up' were only thirty-two. The Fascist University Groups (GUF) were the principal hothouse for rearing new party officials, and provided fifty-four federal secretaries, ten members of the National Directorate, six inspectors of the PNF, two deputy-secretaries, and one National Secretary.

This was the cause for growing criticism of the 'bureaucratization' of the party and the regime from within the Fascist youth movements in the late 1930s and of demands for renewal of the executive class. These signs of unrest and impatience on the part of some of the younger Fascists were mainly limited to university students. They never constituted a challenge either to the regime or to the fundamental principles of the totalitarian experiment which these younger Fascists simply wished to speed up and make more radical through new reforms and social policies designed to reshape the Italian character and hence bring into being the Fascist 'new man'.

The anthropological revolution

At the final Congress of the PNF held in Rome in June 1925 Mussolini had stated

what we describe as our ferocious totalitarian determination will now be pursued with even greater ferocity; it will be the compass and the predominating concern of all our actions. There must be Fascist Italians, just as the Italians of the Renaissance and of Ancient Rome shared unmistakable characteristics . . . by means of a process of unrelenting and tenacious selection we will create the new generations in which each person will have a clearly defined role. I take pleasure at times in the idea of generations created in a laboratory. To create, that is to say, a class of warriors constantly prepared to die; a class of inventors able to reveal the secrets of every mystery; a class of judges, a class of great leaders of industry, of great explorers, and great governors. It is through such forms of methodical selection that outstanding professional cadres are created, and it is they in turn who create empires.[13]

From as early as 1925, therefore, the project for the totalitarian anthropological revolution that Fascism planned to implement through the new political system that was to be established was already fully developed, and the implementation of this project had already been assigned to the party. The new Fascist totalitarian state was to be the laboratory in which the 'new Italian', totally dedicated to the achievement of the imperial ambitions of the Duce and the Fascist Party, was to be created. The regime's whole system of mass organization, from primary schooling to the organization of leisure time, was developed around this single goal.

[13] B. Mussolini, *Opera Omnia*, 35 vols., eds. D. and E. Susmel (Florence, 1951–63), vol. XXI, 362.

The experiment in anthropological revolution was intensified when the regime opened up a new campaign for the 'reform of social behaviour' directed against the bourgeoisie and introduced the racial and anti-Semitic laws at the end of the 1930s. The regime's racial programme had taken coherent and systematic shape after the war in Ethiopia, and the measures against the Jews were a later extension of this. Until the late 1930s the regime had not given particular priority to racism in its policies, although it had frequently emphasized the need to improve the Italian race and in its colonial undertakings had always followed typically colonial and racist criteria and had perpetrated acts of deliberate savagery during the war and against the indigenous peoples in Libya and Ethiopia. Fascism had not originally been an anti-Semitic movement and although it did contain some anti-Semitic groups they had little influence. There were a number of Jews amongst the founders of the *fasci di combattimento*, as well as in the Fascist Party and the government. In 1932 Mussolini had publicly poured scorn on German racism, claiming that pride in the nation gained nothing from 'the delusions of race' and he had denied that anti-Semitism existed in Italy. Many foreign Jews fleeing from Nazi persecution had found refuge in Italy, until anti-Semitic legislation (which originally found support amongst only a handful of fanatics) was officially introduced in 1938. But on 14 July 1938 the government published the *Manifesto on Race* and on 19 July the Demographic Service of the Interior Ministry was renamed the Central Directorate for Demography and Race. On 6 October, with opposition only from Balbo, De Bono, and Federzoni, the Fascist Grand Council approved the *Manifesto on Race* which prohibited Italians entering into marriage with 'elements belonging to the Hamitic, Semitic, or other non-Aryan races', banned foreign Jews from entering Italy and ordered the expulsion of those who had done so, and set out the restrictions to be imposed henceforth on Italian Jews. On 17 November the decision of the Grand Council became the law of the Italian state.

Although the anti-Semitic laws of 1938 were certainly a consequence of Mussolini's alliance with Germany, they were neither requested nor imposed by Italy's Nazi ally. The laws were freely and knowingly imposed by Mussolini for political and ideological reasons that had more to do with his desire to compete with, rather than imitate, German National Socialism. Mussolini's main concern was to emphasize how the 'spiritual' racism of Fascism differed from the 'biological' racism of the Nazis, and to underline that difference he used the slogan that the aim of Fascist anti-Semitism was to 'discriminate not persecute', as if discrimination was not both premiss and part of the persecution inherent in Fascism's totalitarian logic.

Totalitarian 'Caesarism' and the monarchy

As the experiment in totalitarianism took shape, the Fascist state took on a political form that is best described as 'totalitarian Caesarism', in other words a charismatic dictatorship rooted in a complex institutional structure whose foundations lay in the single party and in the subordination and total assimilation of Italian society into the state through the organization and mobilization of the masses. The concentration of power in the person of the Duce had never been the result simply of Mussolini's personal qualities. The Fascist definition of the role and nature of the party and the state meant that the leader must be the central and fundamental feature of the new state to personify the principle of undivided authority on which the totalitarian state was premissed. After 1938 leading lawyers began to argue the need for a new constitution in line with the realities of the new Fascist political system, which they too now defined as a totalitarian state. This need became even more pressing in 1939 when the Chamber of Deputies was finally abolished and replaced by the Chamber of Fasci and Corporations. This reform finally consolidated the Duce's institutional position. A review of legislation since 1939, published in 1941 by the Senate and the Chamber of Fasci and Corporations, devoted a whole chapter to the institutional position of the 'Duce of Fascism, the Head of the Government' who was described as 'The Supreme Leader of the Regime, which now inseparably represents the State'.[14] In a text published by the PNF, the Duce was described as 'the Head of State'.

In this programme for the totalitarian revolution, the monarchy had clearly become redundant. The majority of Fascists would have

---

[14] *La legislazione fascista nella XXIX Legislatura 1934–1939 (XXII–XVII)*, Vol. I (Rome, s.d.), p. 13.

been happy to see it abolished, and although Mussolini confided with only his closest advisers, he too was working in this direction and there is ample and reliable evidence that he was simply waiting for the right moment to get rid of the monarchy, which he considered to be an insufficiently trustworthy institution to include in the Fascist state of the future.

In the so-called 'dyarchy' between the Duce and the king, which after the fall of the regime Mussolini would invoke in an attempt to mitigate his own responsibilities as dictator, effective power was in the hands of the Duce. The king in formal terms remained the head of state, but was either not concerned or not able to prevent or slow down the systematic destruction of the constitutional order. Victor Emanuel III made no effort to oppose the Fascist anthropological revolution, however, even when it assumed its most extreme form with the introduction of the racial and anti-Semitic laws. The prestige of the monarchy also suffered an immense blow when on 30 March 1938 the Senate and the Chamber of Deputies approved by acclamation a law creating the title of First Marshal of the Empire, the highest rank in the military hierarchy, which was bestowed contemporaneously on the king and on Mussolini. As soon as Italy entered the Second World War in June 1940, Mussolini deprived the king of his role as supreme military commander. The army remained loyal to the monarchy, but with some minor exceptions there is no evidence that the military hierarchy ever tried to resist the growing power or the policies of the Duce, who for most of the twenty years of Fascist rule held the Ministries for the Army and Navy. At no time did any senior army or naval officer appeal to the king against Mussolini's decisions, even when these affected the armed forces and the future of the nation most seriously. Nor were the armed forces impermeable to the process of *fascistizzazione* and the influence of the Fascist Party.

However reluctant, the acquiescence of the monarchy and the institutions that supported it when faced by Mussolini and the implementation of the totalitarian experiment was the principal feature of the relationship between 'totalitarian Caesarism' and the monarchy. When after the end of the Second World War the king was called on to give an account of the ways in which the monarchy had tried to oppose the advance of Fascist totalitarianism, the only example he was able to give was that he had succeeded in delaying the introduction of a decree limiting the freedom of the press by a year, from 1923 to 1924. The king himself confessed his impotence in the face of Fascism: 'At that time—he said—it was not possible to oppose the Head of the Government.'[15]

Crisis, defeat, and the end of Fascism

It was military defeat, not the Resistance nor opposition by the monarchy, by the armed forces, by the Church, or economic interest groups, that brought down the Fascist regime. The rest only became factors once military defeat seemed inevitable and once the myth of the Duce had disintegrated.

The Allied invasion of Sicily (10 July 1943) precipitated the collapse of the regime, which by that time had almost completely lost the consensus that it had succeeded in imposing in the course of twenty years of regimentation and repeated triumphs, real or imagined. However, there had been signs that the regime was in crisis even before Italy entered the war. These were evident in growing popular concern about the regime's continuous war-making, that was heightened by the threat of a new world war. But there was also growing resistance to the totalitarian experiment and to the invasive and domineering presence of the Fascist Party in every aspect of public and private life. Rather than protest or opposition, this discontent gave rise to a sense of apathy and resignation, a situation that was vividly described in the report of a police informer in January 1939:

Many are criticizing the Fascist Regime for forcing all citizens to join different organizations which draw them into ever narrower circles that limit and control every form of activity. It is said that this desire to organize every form of individual activity is crushing freedom and suffocates every type of initiative, and people are no longer willing to put up with the restrictions imposed on them and the interference of the Regime in every form of activity, and especially those where outside interference seems least easy to justify. Some now say that this is a system of repression that is becoming increasingly unbearable. For the present, people are putting up with it out of fear and are careful not to show their opposition openly, but it seems likely that were

[15] P. Puntoni, *Parla Vittorio Emanuele III* (Bologna, 1993), pp. 291–8, 321.

some setback to seriously shake the Regime there might well be a violent reaction against this repression.[16]

Concern and hostility towards the intensification of the totalitarian policies of the regime was also increasing in Church circles in the late 1930s. Another Fascist police report of January 1939 stated that in the Vatican 'Mussolini no longer has the prestige he once enjoyed. The Jewish question and the persecution of the Jews lies at the root of this discontent, and they say that, like the decrees of a Roman emperor, these measures could in the future be applied to anyone since there are no longer any constitutional guarantees.'[17]

In a speech to the Lombard Episcopal Conference held in the same month, the Cardinal of Milan declared that the policy of conciliation between the Church and the regime had failed, and he warned of the danger that the 'Fascist religion' was seeking to turn the state into a divinity:

The Catholic Church is confronted today not so much by a new Fascist state—since that was already in existence in the year when the Concordat was agreed—but by an imperialist philosophical and religious system which, although it does not say so in words, implicitly rejects the Apostolic Creed, the spiritual transcendence of religion, the rights of the Christian family and of the individual. The Apostolic Creed and a Catholic Church of divine origin are now confronted by a Fascist creed and a totalitarian state which, just as Hegel had predicted, now claims for itself the attributes of divinity. In religious terms, the Concordat has been stripped of its substance.[18]

As Italian intervention in the European war drew closer, feelings of hostility towards the regime increased in industrial and business circles as well, but again never to the point of clearly formulated political opposition. One of Italy's leading industrialists, Ettore Conti, noted in his diary on 2 January 1940, for example:

We may well be on the verge of war: but never has the country wallowed in such a state of apathy and inertia: never has Fascism been held in lower esteem by the Italians. The failings of the dictatorship are now finally evident to all, even to those who had supported it in good faith. . . . The gradual but constant worsening of the quality of the leadership, the insolence of the

---

[16] Report from Florence, 5 Jan. 1939, in Archivio Centrale dello Stato, Divisione Polizia Politica 1927–1944, b.220.

[17] Ibid.

[18] Cited in P. Beltrame-Quattrocchi, *Al di sopra dei gagliardetti* (Casale Monferrato, 1985), pp. 260–2.

senior officials in every branch, the spread of profiteering combined with the most idiotic constraints imposed on every aspect of private life have turned the Italians into an amorphous herd that has no sense of will, of faith or aspiration.

And with the country in this state, they want to take us to war![19]

The military defeats that piled up as soon as Italy entered the war plunged the regime into a crisis that proved catastrophic. Military defeat caused consensus to disintegrate rapidly, except during a few brief moments of revived enthusiasm aroused by the news of some minor military success. But the crisis of the regime during the war was made more serious by the simultaneous crisis of the Fascist Party. The PNF lost its most militant and convinced members, who immediately enrolled for active service, and at the same time was burdened with new and ever growing assignments on the 'home front'. With the onset of the war Mussolini repeatedly changed the leadership of the party, with no less than four new National Secretaries in the space of three years, which disorientated the entire organization and lowered its standing in public opinion. Another clear sign of the crisis of the regime was the revival of anti-Fascist activities and the clandestine reorganization of the opposition parties in 1942. The strikes in the factories in northern Italy in March 1943 were the result of economic rather than political grievances, but they too played an important role in precipitating the final crisis of the regime.

The regime finally fell on 25 July 1943 when the Duce, who had been abandoned by the majority of the Grand Council, was deposed by the king and arrested. A new government was set up headed by General Pietro Badoglio, who ordered the dissolution of the Fascist Party and began the negotiations with the Allies for Italy's surrender which resulted in the armistice of 8 September.

Shortly after a new Fascist state that called itself the Italian Social Republic (RSI, but it was also known as 'the Republic of Salò') was set up at the instigation of Hitler after German troops had liberated Mussolini. It lasted from 13 September 1943 to 25 April 1945 and was the final attempt to revive Fascism by taking it back to its republican origins. This left Italy divided into two separate states, the RSI in the North and the Kingdom of the South, and marked the start of a civil war between Fascists and anti-Fascists. The former had a variety of

---

[19] E. Conti, *Dal taccuino di un borghese* (Milan, 1946), pp. 673–4.

military and paramilitary organizations (the army, the Republican National Guard, the *Brigate Nere, Decima Mas*), while anti-Fascists joined the different armed partisan groups of the Resistance or the reconstituted royal army in the South. The RSI was run by a Duce who by now believed himself to be politically finished and with no real independence or authority. It was based on a cluster of rival forces and institutions that were constantly competing with one another for political and military reasons, even though they were able to provide some degree of administrative organization and to assert their independence from their German ally, who directly controlled large areas of north-eastern Italy. The volunteers who rallied to the RSI included both old and young Fascists, among them the philosopher Giovanni Gentile, who was killed in 1944, together with men and officers from the regular army. There were also many young people and teenagers of both sexes who had grown up in the climate of totalitarian indoctrination and who were moved by a genuinely romantic form of patriotism. But above all, the Republic of Salò provided the opportunity for the re-emergence and domination of the most intransigent and violent tendencies in totalitarian Fascism. The anti-bourgeois and socialistic tendencies that had gained increased prominence in the final years of the regime now sought to give republican Fascism a new revolutionary and anti-capitalist character. They gave new impetus to the irrational and mystical elements of Fascist militancy that worshipped patriotism, the defiance of death, the ethic of sacrifice, the warrior spirit, and the cult of violence, which became the watchwords of the militia-party re-established by the new Republican Fascist Party. The RSI also revived and intensified the campaign against the Jews by bringing in even more severe anti-Semitic legislation and stepping up the persecution of the Italian Jews. Between 1943 and 1945 more than 7,000 Jews were deported, of whom only 610 ever returned to Italy from the death camps where 6,885 would die.

Completely controlled by the Germans for whom its sole purpose was to provide assistance in the operations against the partisans, the RSI finally collapsed following the victory of the Allies and the Resistance forces which ended with Italy's liberation on 25 April 1945. On 28 April Mussolini was captured and shot: his body, hanging by the feet, together with those of other Fascist leaders, was later put on public display in the centre of Milan.

Italian society under Fascism

Bruno P. F. Wanrooij

While Fascism has often presented itself as revolutionary, its relationship with modernity has been ambiguous. The regime promoted technological innovation, but at the same time wanted to preserve the values of traditional rural society. Thus, within the ongoing process of transformation of Italian society, Fascism tried to check developments which could be a threat to those values. While it favoured progress in a more general sense, it welcomed the emergence of mass society and acknowledged the consequent need for mass organization; on the other hand, it opposed changes in gender relations and strongly disliked the advance of urbanization and its corollary of secularization and cosmopolitanism. The desire to promote progress, yet avoid social change, was at the centre of the Fascist idea of modernity. The contradictions in this approach come out clearly when we take into consideration social practices and material conditions of living. Moreover, measuring the gap between objectives and realizations can be useful to get a better understanding of the limits of the Fascist impact on Italian society.

Fascism and youth

Fascism's claim to modernity and its self-representation as a revolutionary regime were closely linked to its preferential relationship with young people, which had its origins in 1915 when Mussolini, after having been expelled from the Socialist Party and having been abandoned by most of his old comrades, decided to raise the 'banner of youth'. Mussolini had been quick to understand the importance of the war experience for the political formation and psychological development of young people, one of whom recalled later that 'to make war and to become men for us was one and the same thing'.[1] After the war, the Fascist movement gave its full support to the students' request to take over power and presented itself as an expression of the revolt of young people against the ideology and the power of the older generation.

The March on Rome of October 1922 accelerated the circulation within the political élite by bringing young people to power. The average age of the local leaders of the Fascist Party (*Segretario federale*) in 1922 was 31.8, and 35.9 per cent of the Fascist candidates in the 1924 national elections were under 30; Mussolini himself became Italy's prime minister when he was only 39 years old. Once in power, however, the Fascists called for a return to order: students were asked to subject themselves to military discipline and to quell their 'inconclusive instincts of rebellion'. In the future, access to the ruling class was to be the result of serious preparation and of a severe selection for which the reform of the school system, introduced by minister Gentile in 1923, was intended to lay the foundation. The Fascists were keen on maintaining a close relationship with youth, and when Camillo Pellizzi in 1928 publicly denied that youth could be a criterion for preference, the young Florentine Fascist leader Alessandro Pavolini replied that only with the support of young people was it possible to preserve the revolutionary value of Fascism. In 1930 the party leaders intervened in the discussion and indicated some 'firm points about youth', the first of which established that 'The regime is, and intends to remain, a regime of young people also from the point of view of age'.

By that time, a sense of disaffection was widely diffused among students who noticed that the pace of renewal of the élite had slowed down considerably. Various measures were adopted to convince the students that, notwithstanding all this, they had a future in Fascist society. A select group of students were invited to participate in party and trade-union activities. Fascist student groups (GUF) gave, with

---

[1] Giuseppe Bottai, *Diario 1935–1944* (Milan, 1982), pp. 46–7.

the financial support of the party, a new impetus to their cultural activities and offered the students ample possibilities to participate in pleasure tours, sport, and other activities which could gratify their feelings of belonging to a social élite.

The development of the corporatist ideology offered the students the opportunity they had been expecting to gain more influence in politics. Although the Ministry of Corporations had been created in 1926, corporatism became really important only in the 1930s, when the economic crisis was seen as an indictment of the failure of capitalism. In 1932 Ugo Spirito suggested that public intervention in the economy should not be limited to state subsidies for private industry: corporations, in which workers and capitalists would collaborate for the common good, should take over the property of firms. Spirito also proposed to abolish the trade unions which he considered obsolete in a corporatist economy where the problems of class struggle no longer existed. Giuseppe Bottai, who was the Minister of Corporations from 1929 to 1932, on the contrary, took the view that the trade unions were still necessary to represent the workers.

In the political debate which followed, the students often tried to promote a 'leftist' interpretation of Fascism which underlined the contrasts between corporatism and capitalism and assigned to young intellectuals an important role in the construction of a new model of society. As a result criticism of the present was transformed into a programme for the future which linked young people indissolubly to Fascism. For this reason Mussolini himself encouraged the students in their revolt against the increasingly bourgeois outlook of Fascist society and asked them to keep the ideals of revolution alive. The regime succeeded in convincing the students that the revolution had not finished and only needed the contributions of young people to regain momentum. Even the invasion of Ethiopia could in this context be interpreted as an occasion for young people to express their revolutionary valour: 'This is our moment, the moment of our generation, the moment of the young people of Mussolini', wrote one student in the journal *L'Appello* in 1935.

Themes like corporatism, the role of the trade unions in Fascist society—and after 1938 also racism—were at the centre of attention during the *Littoriali della cultura e dell'arte*, yearly national debating contests which started in Florence in 1934 and offered a platform for a relatively free discussion. After the war against Ethiopia, the 'leftist' interpretation of Fascism gained more influence and the trade unions became more active, gaining the support of the young workers, who were more easily convinced by anti-capitalist propaganda. The slogan 'Reach out to the people' encouraged students to become more active. In doing so, some of the students went well beyond the hierarchical approach which the regime had wanted to give to the relations between young intellectuals and workers. After visits to factories, and personal contacts with workers, 'leftist' students started to denounce the violations of labour legislation in the press.

Judging from France the critical attitude of the Italian students, the Socialist leader Pietro Nenni convinced himself that Fascism had failed to consolidate among young intellectuals. The frequent expressions of strong anti-capitalist attitudes persuaded the Communists of the need to change their strategy. Considering the students' requests for social justice as sincere and hoping to be able to transform 'leftist' Fascism into anti-Fascism, in 1936 the Communists launched an appeal to their 'brothers in black shirts'. With this objective in mind, Eugenio Curiel, using his position as editor-in-chief of the Paduan student journal Il Bò, sponsored the participation of students in the activities of the Fascist trade unions.

The new 'legal' strategy of the Communists, however, was only partly successful due to the ambiguity of the Fascist attitude; by allowing the students to campaign in favour of a return to the original revolutionary spirit of the Fascist movement, the political leadership inclined them to accept, at least for some time, the less enthralling reality of Fascist society. More concretely, the development of a corporatist bureaucracy created new jobs for young intellectuals who thus were induced to adopt a more submissive attitude.

The Fascist student groups could be an excellent starting point for a career in the state and party administration, as the example of Agostino Podestà shows. Podestà was born in 1905 and headed the GUF of the university of Pavia from 1924 to 1929. After having served as Segretario federale of the Fascist Party in Avellino (1931), Verona (1932), and Padova (1934), he joined the state service and became prefect in Arezzo (1936), Perugia (1939), Bolzano (1940), and Fiume (1943). Even more brilliant was the career of Aldo Vidussoni, who was born in 1914 and became the national leader of the Fascist Party in

1941, after a career in the Fascist student organizations and in the Party. Students thus often tended to take the slogan 'make way for youth' very personally.

It remained nevertheless necessary for the regime to exercise strict control in order to avoid the emergence of a generation conflict which could hurt the interests of the ruling élite. For this reason, the Fascist leaders wanted to be associated with youth: they kept up a public image of physical fitness and hid the signs of ageing. Moreover, they put the accent on the spiritual values connected with youth, rather than on age. As all good Fascists were supposed to possess characteristics like enthusiasm and optimism they could claim that they had remained 'young'.

The alliance with Nazi Germany, Fascist Italy's participation in the Spanish Civil War, and the introduction of anti-Semitic legislation all contributed to reduce the possibilities for a 'leftist' interpretation of Fascism. The growing impossibility of criticizing the regime 'from within' did not automatically lead to an increase of anti-Fascism, but radically altered the nature of consensus. The young people who continued to give their support to Fascism and who were still numerous during the tragic epilogue of the Republic of Salò did so as an act of faith, because they believed that a return to the revolutionary origins of the movement was still possible, or because they deemed that only in this way could they honour the patriotic values which they cherished.

During the Second World War the myth of youth turned against the Fascists who now found themselves in the unfortunate position of being identified as members of the older generation. Anti-Fascist movements had a growing influence among the young, and in 1942 the Communist leader Palmiro Togliatti observed gleefully that a change of generations had finally come about.

The nationalization of the masses

In the lower classes the myth of youth separated young people from the members of the older generation, who were looked upon as remnants of the past, incapable of appreciating Fascist modernity. Young workers were encouraged to identify with members of the same age group rather than with the other members of the working class. Often, however, their participation in the activities of the Fascist mass organizations was considered a form of betrayal by those who had suffered the violence of the Fascist squads and who refused to adapt to the Fascist lifestyle. During the 1930s generational conflicts started to undermine the idea of class solidarity, which seemed increasingly obsolete.

For the regime the mere repression of anti-Fascism was not sufficient: it aimed at cancelling the very memory of the opposition and was aware that its control over Italian society depended on its capacity to control the political formation of youth. Generally, the education of young people from the lower classes aimed at a passive integration in the Fascist mass organizations which did not leave much scope for autonomy, unlike the student organizations that were supposed to train the future leading class. The Fascist leaders invested both energy and financial resources in setting up new youth organizations, the first of which, the Opera Nazionale Balilla (ONB), was founded in April 1926. By 1937 the Gioventù Italiana del Littorio, which had incorporated the ONB, putting it under the direct control of the Fascist Party, offered children and young people of both sexes, from age 6 to 21, opportunities for leisure time activities, and contributed also to their political indoctrination. Upon entering the organization, young Italians had to swear that they would execute all the Duce's orders without discussion and that they would serve the cause of the Fascist revolution, if necessary with their blood.

Even though participation was formally not mandatory, it was difficult for pupils of primary and secondary schools not to adhere to the Fascist organizations, especially if they liked sports. In the higher age groups, where school attendance was much lower, the organization rate dropped rapidly. Geographical location played a role as well: percentages were generally much higher in the industrialized and densely populated regions of the north than in the south. Finally sex made an important difference: although the numbers in the Fascist women's organizations increased substantially during the 1930s, the organization rate remained higher among boys and young men than among girls and young women. Moralist objections to female appearance in public were a decisive factor in this regard.

The success of the Fascist youth organizations, which by 1937 had more than seven million members, forced even convinced anti-

Fascists to allow their sons and daughters to participate. Many gave in because they feared that a refusal would create obstacles for the careers of their children or make them social outcasts. To allow participation, however, inevitably implied a recognition of Fascism's role in education and made the transmission of alternative values more difficult. The Fascist leaders were well aware of this and were clever enough not to discriminate against the children of anti-Fascists.

One of the most popular measures introduced by the regime regarded the creation of *colonie*. Hundreds of thousands of children, most of them from the urban working-class areas of the north, for the first time in their life spent some time at the seaside or in the mountains, were fed, had fun, and learned the basic principles of Fascist doctrine. The success of the *colonie*, which hosted some 240,000 children in 1931 and reached the number of 800,000 in 1939, contributed significantly to the creation of a mass consensus for the regime.

Sport also played an important role in the nationalization of the masses. Since 1927 the ONB was in charge of the mandatory courses of physical education in primary and secondary schools. Membership of the Fascist Party was a prerequisite for sports instructors who were trained at the newly founded academies in Rome (for men) and Orvieto (for women). Mussolini was aware of the value of sport for political propaganda and nominated loyal Fascists to key positions. After the Olympic Games of Amsterdam 1928, Augusto Turati was designated president of the Italian Olympic Committee. The president of the National Soccer Federation was Leandro Arpinati, ex-leader of the Bolognese squads, who gave a major impulse to the modernization of sports facilities. In the major cities new football stadiums were built, often designed by well-known architects, like the Florence stadium, named after the Fascist 'martyr' Giovanni Berta and designed by Pier Luigi Nervi, which was inaugurated in 1931.

The promotion of sports was successful: during the 1930s the Italian national team, coached by Vittorio Pozzo, won two world championships (Rome 1934 and Paris 1938), plus a gold medal at the 1936 Olympic Games of Berlin. The Fascists used sports to increase Italy's international prestige, to rally public opinion in favour of new national myths, and to educate 'the nation in arms'. In 1933 Primo Carnera became a national hero when he defeated Jack Sharkey and became the world heavyweight champion. Mussolini greeted the victory of this emigrant to America as the victory of 'all sporting and Fascist Italy'. As Patrick McCarthy has recently written, sportsmen like Primo Carnera and the 'flying Mantuan' Tazio Nuvolari, the first Italian driver to win the Grand Prix of Nuremberg (1935), became symbols of a new, more modern and virile Italy, redeemed thanks to the genius of Mussolini.

Totally different was the education of young women who were trained to become good mothers and housewives. These objectives were not always reached: a 1937 survey among Roman school girls showed that only few of them were interested in the 'profession of mother', and a vast majority preferred sport and cinema to domestic chores.

Ruralism and the peasant family

The exaltation of the idea of youth, with its connotations of change, progress, and modernity was in striking contrast with another cornerstone of Fascist doctrine: the ideal of the patriarchal family where roles and responsibilities were strictly related to age and sex. According to the Fascists, a good family was united by work and religion, had a high level of internal cohesion and solidarity, no internal conflicts, and was obedient to the male head of the family. The model was that of the multiple family household of the Tuscan sharecroppers, where several conjugal units (often brothers with their wives and children) lived and worked together under the authority of an older male (generally the father or the oldest brother). This type of family was supposed to guarantee continuity and social cohesion. Sharecropping was described as an almost ideal example of cooperation between capital and labour, as both the peasants and the proprietors had a vested interest in the success of the rural enterprise.

In reality, during the 1930s the system of sharecropping entered a deep crisis: poverty forced families to split up and many peasants left the countryside for the cities. In the Fascist interpretation, however, not poverty, but female whims led to the decision to abandon the *podere* and the patriarchal family: 'When young men get married they are anxious to abandon their parents and to create their own families, because their young wives do not accept the authority of the head of the family, and wish to move to the cities where they can amuse themselves more easily'.[2] According to this interpretation, the causes of the crisis were, above all, psychological and were linked to changes in gender roles which made it impossible for men to resist the pressure put upon them by their wives. Fascist family policies aimed therefore at reconstructing male authority, and opposed the spirit of independence in young people which threatened the survival of the traditional family.

It is true that in the more advanced and prosperous areas the conditions of young women had changed. In Emilia, for instance, according to a study published by the National Institute of Agrarian Economy gender relations had become more easygoing: 'sturdy young men without many artifices make place on their bike for peasant girls who are happy to be carried around from one village to another to have an ice-cream or to go to the movies'.[3] To attribute urbanization to female whims, however, would mean denying the effects of the deep crisis which hit Italian agriculture in the early 1930s and which threatened the survival of many peasant families who had already been living in almost untenable conditions.

Even taking into consideration the rather low standards of the period, housing conditions in the countryside were bad. According to the 1931 population survey, about one-fourth of all Italians lived in one-room habitations. Italy's average habitation rate (number of persons per room) was 1.4, but in overwhelmingly rural regions like Basilicata and Puglia the number went up to 2.6, where a population rate of more than two indicated that habitations were overcrowded. A 1934 survey of rural dwellings in the southern regions of Abruzzo and Molise calculated that 52 per cent were not habitable and needed urgent repairs or should be demolished. In Milocca, in the Sicilian province of Caltanissetta, people shared the one room where they slept and cooked with animals like chickens, dogs, and sometimes even a mule or a pig. In this peasant village all inhabitants had to fetch the water at three waterpits, which in summer frequently dried up.

[2] Quoted in Simona Colarizi, *L'opinione degli italiani sotto il regime, 1929–1943* (Rome–Bari, 1991), p. 103.
[3] 'Una famiglia di mezzadri nel comune di Vignola', in Istituto nazionale di economia agraria, *Monografie di famiglie agricole*, Vol. VI. *Contadini della valle del Panaro (Emilia)* (Milan–Rome, 1936), pp. 14–15.

Conditions were not much better in the North. In Cisliano, near Milan, the general impression conveyed by a 1937 survey was one of extreme poverty: houses were damp, dirty, and overcrowded, and generally consisted of only two rooms on different levels, of which the one at street level was hardly fit for habitation due to humidity. In the mountain areas of Lombardy, during winter, peasants were forced to seek protection against the cold in the cow stable because no other suitable rooms were available. In most rural dwellings electricity, running water, and sanitary facilities were absent or insufficient. Some observers justified this situation by claiming that sanitary facilities were a luxury item unsuited for peasant homes, but even those who acknowledged the need of rural workers to wash themselves were aware that only the least expensive and most basic facilities had a possibility of being adopted.

The workload of women, who had almost complete responsibility for domestic chores, was extremely heavy, especially since in most rural areas women's responsibilities included work in the fields. According to surveys carried out in the 1930s the total number of annual working hours of women in sharecropping areas was often more than 3,500; on the farms of the Alps of Trent it was not unusual for women to work more than 4,400 hours per year, an average of more than twelve hours per day.

The work of women was an important resource for peasant families. Among the day labourers of the Po Valley, women earned more than their husbands by working in the ricefields, picking fruit, or ploughing the earth. Moreover, peasant women often were actively involved in commercial transactions selling flowers, mushrooms, strawberries, or eggs in the market of nearby cities and thus contributing in cash to the family income. Although women worked longer hours than men, their contribution to family activities was less appreciated. Arrigo Serpieri, agronomist and Minister of Agriculture, calculated the value of women's work at only 60 per cent that of men.

In the early 1930s the fall in the price of agricultural products made life ever more difficult for peasants, who in many areas also had to cope with the diffusion of grape phylloxera, which made it necessary to eradicate numerous vineyards. The consequences were disastrous: in 1931 farm workers had to accept a cut in their wages of 24 per cent. Even though prices also declined, it is likely that real income declined even more due to the increased difficulty of finding work. Fascism reacted by promoting a campaign in favour of *sbracciantizzazione*, the transformation of wage labourers into sharecroppers. In reality, as we have already seen, sharecroppers were suffering from poverty as well. Practically all of them were heavily indebted, and many peasants had no money to pay taxes. The situation was made worse by the impression that city dwellers were better off: not only were the wage cuts in industry lower, but also access to welfare and charity provisions was easier. In these conditions the more honest observers admitted that peasant women had excellent reasons for preferring city dwellers as marriage partners and for abandoning the farms for which they frequently carried almost the entire workload.

Migration often seemed the only way out, but the introduction in many countries of restrictions on immigration and the adoption in Italy of legal measures against internal migration made it more difficult to adopt this solution. Already in 1926 the Fascist government had set up a Permanent Committee to study the problem of internal migration with the aim of directing the flow of migrants to regions where the labour force was scarce. The prefects were instructed to adopt measures to reduce the excessive increase of the urban population. Legislation introduced in 1931 tried to regulate seasonal migration flows and its efficiency was enhanced by public security measures providing for special control on non-residents and authorizing the forced deportation of 'idlers and vagabonds'. Finally, in 1939, legislation was adopted which linked the release of a permit of residence to having a stable job, while at the same time a working permit was issued only to legal residents.

Temporary migration had allowed the survival of the rural population, albeit at subsistence level, by increasing the net income in areas where the increase in the revenues from agriculture lagged behind the needs of a growing population. By working for part of the year in the nearby cities or abroad peasants had managed to reach a minimum level of income. Restrictions on temporary migration now forced peasants to give up their small rural enterprises because they no longer had the opportunity for gaining the indispensable extra income.

In the absence of radical measures for the improvement of the living conditions of the peasants, the restrictions on temporary migration backfired, turning temporary migration into permanent migration. The ineffectiveness of the measures aiming to curb the trend of urbanization should not be read only as the result of the contradictions within Fascist doctrine, but above all as the logical outcome of Fascist economic and social policies which favoured the urban middle classes at the expense of the rural poor. As a result, between 1931 and 1936 the urbanization rate was 21.1 per thousand, second only to that of the all-time record of the period 1951–61. Italy was rapidly becoming an urban society.

Given the dismal conditions of rural life, the Fascist appeal for a voluntary return to the countryside was not convincing. The low standard of living in rural areas made the anti-urban bias of many Fascist discourses sound like little more than a rhetorical exercise. Moreover, the transformation of the urban unemployed into peasants was rarely successful. The city dwellers often were unable to adjust to their new conditions. Because many of them did not possess the necessary physical strength and technical knowledge, they frequently ended up joining the masses of the rural unemployed. Like the illegal immigrants who were obliged to leave the cities and to return to their places of origin, those whose relocation to the countryside had been unsuccessful became dependent on charity or party welfare programmes. Thus, ruralization often meant shifting the burden of mass lay-offs in industry from the cities to the countryside.

One of the objectives of anti-urban propaganda was to avoid the concentration in cities of the poor and unemployed who could become a source of social unrest. The desire to eliminate situations which could facilitate the emergence of political dissent also inspired urban planning. The improvement in the living conditions of the poor in this case was only a secondary aim. In Rome, for instance, the demolition of some old town quarters did not have any positive consequences for the original population: many of those who were expelled from the city centre were deported to the twelve new *borgate* built well outside the city, in peripheral areas lacking all urban amenities, including streets and transit connections to the city. The so-called 'popular' building projects which offered better conditions in reality often catered above all to the rapidly expanding category of private and public employees.

Women and the 'battle for births'

As Mussolini had explained in his famous 1927 Ascension Day speech, the return to the countryside was meant above all to counter the negative influence of modern urban society on the birth rate. In the demographic campaign, the cities were described in the most gloomy terms. According to health inspectors, tuberculosis, venereal diseases, and other forms of contagion were rampant in the cities because of the concentration of the population in overcrowded apartments where no distinction was made between sexes and age groups, or between the healthy and the sick; where space was scarce and light, air, and water were insufficient. The consequences of urbanization for the moral conditions of the population were seen as even more negative. Fascist authors accused the cities of corrupting the mentality of the peasants: seduced by hedonism, the peasants who migrated to the cities forgot all moral values and lost the spirit of sacrifice necessary to educate numerous offspring. It is obvious that in this comparison between city and country life the real conditions of peasants hardly played a role.

The 'battle for births' became one of the dominant motives of Fascist propaganda. As the slogan 'number means force' indicates, Mussolini was convinced of the importance of an increased population for the military strength of Italy. However, economic considerations also played a role: an increase in the population meant more competition on the labour market—and therefore lower labour costs—and an increase in the number of consumers. Finally, Italian demographers were convinced that demographic growth had a positive impact on the quality of the population.

With the support of the Catholic Church, the Fascist demographic campaign adopted the principles of 'positive' eugenics, aiming at an increase in both the quantity and the quality of the population, in contrast with the 'negative' eugenics which in Germany and elsewhere led to the elimination of the 'unfit'. The combined effort of the most important political and spiritual authorities makes the failure of the campaign in favour of a rapid increase of the population even more remarkable. In fact, notwithstanding measures like tax exemptions and better career opportunities for fathers of large families and the prohibition of birth control, the regime did not succeed in checking the decline of the birth rate. Especially among the middle classes, normally most loyal to Fascism, few men and women were willing to sacrifice the chances for upward social mobility of their children in order to please the regime. By limiting the number of children, they intended to give them better opportunities.

War and economic crises undoubtedly greatly influenced the decisions regarding the number of children, but maybe even more important was the change in the attitude of women. This explains in part the efforts of the regime to convince women that their place was in the family and in the household.

Recent studies have tried to show that women under Fascism were not only the victims of repression, but also gained new opportunities. While it is true that Fascism, maybe for the first time in Italian history, acknowledged the role of women as social actors, it should be noted that this recognition took place in an authoritarian context and that it did not lead to female liberation. Turning maternity into a civic duty, Fascism put more responsibility on the shoulders of women, without granting them any new rights. In this sense Luisa Passerini has spoken of a 'repressive modernization' the costs of which were borne chiefly by women.

During the 1920s and 1930s a small élite of women, most of them with a middle- or upper-class background, participated in intellectual discussions. Female students, who until 1939 were not admitted to the *Littoriali*, were able to profit from the opportunities offered by the Fascist student press to express their ideas. In their writings Fascism's effort in mobilizing women was often interpreted as an alternative to feminism:

Fascism, without forcing them, led women back to their duties as housekeepers, and reconciled the new duties which were assigned to them with their maternal instincts. Fascism does not want women to be passively obedient to men, but conscious of their responsibilities and of their rights. . . . By bringing women back to their homes, Fascism is not aiming at their confinement because the new modern home has its doors open to the society to which it belongs.[4]

---

[4] Bianca Fleury Nencini, *La donna fascista nella famiglia nel lavoro e nella società* (Pisa, 1936), pp. 4–5.

Housekeeping, procreation, and education were thus transformed into civic duties.

Fascism introduced novelties also for women from the lower classes. On the positive side, the National Foundation for the Protection of Maternity and Infancy (ONMI), founded in 1925, offered many women and children access to health care. The activities of the ONMI helped to create the impression that Fascism had the firm intention to improve the quality of life of Italian women. However, the quality and quantity of medical assistance differed according to region and was virtually absent in the rural south. ONMI admitted only women who complied with its regulations (making, for instance, breastfeeding mandatory) and who were willing to accept visits of control by inspectors. Welfare thus helped to establish public control over the private life of women. The results of the ONMI activities were rather disappointing: the Italian infant mortality rate in the first year of life remained almost double that of the European average.

Generally speaking, for women, integration into the political system meant above all assuming new responsibilities: in order to comply with the new rules of autarchy the peasant women belonging to the organization of the *massaie rurali* were required to raise rabbits, chickens and bees. Women's civic duties were particularly heavy in the colonies, where the presence of Italian women was supposed to protect men against temptations and thus to guarantee the moral superiority of the colonizers: 'The rigid defence of race is the responsibility of the Italian woman who has a proud mind and pure customs, and will admit no racial promiscuity which would reduce her to the level of slavery'.[5]

Convinced that work for wages could not be combined with the duties of maternity, the Fascist leaders opposed female employment in industry and in the service sector, while at the same time exalting the contribution of women to agriculture. Blaming women for male unemployment, Fascism reaffirmed already existing elements of conflict within the working class. The regime, however, proved unable to reduce the level of female employment significantly, except in public administration. Lower wages for women, established by law in 1927, not surprisingly had the effect of making it more attractive for employers to hire them. Moreover, the low level of male wages made

[5] Laura Marani, *Preparazione della donna alla vita coloniale* (Milan, 1938), pp. 4–5.

women's work indispensable for the family. As a result, in the 1930s Fascist Italy continued to have a higher proportion of married female wage-earners than most other European nations, even though the law placed clear restrictions on female employment.

Although most aspects of Fascist population policies received the enthusiastic support of the Catholic Church, Party and Church did not generally share the same objectives; nor did the Church always approve Fascist methods. Catholic moralists feared that the participation of women in the Fascist mass organizations would distract them from their duties in the family and in the household. The participation of girls and young women in gymnastic exhibitions was judged as contrary to public decency. Sport was positive only if it prepared women for maternity. As far as gender relations were concerned, Catholic doctrine insisted that both for men and women sexual activities outside marriage were sinful, whereas most Fascists subscribed to the idea that extra-conjugal sex was part of male nature and considered the visits to brothels of young men as a positive expression of the exuberant sexuality of the Latin male.

Technology, consumption, and the media

The successes of the Italian aviation and the new *autostrade* contributed to establishing Fascism's modern image, but at the same time confirmed the impression of superficiality which often characterizes the regime's attitude towards expressions of modernity. Fascism did little to improve the overall quality of Italian roads. Most *autostrade*—like those between Milan and the Lombard lakes, between Rome and Ostia, and between Florence and the coast—connected cities with holiday resorts, and catered almost exclusively for a high-society public.

Something similar took place in aviation. In the 1920s record-holders like Carlo Del Prete, Francesco De Pinedo, and Ernesto Campanile became popular heroes thanks to their victories in international competitions and their individual exploits. In 1930–1 a squadron of the Italian airforce headed by Italo Balbo crossed the Ocean and toured South America. When in 1933 Balbo reached the shores of North America after a long-distance flight as commander of a squadron of twenty-four seaplanes enthusiasm reached its zenith. Italian immigrants enjoyed the new prestige of their home country and thousands of them participated in the celebrations held in Montreal, Chicago, and New York. The personal success of Balbo was enormous: the mayor of Chicago offered him the keys of the city and 15 July was declared 'Italo Balbo's Day'.

These successes, however, could not cover the fact that the development of civil air transport in Italy lagged behind. The first regular flight, connecting Trieste, Venice, and Pavia was inaugurated in April 1926, soon followed by others, including Brindisi–Constantinople and Venice–Vienna. The number of passengers increased from 3,991 in 1926 to 33,650 in 1931, but remained low when compared with the more advanced European nations.

Speed and technology were not only a privilege of the happy few: in a passive way, many Italians participated in the successes of Italian cars and pilots through the radio and the press. The Fascist leaders were often fascinated by modern technology but at the same time hesitant about the possible effects of its diffusion among the masses as is shown by their use of the new mass media. The Fascists were quick to understand the importance of the radio and movies for propaganda, but feared that the images and impressions of a more affluent and cosmopolitan society might arouse the desire for geographical and social mobility and thus contribute to undermining the values of authority, obedience, and religion, still so important in rural society. The tension between modernizing and traditionalist impulses was expressed clearly in Italian cinema, where films like *Il Signor Max* (1937) conveyed both the fascination with the cosmopolitan world of the Grand Hôtels and the conviction that real happiness could be found only in the family, in work, and in normal life.

Moralists especially feared the enormous popularity of American movies which were accused of fomenting the rebellion of young people and women, by providing images of a country where traditional hierarchies did not count, and where materialism and the cult of success seemed to have cancelled religious values and the sense of sacrifice. The adoption of a new lifestyle by young people who, especially in the cities, openly questioned the rules regulating courtship, and the growing diffusion of flirting were seen as the consequences of these pernicious foreign influences. The so-called modern girls,

lly, were accused of following the American example in their
for sexual freedom.

e 1930s saw a rapid expansion of consumer culture in Italy: new
department stores opened and manufactured soap and toothpaste
became articles of mass consumption, just like the canned tomatoes
of Cirio and Buitoni's pasta had become earlier. Advertising was used
on an ever-wider scale to attract new consumers. The anti-bourgeois
campaign launched in 1938 shows the extent to which Italian society
had changed notwithstanding Fascist opposition to 'Americanization'. The bourgeoisie was attacked because of its self-interested outlook on life, its lack of enthusiasm, and its scarce contribution to the
demographic battle. The campaign aimed at extending Fascist control over civil society and convinced many young Fascists of the revolutionary intentions of the regime. Yet many other Italians loathed
the frequent inroads into their private life, and sided with the Catholic Church in its defence of the autonomy of the family against state
control. However, neither the Catholic Church nor the Fascist State
were able to protect traditional Italian society against the rising tide
of consumer culture.

Victoria De Grazia has written that Fascism tried to promote its
own model of 'restricted consumption', organizing the public as
consumers by using mass organizations like the Opera Nazionale
Dopolavoro (OND), founded in 1925 with the purpose of providing
workers with 'healthy and profitable leisure time activity'. The Dopolavoro card gave access to discounts, but in doing so at the same time
established a hierarchy in expenditures, favouring those products—
like radios and insurance plans—from which the Fascist political and
economic system could benefit. The members of the Dopolavoro
organization greatly appreciated the opportunities to participate in
short trips which allowed them, often for the first time, to visit historical sites or other tourist attractions, and helped them to widen their
intellectual horizon.

The OND was part of a Fascist welfare system, the creation of
which had started in 1925 with the foundation of the ONMI. The
various measures introduced by the regime—including health insurance and insurance against accidents on the job—did not create a
general right to public assistance, but gave special privileges to certain
categories of workers, like public servants. Fascism thus laid the
foundation for the post-war creation of a sectional and clientelistic

system of welfare. Notwithstanding these obvious limits and even though resources were insufficient and unevenly distributed over the national territory, the existence of the welfare system was crucial to the legitimization of Fascist rule.

In the debate about which forms of modernization should be promoted in Italy, the American experience was of course the point of reference. The discussion was not entirely theoretical as the 'Americanization' of Italian society was in full course in the 1930s when American products—from chewing gum to typewriters and from movies to gramophones—invaded the Italian market. Young men dressed '*alla Fox*', and young women wanted to be slim and had their hair bobbed, trying to look like Hollywood stars. As Mario Soldati wrote in 1935, 'America is not just a part of the world. America is a state of mind, a passion. From one moment to another, any European can catch the American disease, revolt against Europe, and become American.'[6]

The limits of consumerism in Fascist Italy appear clearly in the attempts to rationalize domestic work. After the Italian publication of Christine Frederick's ground-breaking *The New Housekeeping* in 1928, a new journal, *Casa e lavoro*, started to propagate the application of the principles of scientific management to domestic chores. Contrary to the situation in Germany and in the Netherlands where the rationalization of domestic work had found practical applications also in popular building projects, in Italy aesthetic considerations prevailed over functionality leading to a radical change in the design of the interiors of middle-class apartments. A good example is the *Cucina elettrica*, the electric kitchen presented at the 1930 Monza Triennial Exhibition. Journals like *Domus* and *La Casa Bella* contributed to educating the taste of new customers.

Rationalization, however, was not only limited to educating middle-class consumers: the Fascist women's movements organized numerous courses in 'domestic economy' in order to teach women of the lower classes how to use the principles of scientific management to run their household with more efficiency, to make ends meet, and thus to fulfil their duties as housewives. In this sense, rationalization helped Fascism to gain more control over the private sphere and contributed to focusing the attention of the political leadership on

---

[6] Mario Soldati, *America, primo amore* (Florence, 1935), p. 199.

the economic role of housewives. Advertisements were also increasingly directed at women because the manufacturers were aware that they took most of the decisions about spending. This celebration of women as thrifty housewives and discerning consumers reinforced traditional gender roles but at the same time contributed to altering the balance of power within the family.

Outside the household, the ideals of rationality were important above all in the industrial sector. Here, however, the attempts to introduce the Bedaux system, which allowed for a strict control of the level of productivity, met with the fierce opposition of the workers who refused to accept higher workloads without the wage increases which elsewhere had accompanied the introduction of new methods of production. Even the most enthusiastic supporters of rationalization admitted that the combination of cost-cutting measures and increased exploitation of the labour force was to the exclusive advantage of the employers. The Fascist state guaranteed these favourable conditions by suppressing workers' unrest using both repressive measures and the newly founded welfare system.

Conclusion: Fascist contradictions

The contradictions within the Fascist model of social and economic development and the contrast between the ambitious declarations of the regime and its relatively scarce achievements can only be understood by taking into consideration the fact that Fascist doctrine was not a purely theoretical construction, but was (re-)elaborated day by day, taking into account the challenges coming both from within and from outside Italy. The contradictions stemmed also from the necessity to reconcile the interests of the various social groups which had given their support to the regime in order to maintain a precarious balance of power.

In a similar way, the plurality of images of Mussolini (Mussolini on the beach with his wife and children in 1923, Mussolini the lion tamer of 1925 challenging the Socialist beast, Mussolini-aviator, Mussolini-athlete, Mussolini–violinist, Mussolini-revolutionary, and Mussolini in tailcoat and tophat as member of the Establishment) allowed different readings of the role of Fascism in Italian society and of the position of Mussolini himself, thus facilitating identification. Depending on the viewpoint of the observer, Fascism could appear revolutionary or conservative, religious or pagan, bellicose or pacific, and attract support for opposite reasons. Far from being an indication of the inherent weakness of Fascism, the polymorphism and the polysemy of Fascist doctrine were crucial to the creation of consensus.

The general objective of the Fascist leaders was to develop an Italian model of modernization, which would combine scientific and technological progress with the preservation of traditional values. This attempt to elaborate an alternative model of modernity received the full support of Catholic intellectuals who dreaded the consequences of secularization, but appreciated the possibilities for evangelization offered by the new mass media. Fascism tried to reconcile two opposite trends: one identifying with modernity ('epochalist' in the terminology of Clifford Geertz), the other with traditional, rural values ('essentialist'). The myth of ruralism, celebrated by the Fascists notwithstanding rapid urbanization and industrialization, was part of this contradictory model of social development. The images of peaceful rural communities and harmonious patriarchal families helped the urban middle classes, who cherished the illusion of progress without change, to dominate the social and psychological tensions engendered by the transition from a rural to an industrial society.

The visual arts: modernism and Fascism

Emily Braun

In 1948 the first Venice Biennale since the fall of Fascism claimed to re-establish Italian art within the main currents of European modernism. But modern art during the *Ventennio* had never been repressed; to the contrary, the regime had supported the artistic avant-garde in word and deed. As Giorgio de Chirico put it, 'For the sake of truth it must be said that the Fascists never forbade people to paint as they wished. The majority of the Fascist hierarchy were in fact modernists enamored of Paris.'[1] Yet in the decades following the Second World War both the vitality of the visual arts and the actual histories of individual artists were lost to ignorance, shame, and the presumption that Fascism, as a totalitarian enterprise, corrupted all forms of creative expression under its auspices. Only since the 1970s have scholars revised the view—put into place by Benedetto Croce—that Fascism was a mere parenthesis in the history of Italian culture. The visual arts thrived under Fascism, leaving a body of works now accepted in the canon of twentieth-century modernism; at the same time, artistic production was inextricably linked to the propaganda imperatives of the regime.

If Fascism is credited with aestheticizing politics by pressing the

---

[1] Giorgio de Chirico, *The Memoirs of Giorgio de Chirico*, trans. Margaret Crosland (London, 1971), pp. 184–5.

THE VISUAL ARTS | 1ɔ,

mass media into the service of aura and ritual, it is also true that aesthetics were politicized in the attempt to create a totalitarian state and Fascist 'new man'. A generation before Fascism came to power, artists and intellectuals yearned to modernize the Italian nation and its culture on a par with Europe. The Italian avant-garde embraced artistic modernism from France and Germany, at the same time as it refuted the rhetoric of art for art's sake in favour of cultural intervention and militant nationalism. Fascism attracted artists who rejected the compromised politics of both Socialism and parliamentary democracy in favour of radical action. They were also driven by a deep-seated fear of professional obsolescence: how would traditional painting, sculpture, and architecture survive in the age of mass politics and mechanical reproduction? Mussolini's speeches played on creative metaphors of 'moulding the masses' and 'constructing new myths', assuring artists an élite position in the hierarchical Fascist state.[2] Artists were able and willing to represent the faces of Fascism in innovative and persuasive ways; conversely, the regime accrued prestige and consensus through its calculated patronage of the fine arts.

The experience of the avant-garde under Fascism alters the long-standing presumption that modernism was the purview of centre and left-wing politics. Not only was the regime highly favourable to international-style architecture, but it readily exploited Russian Constructivist designs for its own propaganda exhibitions, and tolerated cubism, expressionism, and geometric abstraction. Hence, Fascism occupies a particular position with regard to the fine arts: refuting the dictated aesthetics of the Stalinist and Nazi regimes, it built consensus through a pluralist patronage style comparable to that of democratic nations between the wars. A liberal cultural policy ensured the livelihood of the liberal arts, while active state intervention served to distinguish Fascism from the laissez-faire attitude of the Giolittian period. Moreover the regime's position towards artists—free to create but obliged to serve—upheld the view of Fascism as a Third Way between communism and capitalism, intolerant of both anonymity and anarchic individualism.

Fascist culture was no mere by-product of political ideology, but

---

[2] See Mussolini's speech at the inauguration of the Prima Mostra del Novecento, 15 Feb. 1926, reprinted in *Scritti e discorsi di Benito Mussolini*, Vol. V (1934), pp. 279–82.

the chief means of its construction and representation. ~gh ubiquitous monuments, daily rites, and the systematic relay ~rd and image, Fascism aimed at creating a 'total style of life', in ~sonal comportment as well as environmental design. Yet in practice, high culture often drove a breach into the totalitarian fabric and uniformity desired by the regime. Cultural policies made sharp distinctions between the fine arts and base propaganda. Innovative and far-reaching in their control of cinema, radio, youth groups, and leisure organizations, the Fascists upheld the traditional autonomy of painting and sculpture, even while encouraging wider distribution and audience through exhibitions and public commissions. Reducing art to an instrument of indoctrination was anathema to Italian critics, many of whom, such as F. T. Marinetti, Margherita Sarfatti, Giuseppe Bottai, and Cipriano Efisio Oppo, occupied key positions of power and enjoyed direct access to the Duce. As a result, the expression and reception of ideology were often ambiguous in content: artistic intention and actual works of art could be open to conflicting interpretations, and in some instances be critical of the regime. But this was one of many paradoxes generated by the fundamental contradiction of pluralist culture under a totalitarian state: Fascists infused modernism with classical values and usurped visual idioms that derived from ideologies antithetical to their own.

This is not to say that high culture was immune to propaganda: on the contrary, the same autonomy that guaranteed a relative freedom of expression also served to legitimize the regime at home and abroad. Individual initiative, not an enforced party line, produced aesthetic quality, and pluralism was the strongest argument for the purported 'spiritual values' and 'universalizing mission' of Fascism. Italian achievements in architecture and the arts over two millennia were held up, not only as the finest expression of an empire and a people, but of Western civilization on the whole. Linking Augustan Rome to the Third Rome of Fascism, Mussolini drew on an incomparable cultural patrimony to augment his diplomatic weight in the European arena and stir domestic pride. A rhetoric of cultural imperialism justified Fascist bellicose and colonialist policies. The stark separation of high and low also gave truth to the lie of a 'Fascist humanism', by distancing the regime from the 'anti-culture' of Nazi Germany and the Soviet Union, and even the 'venal' capitalism of America. Lastly, the respect afforded to artistic vocations countered the regime's own reputation for brutality while allying intellectuals' fears over the standardization entailed in 'nationalizing' the masses.

The history of the visual arts under Fascism includes the bureaucratic apparatus imposed by the regime, and the individual contributions of those who collaborated in varying degrees. The government regulated professional conduct and used economic incentives to ensure the loyalty of artists and architects. Whereas the establishment of centralized unions and state-run exhibitions guaranteed a veneer of managerial efficiency, the absence of dictated aesthetics gave intellectuals the illusion of personal freedom in evolving a specifically Fascist art. Like Lenin and Trotsky in the early years of the Bolshevik revolution, Mussolini understood that new culture had to rise gradually from the remnants of bourgeois institutions, and he built upon the status quo of competing artistic movements. As long as artists evoked grand themes of *italianità*, *mediterraneità*, and *latinità*—they could pursue any number of visual representations. A famous inquiry conducted by the Fascist minister Bottai in 1926–7 confirmed that the majority of Fascist intellectuals rejected the idea of an art of the state, as well as bombastic neoclassicism and illustrative kitsch. As a result of this beguiling pluralism, various movements openly jostled for state recognition, critics voraciously debated the most appropriate styles, and party officials established their own cultural fiefdoms. The margin of creative freedom afforded by the regime effectively channelled potential dissent among the intellectual class.

To be sure, the relationship between artists and the regime, as well as the quality of creative production, was never static, but changed in reaction to Fascist foreign and domestic policies. During the second decade of Fascism, the conflict between commitment and autonomy fostered bitter factionalism among progressive artists and architects. In 1935–6 Mussolini's colonial campaign in Ethiopia and the subsequent sanctions levelled against Italy brought new pressures to bear: as the nation geared for war and empire, so too did culture. Less open to international trends and formal experimentation under the regime's hard-line policy of cultural autarchy, the arts were also submitted to increasing demands for dogmatic content. Mundane naturalism, rhetorical neoclassicism, and monumental scale became the order of the day. The alliance with Nazi Germany and the legislation of the anti-Semitic laws further polarized views on creative freedom and the legitimacy of modernism as an inherently Italian style, but the regime never reversed its pluralist stance. Here too, the retrenchment of modernism in Italy in the later 1930s bears comparison to developments in France and America, where the conservative rhetoric of a 'return to man', and ideological battles over style led to the enervation of the historical avant-garde. What distinguishes the visual arts under Fascism, however, is how modernist aesthetics were used for anti-democratic politics, and, after 1938, the open persecution of Jewish artists.

The foundations of Fascist culture and the regime's policies were laid in the immediate post-war years, in large part influenced by the avant-garde generation. The first decades of the century saw the rise of Futurism, the first full-fledged Italian modernist movement, whose resounding influence abroad could not be ignored by those intent on producing an innovative culture with international clout. Moreover, Marinetti's political theatre and mass marketing—as well as his rhetoric of violence and virility—provided a blueprint for Fascist political spectacle. Beginning with the Interventionist period, Futurism shared with nascent Fascism the desire to circumvent class conflict through the secular religion of the state. Like Gabriele D'Annunzio before them, the Futurists promoted the cult of 'Italian genius', and the idea that a creative élite, not the masses or productive forces, would shape the new Italy. Though proponents of modernization, the Futurists abhorred the standardization and anonymity ascribed to the 'Bolshevik' model. And although the machine was ubiquitous in Futurist image and texts, the movement never systematically exploited mechanical forms of reproduction, such as photography or cinema, which would have ensured mass audience and distribution. Instead, the Futurists' legacy was one of irrepressible individualism and unwavering allegiance to the *patria*, a combination that inevitably led to instances of conflict and accommodation in its relationship with the regime. Even as Marinetti donned the robes of the conservative Accademia d'Italia, for example, he could use his personal celebrity to assail the Nazi-inspired anti-modernist campaign of the late 1930s. Because of its historic role in the founding of Fascism, the Futurist movement stood for the mythic revolutionary days of Fascism; Marinetti exploited this symbolic capital to ensure the livelihood of the movement throughout the *Ventennio*, though it was never privileged in state commissions or purchases.

Futurism was inevitably altered as many of its key practitioners changed allegiances in the post-war 'return to order'. Yet it continued to carry the banners of youth and modernism in the arts, and proliferated as a national movement with followers all over the peninsula and a new base in Rome. Indeed, it was only in the 1920s that Futurism realized its ambitions to 'reconstruct the universe', extending its practice to stage design, fashion, furniture, murals, and exhibition installations. Of the original Futurists, Giacomo Balla proved the main influence on the younger generation with his brilliantly coloured, synthetic cubist style, and forays into the decorative arts. He also drew mystical renditions of Mussolini in blackshirt for the journal *L'Impero* after the March on Rome. Balla's chief disciple, Fortunato Depero, developed a signature style of mechanistic imagery in stage design and graphics; his innovative advertising campaigns for private companies (most notably for Campari in 1925–33) were among the few opportunities afforded artists in the capitalist economy under Fascism. The other key figure of the 1920s, Enrico Prampolini, established links to the European avant-garde with his Dada-inspired periodical *Noi*, and then as a member of the Paris-based group of non-objective artists, Abstraction-Création. Balla, Prampolini, and Depero represented the Futurist contingent at the 1925 Paris Exposition Internationale des Arts Décoratifs et Industriels Modernes, and were the only competitive presence, given the woefully retrograde Italian pavilion—the first international show for the Fascist regime. Indeed the experience of the 1925 exhibition, with the stunning pavilions by Le Corbusier for L'Esprit Nouveau and Melnikov for the USSR, was a major impetus for the regime's progressive reorganization, in 1927, of the Triennale delle Arti Decorative ed Industriali Moderne.

The Futurist vision of modernity was challenged in many quarters; already, during the war, the former Futurists Carlo Carrà and Ardengo Soffici rejected analytic cubism in favour of a return to the Italian tradition. Theirs was no retrograde revival of past styles, but a reworking of Giotto and the Italian primitives through a modernist lens, specifically, the ironic classicism of Giorgio de Chirico. De Chirico himself had returned to Italy in 1915 after making his career in Paris; the influence of his Pittura Metafisica was tempered through his disciple Carrà, who defined the return to solidly modelled forms in nationalistic terms. The works of de Chirico, his brother Alberto Savinio, Carrà, Soffici, and Giorgio Morandi were promulgated in the Roman journal *Valori Plastici* (1918–22). Though unaffiliated with the

Fascist movement, the journal codified 'plastic values'—an art of tactile volumes and stark cubic masses—as an indigenous style; it also promoted the myth of Italians as a race of great constructors—a myth used by the regime to position artists as the privileged builders of the Fascist state. The art of *Valori Plastici* inspired the uncanny images of Magic Realism, or Neue Sachlichkeit, as it was known in Germany, as well as the dream painting of the French Surrealists. Likewise, the profound influence of de Chirico's early style on art and architecture in Fascist Italy cannot be underestimated: it ensured the legitimacy of a modern style based on an unorthodox, even subversive, use of classical vocabulary that undercut the regime's more pompous invocations of antiquity.

The specific alliance of 'plastic values' with a Fascist art was left to the critic Margherita Sarfatti, Marinetti's chief rival, and leader of the Novecento group. The Jewish-born Sarfatti was Mussolini's mistress for some twenty years; she directly influenced his cultural policies and penned his best-selling biography in 1925. Founded on the eve of the March on Rome, the Novecento group of seven painters rejected the deleterious 'confusion' of the pre-war period, and proclaimed a new social and spiritual order in art as well as in politics. The group's debut exhibition in March 1923 was the occasion for Mussolini's first official remarks on cultural policy: he disavowed 'anything resembling an art of the state', acknowledged the autonomous status of creative endeavours, and assured economic support to the arts. For her part, Sarfatti claimed her artists to be 'revolutionaries of the modern restoration', and argued for an art based on 'new aspects of tradition', establishing the contradictions that would inform Fascist culture well before government policies were put in place.[3]

Despite the opportunism of its conservative rhetoric, the Novecento did realize its aim for a 'modern classicism' in the style of Magic Realism, which characterized the enigmatic narratives of Mario Sironi, Achille Funi, and Ubaldo Oppi and those in the Novecento orbit such as Felice Casorati and Antonio Donghi. This group style dissipated by the mid-1920s, however, when Sarfatti opened the ranks to include artists of diverse stylistic and ideological bent in

---

[3] Margherita Sarfatti, preface from *Il Novecento Italiano: Catalogo della II mostra* (exh. cat., Palazzo della Permanente, Milan), 1929, reprinted in Rossana Bossaglia, *Il Novecento Italiano*, 2nd edn. (Milan, 1995), pp. 110–11.

order to create a national base and make the Novecento de facto the art of the Fascist state. In 1926 the first Mostra del Novecento italiano hosted over one hundred artists, among them Second Futurists and artists associated with *Valori Plastici*. But Sarfatti's ambitions backfired: the heterogeneous profile only underlined the lack of a representative art. Internal quarrels, rival movements, and jealousy over Sarfatti's influence weakened the Novecento, especially after its second exhibition in 1929. Although it was never declared the official art, the Novecento did much to shape the image of Italian art abroad in the 1920s; Sarfatti organized a series of major shows for the European capitals—a form of cultural diplomacy continued by the regime. Artists associated with the Novecento also received the bulk of state purchases and commissions until the mid-1930s. Even after its demise, the Novecento was assailed by intransigent quarters in the Fascist Party, led by Roberto Farinacci, whose xenophobic rhetoric presaged the anti-modernist, anti-Semitic campaign later in the decade.

The regime implemented its own policies and economic support for the arts in the second half of the 1920s. The Fascist Syndicate of the Fine Arts came under the jurisdiction of the Confederation of Artists and Professionals, an umbrella organization that also included syndicates for musicians, architects, and writers. Syndicate membership, which ostensibly required a PNF card, gave artists access to the state's new monopoly over exhibitions and distribution, on local, national, and international levels. Membership (and good conduct) was virtually obligatory for anyone who wanted to work, but the state did not regulate style and subjects, and esteemed artists, rather than hack bureaucrats, occupied positions of authority and influence. The syndicate system rewarded stalwart Fascists, drew the support of the younger generation, and allowed the politically uncommitted, or even opposed, to negotiate their positions. Mussolini continued to stress quality over conformism: 'One may be a Fascist of valour, even a Fascist of the "first hour", but an incompetent poet. . . . The party card does not give talent to those who do not already possess it.'[4] Though the dictatorship controlled the press, art criticism continued unabated: the number of art periodicals increased under the regime, and forums for open debate were commonly featured. By comparison

---

[4] Mussolini, speech of 10 Oct. 1928, *Scritti e Discorsi*, Vol. VI, p. 251.

to literature and cinema, with their narrative forms and mass audiences, censorship in the visual arts was minimal until the Racial Laws.

The new state patronage focused on a hierarchical system of exhibitions, beginning with the provincial and inter-provincial syndicate shows: over three hundred were held between 1927 and 1939, replacing traditional local arts associations and serving as a venue for emerging artists. The Rome Quadriennale, first held in 1931, bestowed national recognition upon established artists and movements with personal retrospectives and group shows. Significantly, a room at the Quadriennale depended on individual lobbying efforts and the judicious balances forged by the secretary-general, C. E. Oppo, rather than dictates from on high. The Venice Biennale, taken over by the state from the city of Venice in 1929, put Italian artists on a par with the international contingents, which were for the most part conservative, given the constitution of their own government committees. The secretary-general of the Biennale, Antonio Maraini, himself a mediocre sculptor, was also the most obsequious of Fascist arts administrators. Under his initiative the Biennale instituted prizes for stipulated subjects of didactic content for the first time in 1930, a form of scurrilous coercion that was publicly denounced by leading artists and critics. Although response was so poor that some prizes were withdrawn, subject competitions increased in the second decade of the regime as a means of attracting neophytes and minor talents. Lastly, the Milan Triennale supported modern architecture and the applied arts in an experimental milieu, with an eye to industrial production, new materials, and building types. It provided a public forum for the younger generation of architects and designers of the Rationalist movement, who were otherwise constricted by the conservative National Syndicate of Fascist Architects.

Ever mindful of consensus, the regime engaged leading artists and architects in propaganda exhibitions exalting the Fascist press, leisure organizations, and the nation's productive forces. Intended for mass audiences, these temporary displays were organized under the auspices of the Ministry of Popular Culture, underscoring the regime's theoretical distinction between crude persuasion and the ennobling effects ascribed to the fine arts. The most highly attended and critically acclaimed event was the Mostra della Rivoluzione Fascista (MDRF) of 1932. Photomontage, dynamic spatial sequences, and evocative lighting and auditory effects were used to create a collective and ritualistic experience of Mussolini's rise to power. With installations derived from Constructivist agit-prop designs, the MDRF represented the epitome of Fascist modernism and the regime's appropriation of foreign styles for nationalist purposes.

Rationalist architects similarly looked abroad to forge an innately Italian style for mass culture exhibitions. Giuseppe Terragni, Edoardo Persico, Giuseppe Pagano, and Marcello Nizzoli contributed the most innovative designs of the period based on photomontage grids and transparent structures and materials. Their installations at the Mostra Aeronautica of 1934 and the Room of Victory at the 1936 Triennale show how economy of means and purist sensibilities were equally useful in conveying Fascist propaganda of discipline and conquest. It should be noted that the Ministry of Popular Culture also ensured the marriage of fine arts and public spectacle in the organization of old master exhibitions for foreign consumption. The unprecedented loans of renaissance and baroque masterpieces to London in 1930 and Paris in 1935 emptied major Italian museums and churches of works that were never before, and never again, removed from their site. The risk to the cultural patrimony paid off, as these 'gifts from Italy' increased Mussolini's popularity abroad, and in the French case sealed a temporary diplomatic rapprochement between the two 'Latin sisters'.[5]

In addition to its politics of display, the regime allocated funds for the purchase of art works in the name of various government ministries, public museums, and the Duce himself. Mussolini's building programme of the 1930s also ensured artists' livelihood in a period of economic depression. Numerous commissions were awarded to decorate government offices, local Fascist headquarters, and entirely new towns, such as Sabaudia and Latina, erected in reclaimed marshland. In 1942 the regime approved the Two Per Cent for Art Law, which mandated a proportion of the expenditure of a new building's construction costs for works of art. This policy had been in place unofficially for over a decade, ever since Bottai's supervision of the commissions for the Palazzo delle Corporazioni in Rome (1927–32). Designed by Marcello Piacentini and Giuseppe Vaccaro, in a

---

[5] *Exhibition of Italian Art 1200–1900* (exh. cat., Royal Academy of Arts, London), 1930 and the *Exposition de L'Art Italien de Cimabue à Tiepolo* (exh. cat., Petit Palais, Paris), 1935.

stripped-down classical style, the project was a model of cooperative labour among artists and of a unifying iconography expounding the benefits of the corporate state. Although the Fascist patronage of public works bears comparison to that of New Deal America, commissions were not determined by committee or by the opinions of local communities, but by the fiat of party officials or the architects in charge. Piacentini, the director of *Architettura*, the Syndicate's official mouthpiece, was the most powerful architect between the wars, and delegated many major projects of the period with characteristic self-interest.

As with painting, modern Italian architecture had its moderate and progressive exponents, and the regime encouraged acrimonious debates over issues of *italianità*. But because of the imposing public function of architecture, the factionalism was more overt and the regime's patronage more consequential. Since Fascism presented itself as distinct from earlier political ideologies, it could dispense with historical revivals and readily embrace the iconoclasm of Rationalist architecture. Yet the need for celebratory monuments also ensured the ready support of rhetorical classicism—of civic buildings replete with arches and columns. In between lay the austere monumentalism of Piacentini, who created a *Stile Littorio* or imperial Fascist style in modernist terms, by eschewing ornament in favour of abstracted façades. The ideological conflicts between novel interpretation and heavy-handed traditionalism played out in the most prestigious commissions, among them, the Santa Maria Novella train station in Florence, the Città Universitaria and the Palazzo del Littorio (never realized) in Rome, and the EUR complex to the south of the capital. Mussolini's imperial ambitions also led to dramatic interventions in the urban fabric of Rome: the excavation of Augustan sites, the demolition of medieval and renaissance neighbourhoods, and the construction of triumphal avenues through the historic core.

The first exponents of a modern Italian architecture were Giovanni Muzio, Gio Ponti, Emilio Lancia, and others of the loosely affiliated Novecento group, based in Milan in the 1920s. Muzio's apartment complex—dubbed the *Ca' Brutta* (ugly house) (1922)—typified the group's use of inverted ornament and unsettling visual movement on the façade. The evocative, even ironic, play with classical vocabulary accounts for the affinities with both Novecento Magic Realism and late twentieth-century postmodernism. The idea of a modern interpretation of tradition was promoted in the journal *Domus*, edited by

Ponti, which was also a prime vehicle for reforming the decorative arts from the craft tradition to industrial production. By the 1930s, Muzio had subsumed the decorative details under a more rigorously geometric style, as in his Palazzo dell'Arte (1933) for the Milan Triennale. While incorporating modern materials and denuded façades, those in the Novecento orbit made the theoretical distinction between the 'pure rationalism' born north of the Alps, and the Italian need for material and spiritual comforts.

The international style, specifically the ideas of Le Corbusier and Walter Gropius, had been introduced through a younger generation of architectural students at the Milan Politecnico—the so-called Gruppo 7—in 1926–7. By 1930 those proposing a distinctly Italianate version of functionalism founded the Movimento Italiano per l'Architettura Razionale (MIAR). Though the organization was soon abolished because of its polemical stance and rivalry with the Syndicate, the Rationalists promoted their ideas through the journals *Casabella* and *Quadrante*, especially in the critical writings of Pagano and Alberto Sartoris. They maintained an uneasy if workable relationship with Piacentini: after his initial opposition to the MIAR, he began to include many Rationalists in important state commissions, especially after his own buildings were attacked by reactionary factions. By the end of the decade, however, building projects decreased, the Rationalists were sidelined, and racist rhetoric polarized the movement. Several of the Rationalists eventually joined the Resistance; both Pagano and Gian Luigi Banfi of the BBPR group died in the concentration camp at Mauthausen.

Italian Rationalism arguably represented the most European-oriented and progressive wing of the visual arts under Fascism, addressing workers' housing and the applied arts as well as civic buildings. As in other nations between the wars, the modernist movement in Italy mediated between historical contextualism and the demands of mass society, between the symbolism of state authority and the use of machine-inspired, standardized forms. The accommodation of functionalist criteria to a Fascist style was not as paradoxical as it seems. The Rationalists could hold up cubic masses, flat roofs, continuous fenestration, and whitewashed walls as indigenous qualities of the Mediterranean climate and architecture. Just how well functional design served the propaganda exigencies of the regime was masterfully demonstrated by Terragni's *Casa del*

Fascio, the party headquarters in Como (1936). Transparent materials, ordered structure, and hierarchical design symbolized the goals of Fascist government, while attending to practical requirements such as the Duce's public orations, mass gatherings, and meetings of Fascist officials. As Terragni himself described the operative metaphor: 'Here Mussolini's concept that Fascism is a glass house into which we can all look gives rise to the interpretation ... no encumbrance, no barrier, no obstacle between the political leaders and the people.'[6]

Regime architecture—in all of its building styles—gave impetus to the mural painting movement, the avant-garde answer to a politically committed art in the 1930s. The 'Manifesto of Mural Painting' (1933) authored by Sironi, and signed by Carrà, Funi, and Massimo Campigli argued that monumental public art subordinated the individual artist to a collective task, and was hence the most appropriate form of Fascist art. The mythic function of murals would transform popular consciousness through an epic evocation of national destiny. Here, however, the mural painters were clear in defending the autonomous qualities of pictorial expression, linking Byzantine mosaics and Giotto's frescos to modernist imperatives of abstract rhythms and two-dimensional design. Trompe l'œil illusionism was rejected as 'nordic' and 'bourgeois'. The debate over mural painting culminated at the 1933 Triennale, where Sironi commissioned thirty artists—among them de Chirico, Severini, Depero, and Prampolini—to decorate the walls of Giovanni Muzio's new Palazzo dell'Arte. The clash of styles and subjects, as well as technical problems in execution, promoted an enormous backlash in the press. Purists from the Rationalist movement denounced the frescos as an anachronistic enterprise inimical to modern architecture, while Mussolini personally intervened to stop the acrimonious exchange between Sironi and Farinacci's reactionary camp. The Triennale affair signalled the beginning of the internecine cultural battles that marked the later 1930s.

Despite the failure of the Triennale, public commissions continued to be the most prestigious form of state patronage. Sironi received the most prominent sites, including the Palazzo delle Corporazioni and the Città Universitaria (1935) in Rome and the Italian pavilion at the 1937 Paris Exposition Internationale des Arts et des Techniques.

---

[6] G. Terragni, *Quadrante*, no. 35/36 (1936).

Sironi was the chief caricaturist for the *Il Popolo d'Italia* and designed the propaganda pavilions of the Fascist press. He embodied the guiding myths of the regime—the Fascist Revolution, the omnipotence of the Duce, and the corporate state—in an archaizing, expressionist style. Typically his murals featured massive figures, set deep into the pictorial ground, gouged, and abraded like archaeological finds. The visual effects of time immemorial served as potent metaphors of Fascist perpetuity, or the 'primordial' destiny of the Italian people. In the words of Mussolini, 'these works dug out from rock and brought forth by Sironi from the darkness of forgotten ages represent the poetic depths of my revolution.'[7] Significantly, the gestural abstraction of Sironi's style carried his career into the post-war period under the rubric of the European Informel, despite the embedded motifs of his Fascist iconography. One of the few zealous Fascists to survive Salò and the war, Sironi remained an esteemed pariah—an oxymoron befitting the leading artist of the regime.

Sironi's peer in sculpture was Arturo Martini, who also used archaic forms to enliven the classical tradition in search of a non-rhetorical Fascist style. Inspired by recent archeological discoveries of Etruscan art, Martini evolved a sculpture of psychological and physical fragility, of fragmented forms and battered surfaces. In a period where marble and bronze bore symbolic weight, Martini exploited the impoverished materials of terracotta and tufa stone. As a result, his monumental public commissions—such as the *Vittoria dell'Aria* for the Mostra dell'Aeronautica (1934) and *Athena*, crowning the piazza of the Studium Urbis in Rome (1935)—were among his least successful. The Etruscan style epitomized another aspect of the antique tradition that was Italic and not Greek, a humble realism opposed to the perfection of the Hellenic canon. Such alternative interpretations, however, were easily absorbed by the state's eclectic patronage and the discourse of Fascist regionalism, which sought the authentic expression of the Italian people in rural and indigenous forms. The originality of Martini proved the exception under Fascism. Instead, official commissions pursued an anachronistic style of virile warriors, typified in the work of academician Romano Romanelli, or the lofty athletes lining Enrico del Debbio's stadium at the Foro Mussolini in Rome (1928–32).

---

[7] Y. De Begnac, *Taccuini mussoliniani*, ed. F. Perfetti (Bologna, 1990), p. 590.

By 1930 several stylistically diverse groups vied for official recognition under the state's eclectic patronage. The intellectuals of Strapaese ('Supercountry') opposed the grandeur of the Novecento, and claimed that authentic Italian culture lay in provincial traditions tied to small town life and the peasantry. A grass-roots movement based in Tuscany and Emilia-Romagna, the Strapaese was fervently Fascist, but resented the inflated bureaucracy and rhetoric of the regime. Its mouthpiece was the journal *Il Selvaggio* (1924–43), run by Mino Maccari, whose biting caricatures indicted pompous party officials as well as American consumer culture. Carrà, Soffici, and Ottone Rosai contributed to the Strapaese circle with landscapes and genre painting rendered in a conservative, naturalist idiom. The most representative artist, however, was Giorgio Morandi, renowned for his disarmingly simple still life compositions. Though Morandi emerged after the Second World War as the foremost Italian exponent of 'pure painting', untainted by Fascism, he exhibited with the Strapaese for over a decade and featured prominently in their writings and intimate circles. For Maccari, Soffici, and others, the resolute sameness of Morandi's works evoked the unbroken continuity of rural life, as well as a proud refusal of passing trends and foreign influences.

Even non-objective art found support under the regime: the 1935 Quadriennale launched the first national show of the Lombard painters Mauro Reggiani, Osvaldo Licini, and Atanasio Soldati, among others. The Italian exponents of lyrical and geometric abstraction were based in Milan and Como, and often worked together with Rationalist architects. Their activities were promoted by the critic Carlo Belli and by the Galleria del Milione, one of the few successful commercial galleries of the period that showed the work of contemporary Europeans. Of a younger generation, the abstractionists typified the ways in which the politically moderate and uncommitted could work under the system with a minimum of lip-service paid to the regime. In their first manifesto of 1934, for example, one reads how non-figurative art disavows the classicism of 'arches and columns' but still evokes the essential Mediterranean, and hence Fascist qualities of 'order, equilibrium, and clear intelligence'.[8] Others such

---

[8] O. Bogliardi, V. Ghiringhelli, and M. Reggiani, 'Dichiarazione degli espositori della prima collettiva di pittori astratti', 1934, reprinted in Paola Barocchi (ed.), *Storia moderna dell'arte in Italia: Manifesti polemiche documenti* Vol. III. *Dal Novecento ai dibattiti sulla figura e sul monumentale* (Turin, 1990), pp. 316–20.

as Fausto Melotti and Lucio Fontana experimented with abstraction in private and on a small scale, while executing figurative sculpture for official commissions.

Many of the abstract artists belonged to the Abstraction-Création group and visited Paris; the painter Alberto Magnelli lived there for most of the 1930s. As with the so-called 'Italiens de Paris' (de Chirico, Savinio, Severini, Campigli, Filippo de Pisis, Mario Tozzi) numerous Italian artists travelled and resided abroad, until the outbreak of the Second World War. As the subjects of exhibitions at home and in Paris—in both state events and commercial galleries—these artists served as cultural ambassadors for the regime at a time when Mussolini was still unaligned with Hitler. Moreover conservative French critics, such as Waldemar George, promoted the 'Italiens de Paris' as models of a new humanism (in opposition to French Surrealism), reinforcing one of the leitmotifs of Fascist propaganda. The 'Italiens de Paris' were figurative artists whose work fell under the rubric of *italianità*, even if images such as de Chirico's Gladiators flagrantly subverted the model of virile 'Third Rome'. De Chirico was no Fascist, but like Severini and others, he lent credence to an ideology he did not uphold, by willingly participating in state exhibitions and commissions while pursuing a career abroad.

The Futurists also promoted their work throughout Europe, including exhibitions in Berlin in 1934 and 1937 that caused consternation among the National Socialists, and drove home to Nazi officials the differences between the two regimes' cultural policies. The most salient feature of later Futurism was *aeropittura*, the painting of aerial perspectives and the sensation of flight—themes that were also taken up in sculpture, performance, and experimental poetry. Balla, Depero, Prampolini, Gerardo Dottori, Fillia, and Benedetta were among the names affixed to the first manifesto of '*Aeropittura*' written in 1929, which proclaimed their pursuit of 'a new extra-terrestrial spirituality'.[9] Benedetta, the wife of Marinetti, was one of several women artists involved in the movement, by contrast to the antifeminist stance of pre-war Futurism. *Aeropittura* spawned two styles: literal views from inside the cockpit based on aerial photography

[9] Balla, Benedetta, Depero, Dottori, Fillia, Marinetti, Prampolini, Somenzi, Tato, '*L'Aeropittura*', Turin, 1929, in B. Mantura (ed.), *Futurism in Flight* (exh. cat., Accademia Italiana, 1990), London, p. 203.

(found in the work of Tullio Crali and Tato) and more abstract compositions that drew on biomorphism and non-objective art. The latter, while more innovative and international, was equally useful to the regime in exalting the transatlantic flights of Italo Balbo and the Ethiopian conquest, or evoking the lay spiritualism of 'Mistica Fascista'. Marinetti's pre-eminence as a cultural impresario assured the prominent display of *aeropittura* in the Biennale and Quadriennale, as well as in mural commissions for post offices and transportation terminals. At the same time, Futurism continued to cut an independent swath through the cultural politics of the regime, especially when it led the charge against the cultural policies of the Nazis in 1937–8. Yet, in another typical contradiction, Marinetti adhered to the Republic of Salò.

Indeed the glaring compromises of the historical avant-garde led many of those who came of age in the 1920s and 1930s to reject the models of both classical nostalgia and technological utopia. They voiced their discontent in referendums and Fascist youth journals of the period.[10] The younger generation favoured figurative styles marked by varying degrees of expressionist distortion and brilliant, anti-naturalistic colours. Typically they worked on a small scale, depicting portraits, interiors, and fantasy scenes that distanced their creative endeavours from those solicitous of the regime. The Sei di Torino group deliberately adopted European post-Impressionist styles to counter the nationalistic discourse of the arts under Fascism. It included one of the few openly anti-Fascist artists of the period—Carlo Levi—who was confined to Lucania in 1935. Others, such as Scipione, Mario Mafai, and Antonietta Raphäel Mafai—labelled the Scuola Romana—were strident nonconformists who nonetheless conducted their careers through the syndicate system. Their intransigence was manifested in their scenes of the Roman *bohème*, and in the influence of the Jewish expressionists Soutine and Pascin. Beginning on the eve of the Second World War, the Milan-based Corrente group expressed subtle forms of dissent in their eponymous journal. They adopted the term 'realism', with all of its inherent ambiguity, to

---

[10] See the referendum conducted by the critic Lamberto Vitali, 'Dove va l'arte italiana', *Domus*, 9, nos. 108–109 (1936–7), which included the responses of the abstract painter Luigi Veronesi, the sculptor Giacomo Manzù and artists later associated with the Corrente group. See also the 'Manifesto di Corrente', *Corrente di Vita giovanile*, no. 20 (15 Dec. 1938).

describe their anti-rhetorical stance, but the romanticizing work of Renato Birolli and Aligi Sassu proved more evasive than socially critical. The exception was Renato Guttuso, whose expressionist-tinged social realism caused a sensation at the exhibitions of the Premio Bergamo and ironically served the doctrinaire cultural politics of the Italian PCI after the war.

The relative freedoms allotted to the fine arts may also be explained by the fact that, as vehicles of sheer indoctrination, they could never compete with the efficacy of the mass media, particularly cinema. The speed and spectacle of the moving image left the painted canvas far behind. Cinema received enormous state subsidies, both for the documentary *Cinegiornale LUCE* newsreels and the commercial film industry. In 1934 the newly established Undersecretariat for Press and Propaganda created a film bureau headed by PNF veteran Luigi Freddi; the following year he established the Centro Sperimentale di Cinematografia (CSC), headed by Luigi Chiarini, whose journal, *Bianco e Nero*, provided a progressive link to international film, including innovative Soviet examples. Cinecittà, the largest film studio in Europe, opened in 1937. The CSC and Fascist investments in cinema produced the acclaimed younger generation of Italian film makers, among them Roberto Rossellini, Michelangelo Antonioni, and Dino De Laurentiis.

Typically the regime allowed experimentation and foreign influence in order to make an internationally competitive film industry. The Fascists exploited a modern style of documentary realism for military and historical feature films, which reached their height of popularity and usefulness during the Ethiopian conquest. They also encouraged light entertainment, especially in the so-called 'white telephone' films centred on homogenized bourgeois values and affluence. These were political insofar as they diverted attention from social realities, but otherwise corresponded to Hollywood comedies and melodramas. Indeed the aim of the regime and film makers alike to forge a specifically Fascist cinema was never realized by virtue of the new medium's de facto internationalism in genres, styles, and distribution.

In both high and mass culture, the Ethiopian invasion prompted the overwhelming triumph of *romanità*, and factions of the PNF became polarized over the issue of creative freedom. The growing conservatism had its most visible repercussions in the state exhibitions after 1936 and in the rise of naturalist-realist narratives. The deepening alliance with Germany, as well as the example of the Degenerate Art show in Munich (1937), encouraged the small but vocal Farinacci camp, whose anti-Semitic, anti-modernist campaign was tacitly approved by Mussolini. Giuseppe Pensabene and Telesio Interlandi, writing in the journals *Il Tevere*, *Quadrivio*, and *La Difesa della Razza*, agitated for a cultural policy based on the Nazi model, while attacking the work of prominent contemporary artists and architects as 'Jewish', and 'Bolshevik'. With the passing of the Racial Laws in the autumn of 1938, anti-Semitism spread to the mainstream press, and its supporters spewed out an even more virulent rhetoric. Jewish artists—among them Corrado Cagli, Roberto Melli, and Antonietta Raphäel Mafai—were excluded from exhibiting and censored on the grounds of their race. Also troubling was the way in which some critics mocked the supposed links between modern art and Judaism, but did not speak out against the outrage of anti-Semitism per se. Moreover, progressives began to turn on each other in a political atmosphere of suspicion and persecution.

In opposition to Farinacci, Bottai maintained a fine balance between enforced aesthetics and artistic autonomy. As Minister of Education, he insisted that illustrative styles were void of propagandistic efficacy, and that 'the political value of every work of art is in direct proportion to its artistic quality'. Paradoxically, his arguments on cultural politics were similar to those forwarded by Breton, Rivera, and Trotsky in the manifesto 'Towards a Free Revolutionary Art' (1938). In 1939 Farinacci founded the Premio Cremona, an annual exhibition organized around prescribed themes, such as 'Listening to the Discourse of the Duce on the Radio' or 'The Battle for Grain'. Bottai, in turn, established the Premio Bergamo, which left the subject stipulations deliberately vague. Under the auspices of the ministry, Bottai also started the journal *Primato* in 1940, continuing the tradition of liberal debate in the art press, and serving as a protected platform for the opinions of younger artists. Even as Bottai carried out the repressive measures of the anti-Semitic laws in the schools, he reiterated that 'art cannot take account of race as a biological fact without declining into a materialist realism promoted under the vague label of classicism. . . . The unlimited vastness of content and plurality of forms gives the Italian artistic tradition a universal value and an influence a thousand times larger than its national territory.'[11]

In Fascist Italy the defence of creative freedom, while protecting high art from blatant obsequiousness, actually became a most trenchant form of propaganda, arguing for the 'humanist' values of the patron state as well as its imperialist policies. Ultimately, the visual arts between the wars were neither parochial nor wholly retrograde, and despite its egregious crimes against humanity, Fascism produced its culture. In painting, architecture, and exhibition design, modernism had its quarter, and thrived as a style and as propaganda. State control of the Triennale and cinema laid the groundwork for the triumph of industrial design and neo-realism, respectively, in the post-war period. Major figures of the Informel—Fontana and Vedova, as well as Fausto Melotti—pursued their abstract idioms under the regime. And the architecture of Giovanni Muzio and Terragni has been claimed by the postmodern generation. If Fascism is fascinating, as critical theorists would have it, it is in large part due to the notable energies that were spent in creating its image.

[11] G. Bottai, 'Modernità e tradizione nell'arte italiana d'oggi' (1939), in Bottai, *La politica delle arti: Scritti 1918–43*, ed. Alessandro Masi (Rome, 1992).

Literature

J. R. Woodhouse

The ferment of innovation and literary commitment, 1900–1920

In 1900 Italy had been united for some forty years. State education was still in its infancy (and not universally free), and illiteracy rates were amongst the highest in Western Europe, though the Coppino Education Act of 1877 had made attendance at school obligatory for children over 6, and one effect of this had been to reduce the percentage of illiterates from 78 per cent in 1861 to under 50 per cent by 1910. Italy's great centuries-old literary culture still remained the inevitable preserve of the urban middle classes, while the majority of its people depended for their livelihood on traditional rural industries. Literary Italian itself was a highly stylized medium, having little connection with the spoken language of the majority, much less with the dialects which most Italians spoke and which were systematically collected and studied as anthropological curiosities by regional academics. The search for a nationally agreed capital city for the new nation—Turin (until 1865), Florence (1865–70), and finally Rome (after 1871)—was symptomatic of Italy's need to acquire a linguistic as well as a political heart.

Yet from the opening years of the century centralizing factors were at work: national service in the armed forces gradually brought about a successful mix of generations of young regional speakers, as young conscripts from all over the peninsula were forced to conform to new norms of linguistic uniformity (if only to achieve mutual comprehension). That trend was boosted by the continued promotion of state education, more vigorously pursued after 1922 and the Fascist takeover; further linguistic consolidation was aided by other unifying factors, notably the gradual increase in radio broadcasting and the popularity of talking films (which, significantly, did away with the previous need, during the showing of silent films, for the presence of a literate member in rural audiences, able to read out loud the subtitles).

The particular reform of state education, which was to bear the name of Mussolini's education adviser, Giovanni Gentile (the riforma *Gentile*) gave further impetus to popular literacy, not unexpectedly exploited by the regime for propaganda purposes, most visibly in the second major reform, the Schools Charter (*Carta delle scuole*), promoted by Giovanni Bottai in 1939, which was mainly concerned with the inculcation of Fascist ideas, by means, for example, of the prescription of only those literary texts which were politically acceptable. By 1943, at the end of twenty years of Fascist rule (the so-called *Ventennio fascista*), literacy rates were aligned with other Western European nations, and the new mass education had provided Italy with a generation of fresh audiences for the growing body of, by now, less than élitist writers, who had simultaneously sprung up with the new readership. The novel and often liberal agenda of certain authors, along with an amalgam of political commitment and popular linguistic expression, ensured their own persecution by Fascist censors, but with the fall of the regime, strong left-wing reaction guaranteed that after the Second World War writing would never again revert to its old élite structures.

Considering its relatively narrow base, the literary scene in Italy at the opening of the century was singularly distinguished by a climate of experimentation and innovation which continued unabated for the following fifty years. Giosuè Carducci (1835–1907), the fiery professor of Italian literature at Bologna, and his self-styled circle of pedant friends (*Gli amici pedanti*), had already opposed (by their cultivation of ultra-classical attitudes) what they considered the empty decadence and sentimentality of late Italian Romanticism. Their austere revolution effectively succeeded in interrupting the development of Romantic literature within the peninsula. Instead, their literary themes, their reviews in journals, the literary language of their compositions, and even the metre of their poetry were conditioned by a neoclassical, almost deliberately pagan approach. Typically Carducci's *Odi barbare* (Barbarian Odes) bore that title because, with apparent incompatibility, the poet used traditional classical metres (dependent in Latin and Greek on the *length* of syllables) in combination with Italian vocabulary and sentence structure (dependent in Italian upon *stress* accents). Certainly, until the beginning of the twentieth century, Carducci's radical influence was immense, not only in the literary field, but also in the area of politics (he was a fiercely anticlerical European liberal, but within the peninsula he was also regarded as the standard-bearer of nationalism).

By the time Carducci won the Nobel prize for literature in 1907, Gabriele D'Annunzio (1863–1938), who as an adolescent had idolized the older man's poetry, had gone beyond the master. Instead of Carducci's austere, almost puritanical brand of neo-paganism, which revivified the old Roman myths and virtues, D'Annunzio, also an enthusiastic classical scholar in his youth, followed rather the more sensual path of his fellow-Abruzzese, Ovid, and wrote what critics and public considered stylish if scandalously immoral poems and novels. D'Annunzio also aspired to establish a new dramatic theatre for Italy, and he firmly believed that all of his innovations required an inimitable and, if necessary, iconoclastic new linguistic medium, which he was ambitious to create. In this final revolutionary objective, D'Annunzio was silently aided by the less boisterous authority of his fellow poet, Giovanni Pascoli (1855–1912), who, however, in his turn was keen to make the Italian literary language simpler and more realistic. Pascoli succeeded Carducci in the latter's Chair of literature at Bologna (D'Annunzio had earlier turned down the offer) and Pascoli's personal themes and largely rural settings, expressed in more authentic language and in verse which was much less politically or socially committed, touched a chord with a wide public, and had a powerful linguistic and stylistic influence. These three writers, known collectively as *Le tre corone* (The three crowns), between them laid the basis for much of the creative writing of the coming century, largely because of the work they had written before 1900.

After the death of Pascoli in 1912, hardly a year passed in Italy without the creation of some fresh literary movement, the publication of an innovative cultural journal, or the emergence of new affiliations of writers loosely classifiable in schools. And though by 1910 D'Annunzio's literary vein was almost exhausted, nevertheless his dynamic aestheticism, his widely publicized oratory and journalism, his heroics during World War One, and his anarchic politics guaranteed that his name and his writings were kept constantly before the public. After World War One, D'Annunzio quickly showed his disgust at Italy's political leadership and their handling of the Versailles peace talks. His reaction to what he called the 'mutilated victory' was to seize the Italian enclave in Yugoslavia, the port of Fiume. D'Annunzio made sure that he was fashionable enough under Mussolini's regime to continue to have a permanent, if more self-centred influence on the political scene and on politicians (who, for a quiet life, were forced to subsidize his extravagant palatial home and his Renaissance lifestyle). In one apocryphal story, Mussolini is said to have commented that D'Annunzio was rather like a broken tooth: he had either to be eradicated or to be covered in gold; Mussolini chose the second alternative.

The political clashes between left- and right-wing forces, which surfaced sporadically during the first two decades of the century were reflected in writers' attitudes. In the earlier part of the century contributors to the more reactionary journal, *La Ronda* (1919–23), wrote articles which attacked surviving followers of the earlier and livelier *La Voce* (1908–16) (whose political supplement had urged factional involvement), and firmly opposed supporters of the more avant-garde if short-lived *Lacerba* (1913–15). One leading contributor to *La Ronda*, Vilfredo Pareto (1848–1923), famously defended the violence he saw inherent in Fascism; other adherents attacked the degeneracy in Italian letters brought about, they said, by Futurism. Still other conservatives opposed even the innocuous linguistic innovations of Pascoli. Not untypical of those complainants was Vincenzo Cardarelli (1887–1959), a traditional but elegant imitator of the nineteenth-century Italian classics (especially of Leopardi), whose linguistic conservatism made him regret the fall of the Latin [h] from such words as *(h)umanità*.

Until the First World War, and then its immediate and contentious cultural aftermath, such conflicts gave rise to the concept of literary commitment, akin to political commitment, which became strongest in the opponents of the regime. The word for that commitment was *impegno*, and later, in post-1945 Italy, this was the term that would impose itself as a widespread literary (and literary–critical) fashion, most typical of left-wing writers. *Impegno* was and is an enormous influence on Italian criticism and literature, and has been a constant of twentieth-century Italian literary movements, effectively preventing objective assessments of most authors, and even today dividing universities inside the peninsula and individual departments within each university into left-wing and right-wing critical schools.

For some two years or so into the regime, ultra-conservative and Fascist opinions could effectively be opposed in liberal and left-wing publications, such as the nascent socialist *Ordine nuovo* (1921–5), edited by Antonio Gramsci (1891–1937), or the liberal *Energie nuove* (1918–20), *Rivoluzione liberale* (1922–5) and *Il Baretti* (1924–8), journals of the martyred Piero Gobetti (1901–26). Gobetti, an enthusiastic young liberal, was punished for his political beliefs, beaten up on three occasions by Fascist squads, and forced to take refuge in Paris. He never recovered from his beatings and died in the French capital, just two years after the equally infamous murder of the Socialist deputy Giacomo Matteotti. Meanwhile *La critica* (1903–44), the long-lived journal edited by Benedetto Croce (1866–1952) (albeit more philosophical than literary), always kept up a rational, and inevitably anti-establishment, policy, which made Croce himself anathema to the Fascists, and ensured the removal of his name from the registers of every Italian academy, with the honourable exception of *Arcadia*.

By 1928 the regime had hardened its approach: Antonio Gramsci had been imprisoned, despite his parliamentary immunity (as communist deputy for Venice), Gobetti was dead, and other writers were being condemned to internal exile. The earlier, democratically inclined journals were rapidly replaced by other reviews, including *Il Selvaggio* (The Savage) (1924–43), and *Novecento* (Twentieth Century) (1926–9), which carried more Fascist messages. Between the liberal periodicals of the earlier years and the right-wing, often propagandistic, journals which took their place, several reviews succeeded in keeping alive more radical literary values. *Solaria*, founded in 1926 by Alberto Carocci, just a year after repressive laws were introduced to limit the powers of the press, succeeded in maintaining an internationalist literary outlook, with the names of James Joyce and Franz Kafka recurring on its pages until 1934. In that year it was suppressed, after attempting to publish the innocuous first novel of Elio Vittorini (1908–66), *Il garofano rosso* (The red carnation), regarded by the Fascist censor as socialist in its political approach (and in its title). *Solaria* dedicated two double numbers of 1929 and 1930 to Italo Svevo (1861–1928) and Federigo Tozzi (1883–1920), an important literary manifesto at the time, not least because Svevo's sceptical irony and Tozzi's anti-D'Annunzian stance as critic and writer would not have been well viewed by the regime.

Not all authors were allowed even such limited freedom as the writers of *Solaria*. In particular, political opponents of the regime who were also renowned littérateurs were treated with increasing ruthlessness, and first-rank writers such as Carlo Levi (1902–75), Cesare Pavese (1908–50), and Emilio Lussu (1890–1971) were famously sent into internal exile (*confino*), though Lussu soon escaped to France. Other writers and critics, among them Gramsci, were simply kept in prison, and some, including Ignazio Silone (1900–1979), left the peninsula for the duration of the Fascist regime, and published their work abroad, sometimes in the language of their adopted country. Towards the end of the regime one journal in particular, *Corrente* (Current) (1938–40), before its swift repression, began to express anti-Fascist views developed by young left-wing thinkers, many of whom were later to enrol as Resistance workers. Another late arrival was the journal *Primato* (Supremacy/Pre-eminence) (1940–3), under Fascist control, and founded by the then controversial Minister of Education, Giuseppe Bottai (1895–1959), in a broad attempt to illustrate how Fascism differed from Nazism. In what seemed a move unfavourable to the regime, Bottai published in *Primato* the horrifying *Fantasie* of the painter Mafai, in which Fascist authorities are depicted as torturers. Bottai's editorship of *La critica fascista* (Fascist criticism) had also been mild, and untypical of the hierarchy; his equivocal views were most evident when he awarded a prize to the committed left-wing artist Renato Guttuso for a painting representing Europe tortured by Nazism.

It is curious to reflect how political corruption at the head of the state coincided with a preoccupation with neurosis in those leading literary members who continued to insist on self-expression. Italo Svevo (1861–1928) was mainly concerned in his 'Freudian' novels with psychological abnormalities. Scenic portrayals of schizophrenia characterized the (usually) pessimistic work of Luigi Pirandello (1867–1936). The dying embers of Futurism cast a mad light on that group's final attempts to demonstrate their originality, though their leader, Filippo Tommaso Marinetti (1876–1944), gradually succumbed to the blandishments of the regime, turning his old revolutionary ideas on art and literature into socially acceptable accompaniments to fashion and design. Alberto Pincherle changed his name to Alberto Moravia (1907–90), and achieved immediate fame with his first novel *Gli indifferenti* (1929), in effect a study of the breakdown of human relationships, the sheer boredom of participating in bourgeois family life. Depressed and bored in his turn, Cesare Pavese was to commit suicide in 1950, after successfully publishing a series of novels and short stories, notably *La luna e i falò*, which verged on the maudlin in their repeated themes of introspection, alienation, and disillusionment. Dino Campana (1885–1932), afflicted with chronic nervous debility but potentially Italy's finest poet of the period, died with his talent not fully expressed after a lifetime spent in and out of psychiatric clinics. His beautiful anthology *Canti orfici* of 1914 was influential, but, he considered, too difficult for the average reader (he would sell copies on the street, tearing out difficult pages if he judged a buyer too unintelligent to comprehend the poems they contained; some 'readers' received only the book's covers).

The domination of poetry and the hermeticist revolution

The most important literary expression of the inter-war period was the new wave in poetry, which was to give Italian literature worldwide renown and two Nobel prizes. Blows had earlier been struck against the academic and establishmentarian tradition by the *Crepuscolari*, the poets of the 'twilight of Romanticism', the loosely-knit group of ironic, melancholy, and unheroic writers whose most distinguished exponents were Guido Gozzano (1883–1916) and Sergio Corazzini (1887–1907), both of whom, like other colleagues in their 'school', were afflicted by pulmonary tuberculosis, the deadly inevitability of which profoundly affected their fine, if brief poetic careers. Significantly, Gozzano's best poems, the anthology known as *I colloqui* (1911) are internal 'Colloquies' with himself. Neither he nor his fellows could nourish any of the ambitions of the physical, fashionable D'Annunzio and his followers. Thus in his witty *L'altro* (The Other) Gozzano forgives God for his failures to help him personally, but meditates that the Almighty could have done a lot worse—he could have made him a member of the species *gabrieldannunziano* instead of *guidogozzano*. Gozzano's style, the antithesis of that employed by most of his contemporaries, often deliberately descends into ironic bathos, like 'that of a scholar corrected a bit by a maid-servant', as he remarks in the same poem.

More vociferous attacks were launched on all traditional art and literature by the movement which took its watchword *Futurism* from the influential manifestos of the extremely wealthy Filippo Tommaso Marinetti. The first manifesto was published on 20 February 1909, and for the occasion Marinetti rented the front page of *Le Figaro*. The noisy revolution of the Futurists, allied to the linguistic innovations introduced by Pascoli and D'Annunzio, meant that by 1920 it was no longer possible to gain a poetic reputation in Italy through literary styles which had for centuries characterized Italian. Marinetti's *L'immaginazione senza fili e le parole in libertà* (Wireless imagination and words in liberty) of 1913, had broken with the previous logic of language. In 1909 he had used his preface to the anthology *Revolverate* of G. P. Lucini (1867–1914) in order to attack conventional Italy, country of intellectual and moral tyrannies, against which it was a sacred duty to fight with the arm of poetry 'a free poetry, emancipated from all the traditional ties, in rhythm rather with the symphony of committees, workplaces, automobiles, aeroplanes'. Marinetti's 1915 essay on the prophylactic qualities of war, *Guerra sola igiene del mondo* (War, the only hygiene of the world) rejected the 'stammering and botanical sentimentality of Pascoli. . . . Our deplorable Fogazzaro's emetic milky-coffee air of the sacristy' and D'Annunzio's morbid nostalgia, obsession with sex, mania for academic reminiscences, and relish for collecting and poetizing the bric-a-brac of history. But D'Annunzio's influence, at least, was to outlast that of Marinetti, whose reputation he easily eclipsed during the First World War, and whom he had famously expelled from Fiume in 1919 because of the Futurist leader's intransigence and anti-monarchical politics.

In ways more obviously averse to the regime, the bombast and superficiality of Fascism were privately and intellectually countered by two poets in particular: Eugenio Montale (1896–1981) and Salvatore Quasimodo (1901–68), both Nobel prize-winners, respectively in 1975 and 1959. To their own two names Quasimodo was later to add that of the veteran Giuseppe Ungaretti (1888–1970) as one whom he considered another leader of the hermeticist school of poetry. *La poesia ermetica* (hermetic poetry) (1936) had been the title of a collection of essays by the influential critic Francesco Flora, implying, with a critical opacity all his own, that the new poetry was of an obscurantism akin to that inspired by Hermes Trismegistus, (the spurious post-Christian gnostic and proponent of neo-Platonic philosophy, particularly fashionable during the Florentine fifteenth century). The complexity of the hermeticist movement cannot be compressed into a few paragraphs, but its importance, and the greatness of its finest exponent, Montale, require here a slightly extended mention.

The language and style of the *ermetici* was certainly not universally comprehensible, but in its very difficulty it served as a private reaction to Fascist literary conservatism and populism, as well as a rejection of the academic tradition which Carducci had upheld and which in their own esoteric ways the influential D'Annunzio and Pascoli had continued. If the ebullient Futurist revolt had led its followers into a literary cul-de-sac, the hermeticists responded more austerely, trimming their poetry to the barest essentials, avoiding the formulaic noises of the Futurists and the wordy exaggerations of the D'Annunzians. A famous harbinger of their more severe reaction was Ungaretti's *Mattino* (Morning) of 1917:

M'illumino
d'immenso.

[I illuminate myself with immensity.]

Without a title the lines might seem something from *Pseuds' corner*, but together, title, light, and immensity have an undeniably evocative effect. The main importance of the lines rests with their deliberate avoidance of verbose rhetoric or Futurist gibberish; here began Ungaretti's ambition to give back dignity and logic to the poetic word. His youthful production is easier; in those early compositions he reflects such realities as life in the trenches during World War One. These and other poems were included in the 1923 collection *Il porto sepolto* (The Hidden Port), for which Mussolini wrote the preface. As if to underline his cosmopolitan character, Ungaretti married Jeanne Dupoix in 1919, and spent several years in Paris, occupied for some of that time in writing articles for Mussolini's newspaper, *Il Popolo d'Italia*. Ungaretti had a great love of travel, and his poetry reflected experiences on three continents as well as mirroring the profound influence of the

French decadent poets. In later anthologies Ungaretti experimented with form and theme, many poems being inspired by the death of his 9-year-old son in 1939, an event which thereafter imbued his compositions with an obsessively religious and melancholic atmosphere. His final attitude to the Fascist regime was ambiguous: in 1936 he had left the political discomfort of Italy for Brazil, where he had been offered the Chair of Italian in São Paolo, only to have to return to Italy in 1942 when Brazil entered the war. Back in Rome the Fascist hierarchy made him a fellow of their newly created Accademia italiana, and gave him a Chair at Rome University. With the fall of Mussolini, Ungaretti was seen by the Left as tainted, and viewed askance, and he never truly regained popularity in Italian critical circles.

Salvatore Quasimodo's most famous poem, *Ed è subito sera* (And suddenly it's evening), which was to give the title to his collection of 1942, is like many produced by the hermeticist school, impossible to translate adequately:

Ognuno sta solo sul cuor della terra,
trafitto da un raggio di sole,
ed è subito sera.

[Everyone stands alone on the heart of the earth, transfixed by a ray of sun, and suddenly it is evening.]

The poet evokes in these three lines (already pared down from a longer composition) so many imaginative ideas: loneliness, nature's warmth, and man's origins, the light of reason (and of hope), the pitiless glare of the day, the transience of life and ambition, the advent of evening and death. Quasimodo was to go on to produce influential if uneven collections, and, notably after the fall of Mussolini, became associated (in lucky hindsight) with opposition to the regime; unlike Ungaretti, Quasimodo was heavily favoured by left-wing critics who after World War Two promoted both him and Elio Vittorini as popular and fashionable heroes. The award to him of the Nobel prize in 1959 was not without controversy.

Part of the controversy arose because of the superiority of Quasimodo's contemporary Eugenio Montale who was ignored by the Nobel committee. *Ossi di seppia* (Cuttle-fish bones), Montale's first collection of poems, took its title from a D'Annunzian allusion in

Alcyone, and many themes and moods from the same collection. Nevertheless the *Ossi*, begun around 1916 but published in 1925, were essentially, in tone and philosophy, heir to the *Canti* of Giacomo Leopardi (1798–1837), though Montale's writing has an edge and a toughness which makes him sound more ironic and at times more positive than his great predecessor. From that already fine anthology of youthful work, Montale went on from strength to strength, winning the Nobel prize in 1975, and further dominating Italian poetry until his death in 1981. His nonconformity and his questioning of received ideas had earlier made him anathema to the Fascists, who secured his dismissal from his post as Director of Florence's Gabinetto Vieusseux library for a refusal to join the party. His collection of 1939, *Le occasioni* (Occasions), was an indictment of the regime: the oppressive weight of the dictatorship in Italy, the rise of the Nazis, the invasion of Ethiopia, the Civil War in Spain, all expressed with a complexity and concision too difficult for the average Fascist censor to comprehend, but an inspiration to liberal-minded intellectuals. After 1945 Montale's poetry became more prolific and continued to voice liberal opinions, refreshingly free from the dogmatic bias of critical schools, and expressed with rare beauty of form.

D'Annunzio, Pirandello, and the new theatre

In the theatrical world, as in so many other genres, it is necessary to return briefly to D'Annunzio, for here also D'Annunzio gave another lead, experimenting with his subjects as well as with styles and forms in order to break the bourgeois theatrical mould, this last an ambition which he shared with his mistress, the great actress Eleonora Duse, nauseated, she wrote, by having continually to play *La Dame aux Camélias*, or its other equivalents. D'Annunzio's best play, *La figlia di Iorio* (Iorio's Daughter) was produced in 1904; combining ancient folklore and classical dramatic ideas in a unique piece of writing, it was incomparably better than his other theatrical efforts, including those produced in France and in French during his self-imposed exile there (1910–15). Other playwrights equally concerned with revolutionizing the Italian theatre fell short of their ambitions: Luigi Chiarelli (1844–1947), Luigi Antonelli (1882–1942), and Rosso di

San Secondo (1887–1956) wrote in the mode of the so-called *teatro del grottesco* (Theatre of the grotesque), which echoed some of the contemporary Futurist debates and offered some novel elements to their greater contemporary, Luigi Pirandello. Ugo Betti (1892–1979) deserves a mention here as an important witness of the regime, though, as a high-court judge, dispensing Fascist justice, he wrote little at the time, rather storing up dramatic memories and creative ideas until the end of the Second World War before publishing his eleven semi-political, semi-existential dramas.

But in the world of drama, Luigi Pirandello towers above other contemporaries. He ignored the noisy irrationality of some contemporary experiments, and found his own key to a new theatre in the highly literary and intellectual exploitation and dramatization of recent psychological discoveries and techniques, particularly those associated with the newly diagnosed illness of schizophrenia, a condition he studied at first hand during his wife's chronic affliction with that malady. His theoretical essay on *Umorismo* (Humour) (1908) pointed the way ahead to a successful application of his main idea (and theme) that all truth is relative (and its concomitant that masking the truth is a natural state of mankind). But his austere and unconventional plays had to await the blessing of Parisian audiences before Mussolini, realizing Pirandello's value as an asset for nationalistic propaganda, helped him set up his own *Teatro d'arte* (1925–8), and brought this cosmopolitan Sicilian back briefly to Italy. Pirandello undeniably caused a revolution in the theatre and a more general upheaval in people's reflections on life and drama; among his many plays his most popular (and arguably his best) compositions are visible in *Sei personaggi in cerca d'autore* (Six characters in search of an author) (1921) and *Enrico IV* (Henry IV) (1922).

The new prose writing

Pirandello excelled, too, in the art of writing novellas, and put together a great number of short stories, often using themes and ideas from them in adaptations which later supplied plots for longer dramatic works. He was also the author of seven novels, each of which is still readable and interesting, and he is justly famous for one novel, *Il fu Mattia Pascal* (1904) (The late Mattia Pascal). The new important psychological insight, made fashionable by the Viennese school and visible in the work of the German-educated Pirandello, also had an impact on an important contemporary of his: the Triestine writer Ettore Schmitz (already met here under his pen name, Italo Svevo), whose three pioneering novels could have introduced into Italy the notion of the anti-hero and the literary importance of Freudian psychology. There were many Italians eager to innovate who might currently have been ambitious to write revolutionary twentieth-century fiction. But in a nation where fashionability was (and is) all-important, Svevo remained unfashionable, and his new ideas, treated at the time with scant regard by his Italian contemporaries, had little immediate influence. His novels, *Una vita* (A Life) (1892), *Senilità* (As a Man Grows Older) (1898), and *La coscienza di Zeno* (The Confessions of Zeno) (1923), this last easily his best work, were ahead of their time, though recognized and appreciated by James Joyce (domiciled in Trieste for long periods during the first quarter of the century), and later eulogized intelligently by Eugenio Montale. It is arguable that, partly because of Svevo's fellow-writers' inability to recognize his genius during his lifetime, it was to be in the field of poetry that Italian authors did their best work.

After the relative quirkiness of Italo Svevo and Luigi Pirandello, it is possible to generalize rather more about the prose fiction of the inter-war years. By then, if one excepts D'Annunzio's imaginative journalism, the old maestro had almost ceased to write creative prose fiction. His innovatory aspirations were still visible when in 1909 his *Forse che sí forse che no* (Maybe, maybe not) used the new craze for flying as its quasi-futuristic background (and can still entice readers with its purple passages), while his fantasy-ridden and autobiographical *Notturno* (Nocturne) (1916–22), written 'by touch' on 10,000 strips of paper, is a startling analysis of his physical and spiritual state when, permanently blinded in his left eye during a flying accident in World War One, he was confined to a lightless room for three months in order to save the sight of his other eye, and was forced to use inch-wide strips of paper as a guide for the pencil between his fingers. Into that analysis the poet also wove auditory images from the watery Venice just outside his windows, and, with a stream of consciousness technique all his own, blended reminiscences from his earlier life. The unconventional volume was to give rise to a new style of writing,

'Nocturne prose', imitated by his followers and, because of t.. informality of its syntax and language, becoming a powerful influence on other writers who followed him.

The Fascist censors found it easier to understand prose rather than verse, and, officially or otherwise, an atmosphere of political conformity was created in prose narrative as they imposed their homogeneous rules. One writer who more obviously and spontaneously conformed to the Fascist cultural atmosphere, was Riccardo Bacchelli (1891–1985), whose work imitated the style and attitudes of his nineteenth-century model and ideal, Alessandro Manzoni (1785–1883). Bacchelli wrote some of the longest novels published outside Russia, and was at his best when fictionalizing history as romantic episodes, many of them shot through with Catholic piety—the type of Manzonian escapism which the regime favoured. Other conforming novelists also made a reasonable living in Fascist Italy. Whereas in 1926 Mussolini opposed the award of the Nobel prize to the freethinking Matilde Serao (1857–1927), the award went to Grazia Deledda (1871–1936) (coincidentally then married to a government official); she wrote uncommitted stories of provincial life in Sardinia, *Racconti sardi* (1894), and novels such as *Elias Portolu* (1903) and *Marianna Sirca* (1915), two works renowned at the time, and still holding interest for the modern reader if only for their folkloric and curiosity value.

Deledda's Nobel prize highlighted what might seem at first glance a remarkable phenomenon: that at such a time of nationalist and centralist political fervour there was a whole crop of writers whose subject-matter concerned their regional and often popular origins. But the Fascists were not slow in recognizing the value of regional (and municipal) attachments and loyalties (*campanilismo*), and favoured local cultural initiatives. Vasco Pratolini (1913–91) exploits his native, and, in the inter-war years, ultra-provincial Florence, Elio Vittorini and Vitaliano Brancati (1907–54) concentrate their best efforts on Sicily, Cesare Pavese makes a literary return to his roots in Piedmont's Langhe, and Francesco Jovine (1902–1950) turns his narrative skills to the province of the Molise. Provincial writers also helped to focus attention on the importance of the working-class or peasants, and to emphasize the difference between urban and rural society, between North and South, between language and dialect. Such interest in the regions would in the post-Fascist epoch

he political desire to organize the country into
strative areas.

; who went abroad, voluntarily or perforce, to publish
w their fierce independence of the conformist norms
though much of this type of work had to wait until
1d World War for publication in Italy. Emilio Lussu and
Ignazio Silone were striking examples of good writers who published
influential work outside the peninsula, in France and Switzerland,
respectively. Lussu's *Un anno sull'altipiano* (A Year on the High Plateau) is one of the best Italian memoirs to come out of the First World
War, and a good antidote to the propaganda of the Fascists (and
earlier of D'Annunzio). Silone's fine, if harrowing novel, *Fontamara*,
written in Switzerland, at Davos, in 1930, provides a bitterly satirical
view of the conditions of the rural poor under Fascism in its tale of
life in a southern Italian village oppressed by Fascist functionaries
and by a corrupt social hierarchy supported by the regime.

It seems hardly credible nowadays that in 1940 Alberto Moravia
managed to publish his thinly veiled critique of the regime in the
short stories of *I sogni del pigro* (Dreams of the Lazy Man), and even
less likely that, as late as 1941, he could publish *La mascherata* (The
Masquerade), his allegorical satire on dictatorship, but the obtuseness
or sympathy of the censor is usually held responsible for letting these
works through the net; the second edition of *La mascherata* was
suppressed. Despite his shortcomings, notable in his repetitive
themes and insubstantial plots, Moravia must be included amongst
the century's leading Italian prose writers. Unconsciously he antici-
pated the new prose in his *Gli indifferenti*, published when he was 22
years of age, in which he expressed his youthful contempt for the
Italian middle class, and, obliquely, for Italy's traditional literary style.
He declared, for instance, that he had added punctuation only after
the book was written; his language was deliberately racy, his descrip-
tions realistic and uninhibited. Moravia gained for himself a more
cosmopolitan aura by spending time after 1935 travelling abroad as a
journalist and lecturer. To the younger generation Moravia's technical qualities as a writer, along with his socio-political direction,
seemed akin to those of his American contemporaries: his themes of
rebelliousness and anti-bourgeois behaviour appealed to young
readers, and his lack of sentimentality, his preoccupation with sex,
and attention to often sordid reality were attractive to a large section

of Italy's growingly literate public. The popularity of his work also helped to prepare that same public for the advent of neo-realism after 1945, a tendency exploited mainly on the cinema screen, but also discernible in the realism of much post-war prose fiction.

An undogmatic conclusion

Such a revolutionary period of literary and political growth cannot be compartmentalized dogmatically: although the Fascists began, as early as 1922, to oppress their opponents and impose a censorship (and in consequence some kind of literary conformity), at no time in its history had Italian literature been so imbued with influences from abroad. Superficially Mussolini's xenophobic policies seemed to work, but even that most conservative critic, journalist, and literary polygraph, Emilio Cecchi (1884–1966) was a renowned international traveller, journalist, and lecturer, and an expert critic of Anglo-Saxon literature. The leading poet of the 1920s, Giuseppe Ungaretti, claimed by Quasimodo to be the unwitting creator of the new poetic movement, hermeticism, boasted in his verse of his cosmopolitan wanderings in Africa, South America, and Europe; he was born in Egypt, educated in Paris, and became a university teacher in Brazil.

Despite the censorship, radically influential translations abounded, particularly from American literature, though it is true that the translation by Cesare Pavese of John Dos Passos's novel, *The Big Money*, done in 1937, was required by a whimsical censor to have its proper names anglicized, while Elio Vittorini, Pavese's future editorial colleague, found the first edition of his own volume of translations (from no less than fifteen American authors) was suppressed. Yet most major American authors were translated into Italian and found ready sales. It is probable that in the work of American writers, such as Steinbeck or Hemingway, the young Italian intelligentsia discerned ideals of liberty which compared favourably with the conditional liberties experienced under Fascism. It was also true that American English seemed a less élitist, more democratic vehicle of expression than their own indigestibly classical texts; a new lightness of spirit and expression seemed to come through in the translations. Later Italy's most accomplished post-war novelist, Italo Calvino (1923–85), maturing during the *Ventennio*, commented that, for his own, youthful generation, Ernest Hemingway was a god; literary merit counted for less than libertarian spirit.

In many ways the unconventional Moravia symbolized the relative lack of influence which Fascism had upon Italy's literary culture. Under the regime censorship was undeniably imposed, indeed tightened as time went on, but it is also true that, almost by oversight, left-wing thinkers and writers were permitted limited freedom, which in turn allowed some kind of preparation for the post-war revanche of communism and socialism. While it is a fact that the left-wing thinkers, official and unofficial Socialists and Communists, were consistently weakened by their political disagreements, and never managed to overcome the intelligent opposition of the Christian Democrats and their allies, at least the ranks of the Left were strengthened after 1945 by a kind of literary-critical unity. And by then, ironically, the unofficial censorship implicit in left-wing prejudice, more effective than anything the Fascist censor could have dreamed up, was stronger in suppressing the work of those writers considered as former collaborators or right-wingers; even those long dead suffered from this new kind of dogmatic censorship, D'Annunzio being perhaps the best example.

Social and political thought, 1890–1945

Richard Bellamy

'We don't like Italy as it is today.' As the intellectual entrepreneur Giuseppe Prezzolini observed, Giovanni Amendola's pithy remark of 1910 summed up the sentiments of a whole generation of social and political thinkers. Despite their very different methodological and ideological perspectives, they agreed to a remarkable degree that the unified Italy had not realized the hopes and aspirations of the Risorgimento period. At its best, the resulting disillusionment produced an incisive if invariably polemical critique of Italian political institutions that not only unmasked the divide separating the 'legal' from the 'real' Italy but also served to deepen the analysis of liberal democratic systems more generally. At its worst, this dissatisfaction produced a nihilistic and cynical antagonism to most features of modern societies, combined with a dismissive contempt for the concerns of ordinary people.

The main preoccupation of Italian social and political theorists was with the Machiavellian issues of 'force' and 'consent'. The Italian state's lack of 'force' was manifested in its inability either to defend and promote itself externally or to uphold law and order internally. The absence of 'consent' allegedly arose from a failure to 'make Italians', with the result that few people identified strongly with the new state. Relatively little attention was paid to the key questions of liberal democracy, namely the protection of individual liberties and the accountability of governments. These were dismissed as pseudo-problems that were meaningless and impossible to adequately conceptualize or achieve in themselves, only making sense as aspects of the state's primary task as the focus of the collective strength and will of a people. Indeed, the view that Giolittian Italy had failed to either act sufficiently forcefully or promote a suitably strong consensus had a tendency to shade into a critique of liberalism and democracy *tout court*. Ironically, a more favourable appraisal of both the Giolittian era and liberal democracy only occurred when the Fascist regime transformed such positive opinions in their turn into an oppositional perspective. Thus, this chapter shall first survey the various critiques of Italian liberal democracy up to and immediately following the First World War, then examine the attempts to produce alternatives of both a fascist and communist character, finally exploring the revaluation of both liberalism and democracy produced by the Resistance.

The critique of liberal democracy

In Italy, as elsewhere, late nineteenth-century philosophical culture was dominated by two schools of thought—idealism and positivism. The former drew not only on Kant and Hegel but also had native roots, particularly Vico, and encompassed thinkers as diverse as the liberal Catholics Vincenzo Gioberti and Antonio Rosmini and the anticlerical Neapolitan Hegelians Francesco De Sanctis, Angelo Camillo De Meis, and Bertrando and Silvio Spaventa. The latter was similarly eclectic, looking to the thinkers of the French and British Enlightenments, their nineteenth-century heirs, notably Auguste Comte, J. S. Mill, and, towards the end of the century, Herbert Spencer, and certain Italian followers, such as Antonio Genovesi, Cesare Beccaria, and Carlo Cattaneo. It too covered a broad spectrum of positions, from largely 'methodological' positivists such as Pasquale Villari, whose main concern was to promote the 'scientific' and empirical study of socio-economic processes, to 'systematic' positivists such as Roberto Ardigò, who espoused a materialist epistemology and saw positivism as a complete philosophy.

The idealists were the most influential school in the first decade of the newly united Italy, most particularly through their links with the ruling Historic Right, in whose administrations De Sanctis and Silvio Spaventa served. Predominantly from the South and inspired by the

Hegelian doctrine of the ethical state, they were largely concerned with constructing a 'legal' Italy capable of exercising moral authority over its citizens. By contrast, the 1870s to the 1890s were the decades of the positivists, whose attention was focused on the social conditions of the 'real' Italy. Although mainly from northern Italy, thanks to the studies of Pasquale Villari, Sidney Sonnino, and Leopoldo Franchetti this issue came to be epitomized above all by the 'Southern Question'.[1] In general, the positivists of this generation had greater faith in the progress of society than the idealists. Whereas De Sanctis, De Meis, and Silvio Spaventa, for example, believed the state, guided by the intellectual class, had the crucial if daunting task of educating the lower classes and creating a national political culture, the positivists hoped this transformation could be brought about by the processes of modernization—albeit with the state facilitating the development of southern industry by deregulating agrarian contracts, removing protectionist customs duties, and tempering some of the operations of the free market with discreet social measures.

However, in other respects the positivists shared many of the views of the idealist camp. They were similarly contemptuous of the transformist politics that followed the fall of the Right, seeing it as a crucial block to any constructive reform, and often became critical of all parliamentary democracy as a result. Their emphasis on the South as somehow encapsulating Italy's problems also led them to share certain conservative prejudices of the neo-Hegelians, encouraging them to ignore the new and rather different issues raised by the growth of an urban working class in the north and to favour somewhat anachronistic policies that idealized the potential position of a new class of independent peasant proprietors which they somewhat naively expected to emerge from the introduction of more capitalist farming methods. Finally, despite differences in method and approach, they were likewise preoccupied with 'making Italians', seeing social and economic improvements in largely moralistic terms. This latter aspect was particularly evident in Ardigò's concern with human psychology, which fed into the Italian school of positivist

---

[1] P. Villari, *Le lettere meridionali* (Florence, 1875); L. Franchetti, *Condizioni politiche e amministrative della province napoletane* (Florence, 1875), with an appendix by Sonnino on 'La Mezzeria in Toscana'; and L. Franchetti and S. Sonnino, *I contadini in Sicilia* (Florence, 1877).

criminology, represented above all by Cesare Lombroso. Though he adopted occasionally contradictory opinions on specific topics, Lombroso's basic thesis was that penalties had to match the psychological type of the criminal rather than the crime. Though he employed racist theories as well, he saw social conditions and political institutions as prime influences on human behaviour. For example, in his 1895 book on *Anarchists* he argued against the use of the death penalty or other severe punishments for them on the grounds that their activities were in large part products of Italy's backwardness and injustices.

The writings of the positivists of the 1870s and 1880s bequeathed an ambiguous legacy to their successors in the 1890s. The attention paid to social reforms combined with the progressive and modernizing sympathies of this generation of positivist writers was to pass into socialism, mixing in various ways with Marxism to become the ideology of the Italian labour movement. The major socialist writers of the 1890s—Filippo Turati, Achille Loria, Napoleone Colajanni, Enrico Ferri, and Saverio Merlino—all espoused a complex (and at times contradictory) mix of Darwin, Spencer, and Marx (the subtitle of Ferri's *Socialism and Positive Science* of 1894). Their espousal of reformism stemmed from the resulting belief in the need for an evolutionary approach, that involved passing through the capitalist stage, and the empiricist desire to find practical solutions to specific problems, whilst their emphasis on moral leadership reflected the traditional concern of the intellectual élite with educating the masses. Yet the result was to lay them open to attacks from the Left for collaborating with a flawed political system and promoting bourgeois capitalism rather than the interests of the proletariat, and from the Right for typifying the materialistic, populist, moderate politics they associated with *Italietta* or 'little Italy'.

The intellectual reaction against reformism from around 1900 is standardly associated with the attack on positivism by a new generation of idealist thinkers. It is portrayed as a reactionary assault on the materialism of the modern world linked to a vague yearning for spiritual values. As we shall see, this characterization is certainly partly true, even if ironically there was a partial reconciliation of the Catholic Church with Italian democracy in this period, with the publication of *Rerum Novarum* in 1891. Catholic modernizers, such as Romolo Murri and Ernesto Buonaiuti, however, found little sympathy from either the Church or the fiercely anticlerical idealist school. The acutest critiques of Italian democracy, though, came from the positivist camp and from the Left.

The most incisive and theoretically important of these critical analyses stemmed from the élite theories elaborated by the positivist thinkers Vilfredo Pareto and Gaetano Mosca. Despite superficial similarities in their views, their criticisms were very differently motivated. Born in Paris in 1848 and initially based in Florence prior to taking up the Chair of Political Economy at Lausanne University in 1893, Pareto was a classic liberal deeply influenced by Spencer and more particularly J. S. Mill. For much of the 1890s, he expressed support for the cause of organized labour. He saw 'popular socialism' as a legitimate reaction to the 'bourgeois socialism' practised by the Italian political class gathered around Crispi and his successors, which employed state monopolies and economically disastrous protectionist tariffs to buy votes and adopted increasingly coercive measures to dampen unrest. He also sympathized with individual socialists, such as Colajanni, sharing many of their progressive hopes. However, a convinced economic liberal, he had never accepted either the efficiency or legitimacy of state intervention in the economy, regarding it as merely increasing political power and patronage. His coruscating deconstruction of *Socialist Systems* in 1902 and his later Fascist sympathies arose largely because he felt that from 1900 the balance had swung the other way. Instead of counterbalancing 'bourgeois socialism' in ways that might have established a liberal economic system, 'popular socialism' simply threatened to take its place. Its apparent democratic credentials notwithstanding, socialist ideology, particularly its reformist variant, was simply a mechanism for promoting the interests of a particular group of politicians. By contrast, Gaetano Mosca, who was born in Palermo in 1858, belonged to the conservative southern intelligentsia. Unlike Pareto, he doubted the capacity of the lower classes to participate in politics and had little insight into the plight of northern workers. Whilst attacking the governments of the so-called Left, he idealized those of the Right as the work of public-spirited citizens.

These differences were reflected in their respective versions of élite theory. Both argued that irrespective of the form of government, be it monarchy, aristocracy, or democracy, a relatively compact minority always ruled. Moreover, they also agreed that mass democracy in many ways extended rather than constrained the possibilities for élites to govern. Yet though Mosca in particular bickered continually over who took precedence in having formulated this thesis, they developed it in quite different ways. Pareto's argument, given most fully in the massive *Treatise of General Sociology* of 1916, may have dispensed with the earlier Italian positivists' faith in the progressive evolution of modern society but shared their emphasis on social psychology rather than social structures. A rigorous mathematical economist, who pioneered modern welfare economics, Pareto believed the prime question confronting the social scientist was why individuals were invariably moved by 'non-logical' motivations rather than self-interested 'logico-experimental' instrumental reasoning. He believed the answer lay in humans being motivated by a number of basic emotional 'residues' which could then be manipulated by certain sorts of argumentation, which he called 'derivations'. Though he enumerated some 52 residues, the most important were 'the instinct of combinations' and the 'persistence of aggregates'. Pareto believed the rise and fall of governing classes reflected altering balances of these two residues within the élite, with the first favouring the cunning needed to rule through consent, the latter a more conservative desire for strength. He argued that societies tended to alternate between periods of prosperity, when the skills of persuasion were at a premium, and of austerity, when policies of law and order were demanded. He linked the Giolittian period with the former, suitably situated between the periods of coercive rule of Crispi and Mussolini. Reformist socialism, on this account, was simply an ideology or 'derivation' employed by the prevailing ruling class to maintain their power. Like democracy, with which it had an affinity, it was well suited to élites employing the consensual methods of the 'instinct of combinations', giving their rule a veneer of popular legitimacy. In common with other anti-democrats discussed below, Pareto was more sympathetic to revolutionary syndicalism, which in his view reflected the forceful 'persistence of aggregates'. However, he believed its claims were just as illusory, amounting to little more than rhetorical gestures to legitimize a counter-élite's bid for power. Though he initially welcomed Fascism, it was as a confirmation of his social theory rather than because of agreement with its ideals. He remained an economic liberal and had no sympathy with the syndicalist strand in Fascist ideology. However, his disillusionment with democracy had led him to the paradoxical belief that a free market involving minimal state intervention could only be maintained by an authoritarian state that did not have to bargain with democratically entrenched vested interests. Had he lived, Mussolini would soon have disabused him in this regard and he would undoubtedly have been as critical of the Fascist regime as he had been of Giolitti.

Though Mosca shared Pareto's doubts about both popular sovereignty and socialism his account of the ascendancy of a political class was more truly sociological. Minorities always rule because they form a more coherent group, able to act with greater consistency and coherence and to organize themselves better than the necessarily more diffuse and inchoate majority. He agreed with Pareto that universal suffrage promoted the corrupt and devious political skills of the flatterer, the wheeler-dealer, and the populist demagogue. He also believed that terms such as 'popular sovereignty' and the 'common good' were simply ideological 'political formulae' whereby a ruling class legitimized its position. However, he departed from Pareto in believing that ideally the élite should be, and in fact often was, the most capable. However, the qualities making the group best altered as societies evolved. Thus, the rulers of the industrial age required rather different talents to those of the feudal era, where military prowess was at a premium. A deputy from 1909 to 1919, he opposed the introduction of universal suffrage in 1912 but ultimately accepted the need to come to terms with mass democracy and to concentrate not on its debunking so much as its reworking so that it would produce a democratic meritocracy committed to liberal values and possessing the administrative skills essential for the efficient and just government of contemporary societies. Crucial to this scheme was his doctrine of 'juridical defence'. Mosca argued that a political system had to be so designed as to mix the 'aristocratic' and the 'democratic' tendencies within any society, producing in the process a balance between the 'autocratic' and 'liberal' principles of government. Unlike Pareto, he saw electoral competition between élites and an openness to demands and recruitment from the lower strata as mechanisms for reducing rather than exacerbating corruption. For they ensured that rulers could further their own interests in governing only by taking account of the interests of the ruled in good government.

The idealist revolt against positivism echoed many of these criticisms of mass democracy but linked them to an attack on the materialism of the positivist method. By far the most prominent figure in this movement was the philosopher Benedetto Croce. The nephew of Silvio Spaventa, with whom he lived following the tragic death of his parents in an earthquake, he first came to prominence through his critique of the evolutionist Marxist theories of Loria, Ferri, and others in the 1890s. Croce had been encouraged to study Marxism by Antonio Labriola, a philosophy professor at Rome University and former student of Bertrando Spaventa. In a series of influential essays published first in French by Georges Sorel between 1895 and 1898 and then in Italian by Croce in 1902 as *Essays on the Materialist Conception of History*, Labriola argued that Marxism was above all a theory of revolutionary praxis which involved raising the consciousness of workers concerning their exploited condition within capitalist societies. He inveighed against the reformist conceit that revolution was a process inherent within the very development of industrial societies. Croce had agreed with Labriola that Marxism was above all a practical philosophy geared to political action. He even dubbed Marx 'the Machiavelli of the proletariat'. However, he questioned the coherence of certain Marxist propositions, notably the law of the falling rate of profit, and disputed both the materialist ontology and the utilitarian morality which he believed underlay Marxism. Instead of helping Labriola promote a more critical, sophisticated, and revolutionary Marxism, he briefly became Italy's foremost critic of Marx.

The most intellectually lively and revolutionary branch of Italian socialism was at this time the syndicalist movement. Inspired by Sorel, it also spawned an important Italian literature, including contributions by Enrico Leone, Arturo Labriola, Paolo Orano, and Sergio Panunzio. Belief in the inevitably corrupt and transformist character of parliamentary democracy was once again fuelled by the southern origins of most of the main syndicalist intellectuals. Fiercely workerist in orientation, syndicalism focused on unions and spontaneous activism centred on the myth of the general strike. Once again, a moral transformation was emphasized over social and political reform. Deeply antagonistic to reformist compromises with bourgeois democracy, syndicalists also disputed the Leninist strategy of organizing revolution via a vanguard party. Though Croce admired Sorel's austere morality, he had little time for the movement's other adherents. Indeed, its essentially negative and anarchic tendency led to it attracting the very extreme and, as he eventually thought, irrationalist forces of the Right he was soon to regard as his prime opponents. Rising to prominence with the general strike of 1904, it was declared heretical at the Florence Socialist Party conference of 1908. Nevertheless, their breakaway organization, the Italian Syndical Union (USI) did pretty well, claiming 800,000 members in 1920. Many, such as Panunzio, Orano, and Angelo Olivero Olivetti, later joined Fascism.

From 1900 Croce devoted himself to elaborating his own distinctive Philosophy of Spirit. Along with his collaborator, Giovanni Gentile, who had also written an influential idealist interpretation and critique of Marx in 1899, he employed his review La critica to promote a revival of the idealism of De Sanctis and Spaventa. Croce's idealism had its roots in the contention that human creativity, thought, and morality not only were not instrumental in character, even if practical action was, but were also distinct from each other. Thus, his first major work, the Aesthetic of 1902, was devoted to defending art as the 'pure expression' of artistic 'intuition' rather than the desire to communicate a given idea—the role of philosophy—or a practical programme—the realm of politics.

Influenced by Gentile, Croce historicized this doctrine as a dialectic of distinct moments of the Beautiful, the True, the Useful, and the Good. The first two represented the theoretical aspects of spirit, the last two its practical aspects. Whereas the second and fourth included the first and third respectively, the latter pair were totally independent from the former. Thus, it was possible to write a philosophy of art but art was not itself philosophy. Likewise action that was practically useful was not of itself moral but could only be assessed as such after further and entirely separate reflection. However, Croce did not believe there were absolute standards of Beauty, Truth, Utility, and Goodness either. Rather, these were all matters of historical judgement in the light of prevailing circumstances and their suitability as responses to the particular issues they were addressing.

Croce's historicist belief that present action always entailed an engagement with conditions inherited from the past seemed to make his doctrine more positivist and conservative and less radically idealist than many had initially supposed, including his friend Gentile. Indeed, he was partly moved in this direction by what he came to see as the irrational and voluntaristic tendencies of certain thinkers whom he had initially greeted as fellow-travellers. Chief amongst these were the Florentine intellectuals Giovanni Papini and Giuseppe Prezzolini, whose journal *Leonardo* Croce cautiously welcomed as a suitable expression of youthful iconoclasm, and the various nationalist writers gathered around Enrico Corradini's journal *Il Regno* and the poet Gabriele D'Annunzio, whose work Croce was one of the first to praise. The first group had seen Croce's aesthetic as an anti-naturalist paean to the human capacity for self-invention, the 'Man-God' as Prezzolini's review was entitled. However, Papini's 'magical pragmatism' and his relentless debunking of all attempts at a systematic philosophy, including Croce's own, soon created strong divisions between them. When Papini broke with Prezzolini and founded the proto-futurist *Lacerba*, he along with D'Annunzio became a byword for a certain Nietzschean 'decadence' and irresponsibility that Croce saw as amongst the chief ills of the modern age. Likewise, Croce's conservative desire to revive a sense of 'Patria' and a strong state capable of maintaining law and order, combined with his criticisms of socialist reformism and an aristocratic liberal concern over mass democracy, all aligned him with the second group. But, as he put it in an important essay of 1911, a patriotic faith was one thing, ill-considered nationalist programmes for imperial expansion quite another. To his dismay, he found Gentile apparently endorsing both the extreme tendencies he was attempting to reject. He used Prezzolini's new philo-Crocean journal *La Voce* to launch an attack on his collaborator's 'actualist' philosophy. The crunch came with the First World War. Whereas Papini, D'Annunzio, and Gentile saw it as a purifying bloodbath that would foster a spiritual regeneration of the Italian people and allow the convention-breaking qualities of the superior sort of individual to flourish, Croce advocated neutrality and doubted Italy's capacity to fight. He saw intervention as an unholy alliance of the decadent irrationalists, with their empty quest for national and individual glory, on the one hand, and the democratic populists, moved by a utopian commitment to the illusory and abstract ideals of a war to end all wars and international solidarity, on the other.

Revolution and reaction

Croce was right, the war did place Italy's fragile economy and democracy under tremendous strain, with the Red Years of 1918–20 being swiftly followed by the Black reaction and the Fascist seizure of power in 1922. From the perspective of social and political theory, the most significant event in the former period was the factory occupations in Turin and the theorization of them by the Marxist thinker Antonio Gramsci. Of Sardinian origin, Gramsci had come to Turin to study linguistics at the university but quickly became involved in socialist circles and embarked on a career as a political journalist. Gramsci had already achieved a certain notoriety through having appeared to side with Mussolini's faction by advocating entry into the war and in greeting the Russian Revolution as going against Marx's *Das Kapital*. Gramsci argued that revolution arose not as a direct result of changes in the mode of production but through workers becoming conscious of the available opportunities for revolt and having the desire and capacity to exploit them. He saw intervention as a way of creating the appropriate revolutionary spirit and conditions. Though influenced by revolutionary syndicalism, the chief inspiration came from Labriola and Croce. His revisions notwithstanding, he remained firmly within the Marxist camp both theoretically and politically. The material base might not determine the superstructure but it certainly conditioned it, whilst the party played a central organizational role as against the unions.

This underlying orthodoxy is apparent in Gramsci's view of the factory councils. These originated from the internal factory commissions that were set up after the war. Gramsci saw them as potential Soviets, offering a new form of workers' democracy suited to a modern industrial economy. He believed participation in the management of the factory gave workers a sense of their place within the system of production and exchange. He envisaged an international network of factory councils, which would replace the market as the means whereby supply and demand could be tailored to each other. Along with Palmiro Togliatti and Umberto Terracini, he used their journal *L'Ordine nuovo* to militate for the development of a whole system of factory councils and, crucially, provide them with the intellectual leadership of the party. When northern factories were occupied in September 1920, he made the councils the key organ of the movement.

The occupations ultimately collapsed, in part due to lack of support from the unions and the Italian Socialist Party (PSI), and in 1921 Gramsci and his colleagues joined the secessionists from the PSI in forming the Communist Party of Italy (PCd'I). Gramsci was in Moscow at the time of the March on Rome as the PCd'I delegate to the Comintern, but soon began to analyse the Fascist phenomenon. He now developed his earlier insights into the role consciousness played in the creation of a revolutionary praxis. Gramsci believed that contemporary production line methods and the big monopolistic corporations with which they were associated had created the objective conditions for communist forms of social and political organization to emerge. However, he also argued that the mature liberal democracies of advanced capitalist societies had much more sophisticated ways of winning the consent of the populace to a system that actually worked against their interests than were available in less developed countries. Ironically, therefore, the weakness of Russia's political institutions had allowed Lenin to mount a political revolution even though the economic circumstances had yet to obtain. The Fascist seizure of power and the direct use of the state to defend capital similarly testified to the relative backwardness and fragility of Italy's economy and democracy. In Britain and the United States industrialists had been able both to create a new kind of factory worker without recourse to state coercion, and to evolve forms of mass democracy that obtained the passive allegiance of workers to the political system. He believed a revolutionary strategy suited to Italy's *sui generis* situation now had to be elaborated—one which built links between the northern workers and the southern peasants and established tactical alliances with other parties opposed to Fascism.

Gramsci regarded the goal of such linkages as the forging of a collective revolutionary consciousness rather than reformism. However, many of the existing PCd'I leaders feared tactical alliances with non-workers would dilute the revolutionary commitment of the Party. His argument, though, was more in tune with Comintern thinking than theirs and in 1924 he was elected a deputy and returned to Italy and formed a new Party leadership. Following Mussolini's withdrawal of parliamentary immunity, he was arrested and sentenced to twenty years, four months, and five days of imprisonment in 1928. From 1929 he worked on the *Prison Notebooks*. These elaborated many of his earlier ideas. Of particular importance was his notion of 'hegemony' or ideological power. As noted above, he saw the capacity of liberal regimes to win the consent of the populace as requiring a modification of revolutionary tactics. A 'war of position' had to be fought within the institutions of civil society so as to win people over before a successful 'war of movement' or frontal assault could be mounted on the state. He defended the Marxist credentials of this thesis via a critique of positivist historical materialism inspired by a critical reading of Crocean historicism. Seriously ill, he suffered a series of strokes and died in 1937 shortly after receiving an unconditional discharge.

Many of Gramsci's views were devised as self-conscious reversals of Fascist positions. Whereas he saw Fascism as a totalitarian ideology imposed from above via the forced organization of people within its corporate structures, he sought to make Marxism an equally all-encompassing and 'total' conception of the world but one that would emerge from below through the democratic organization of workers within civil society. Many commentators doubt whether Fascism can be dignified with having anything as coherent as a philosophy. Indeed, Mussolini's success was in part to make it an anti-party that harnessed the support of groups as disparate as the irrationalist iconoclasts around Papini and D'Annunzio, certain revolutionary syndicalists, the disaffected petty bourgeoisie and conservatives desirous of a return to law and order—though these last, who initially included both Mosca and Croce, gradually deserted him from 1925 onwards. However, at least two thinkers tried to give him a theory. Giovanni Gentile, who joined the party in 1923, sought to align Fascism with the neo-Hegelian's doctrine of the ethical state. He hoped thereby to provide it with a lineage going back to the Risorgimento period that allowed him to designate it the true heir of the Italian liberal tradition. But he also gave this doctrine a personal twist deriving from his own 'actualist' philosophy. The subjectivist extreme of idealism, in politics this led him to identify the force of the state with the consent of the people—a position that conveniently justified the Fascist seizure of power. He saw the state as the expression of the collective will of the people, with corporatism the most suitable means for organizing this will. The state's role was not that of a mediator between individuals, as most liberal doctrines suggested, but existed within each individual as the expression of his or her true interests. Fascism had an almost mystical and spiritual quality for Gentile—a position his followers Ugo Spirito and Arnaldo Volpicelli attempted to radicalize in the direction of a Sorelian revolutionary syndicalism.

By contrast, the other main Fascist theorist, Alfredo Rocco, operated from positivist and explicitly reactionary premises. A prominent Nationalist thinker and jurist, he had worked out most of his ideas before the war. He viewed the nation as a quasi-biological organism with which the individual could be almost totally identified. A fierce critic of liberalism, which he associated with an egoistic economic individualism, his ideal was a form of industrial *ancien régime*, comprising a strong state governed by the new feudal class of the industrialists. He advocated replacing 'disorganized' capitalism with a corporatist state of hierarchically organized socio-economic groupings that allowed industrial leaders to discipline the individual to boost national production and engage in imperialist expansion. When the Nationalist Association merged with the Fascist Party in 1923, he quickly rose to prominence. As Minister of Justice from 1925–1932 he was, with Giuseppe Bottai, instrumental in putting this corporatist doctrine into law in the 'Charter of Labour' of 1926. Indeed, positivism was generally more influential than idealism on Fascism. For example, the ideas of Ferri and Lombroso largely shaped the design of the Fascist penal code. However, on the whole Fascist theory limply followed rather than directed Fascist practice, with the legal Italy separated as never before from the real Italy.

Opposition and resistance

Given Gentile's prominence as the ideologist of Fascism it was entirely fitting that Croce should lead the opposition, drafting a famous reply to Gentile's Manifesto of Fascist Intellectuals of 1925. Like many Italian liberals, he had initially supported Mussolini in the regrettably common belief that Fascism was better than socialism. Once it became clear that Fascism aspired to create a new type of regime rather than merely strengthening the hand of the liberal state, he quickly changed tack. He found Gentile's conception of the ethical state particularly repugnant. Invoking his important distinction between ethics and politics, Croce argued that civil society was the realm of ethical life whilst the state was simply a utilitarian institution concerned with efficient governance. Consent might be forced but only in the sense that to be durable it had to reflect the force of circumstances—including the demands and needs of citizens. In his histories of Italy from 1871 to 1915 and of nineteenth-century Europe, he sought to defend the practice of liberal institutions, attributing their collapse to irrationalism and materialism. He also now presented his historicist philosophy as a 'metapolitical' 'religion of liberty'. Human history, he now claimed, resulted from individuals reconceptualizing the world in new ways and so preparing the ground for innovative action to alter the world in the future. Put another way, Croce now argued we changed the world via the different ways we came to understand it.

Although Croce defended traditional liberal political and economic institutions, such as representative democracy, the rule of law, and the market, he regarded their relationship to liberalism as historically contingent. Thus he took issue with the free market economist Luigi Einaudi, arguing that even socialist economic measures could serve liberal purposes in certain circumstances. However, he also disputed the view of the socialist liberal Carlo Rosselli, who argued liberty was necessarily linked to social justice as the means for realizing it. For Croce, individual liberty was the crucial concept and included the freedom to interpret justice in differing ways according to changing historical circumstances.

Nonetheless, Rosselli's position was extremely important within the non-communist anti-Fascist movement. In the 1920s, a similar argument was developed by Guido De Ruggiero, and Piero Gobetti. Gentile's star pupil, De Ruggiero sided with Croce, producing his *History of European Liberalism* in 1924, whilst the precocious 23-year-old Gobetti first published Rosselli's thesis in his Turin journal *La rivoluzione liberale*. Both thinkers had been tremendously impressed by the socialist movement and unlike Croce had sided with it against the Fascists from the first. Historicist liberals like Croce, they were arguably more aware than he was of the importance of industrial labour within modern economies and hence of the legitimacy of its claims. Though Gobetti was sympathetic to the Russian Revolution, learning Russian in order to follow it more closely, he—like De Ruggiero—was nevertheless antipathetic to forms of collectivism that crushed rather than fostered individuality. Whereas Rosselli sought to liberalize socialism, they wished to socialize liberalism—most importantly by linking it to a mass movement. This last aspiration was ultimately a failure. Again like Croce, they became interested in Protestantism, attributing (albeit to differing degrees) the absence of a liberal spirit amongst Italians to the pervasiveness of Catholicism. Though Croce argued Fascism was but a 'parenthesis' in Italian history, for Gobetti it was Italy's 'autobiography'—testimony to the absence of a moral revolution amongst the Italian people.

During the Resistance, the Party of Action revived the theme of 'Justice and Liberty'. Rosselli and his brother had been killed on Fascist orders in 1937 and Gobetti died in exile aged only 25 in 1926. Their arguments, however, were picked up and developed by Guido Calogero, the major figure in the movement, as well as Augusto Monti and Norberto Bobbio. However, it remained influential only amongst fellow intellectuals. Instead, the two dominant ideologies of post-war Italy were to be the two religions of Communism and Christian Democracy. Both parties became partially reconciled to liberal democracy, the one under the leadership of Togliatti in the Gramscian spirit of a strategic manoeuvre whilst building a counter-hegemony, the other, though tainted with acceptance of Fascism via the Lateran Treaty, led by Alcide De Gasperi to a similarly pragmatic acceptance that no realistic alternative existed. Regrettably, ideologists of each side were to continue to concentrate more on the ideal than the real Italy, placing moral uplift above institutional, social, and economic reform.

Epilogue

Adrian Lyttelton

The fall of Mussolini on 25 July 1943 was greeted with spontaneous rejoicing by the majority of Italians. Their mood reflected not only disillusionment and disgust with his dictatorship, but the hope that the sufferings of war which he had brought on Italy would soon be over. Instead, it was the prelude to the most savage and destructive conflict which Italy had known since the Thirty Years' War.

The king, his military advisers, and his prime minister Field Marshal Badoglio were all deeply compromised with the regime which they had overthrown. Even loyal monarchists had grown impatient with Victor Emmanuel's indecisiveness, and regarded his action against Mussolini as long overdue. Even so, the king and his allies could have regained some political credit if they had shown themselves capable of skill or courage in the hour of crisis. Instead, the outcome showed that acquiescence to Fascism had fatally weakened their capacity both for realistic assessment of the situation and for making decisions. While negotiating an armistice with the Allies, the government and the Supreme Command failed to make any effective plans for action once it had been signed. Until the last moment, they tried to keep their options open, and seriously considered repudiating the armistice on the day it was announced. Badoglio cancelled an agreement which would have allowed the American 82nd Airborne Division to land on the airfields near Rome and help the Italian army defend the city. The last directive issued to commanders stressed that they were 'in no case . . . to take the initiative in hostilities against German troops'.[1]

---

[1] E. Agarossi, *A Nation Collapses: The Italian Surrender of September 1943*, tr. H. Fergusson (Cambridge, 1943), p. 97.

The armistice of 8 September 1943 dealt a moral blow to the monarchy from which it never recovered. Left without instructions, an army of one million men evaporated almost overnight. The large Italian forces in the Balkans surrendered to the Germans, with the exception of a few scattered groups who escaped to Italy or joined the local partisans. Seven hundred thousand Italian soldiers were interned in Germany. On the island of Cephalonia, 5,000 men of the Acqui division, which had resisted the Germans with bravery, were brutally massacred after their surrender. The 8th of September has become a symbol not only of the final dissolution of the monarchic state, but of the death of the nation itself. In the absence of any kind of effective moral leadership, it is not surprising that local and family loyalties and self-preservation emerged as the dominant imperatives for both soldiers and civilians. In many cities, air bombardment and food shortages had led to chaotic mass evacuation and a breakdown of organized society.

Opposing political interpretations of the crisis of the 8th of September have tended to see it either as the death of the old authoritarian, oligarchic Italy which left the way open for a democratic resurrection, or as a rupture in the fabric of the national community which has never been repaired. But both interpretations, though they indicate real problems, seem too simple.

In one respect, the significance of the 8th of September cannot be overrated. It marked the end of Italy's great power ambitions, and the temporary loss of its independence. Too many Italian histories of the period have concentrated on the domestic struggle between Fascists and anti-Fascists without a clear analysis of the policies of the occupying powers which determined the context within which they operated. Both on the Allied and even more markedly on the German side, the rivalry between competing agencies of government made the situation more complex, and at the same time allowed the Italians some room for manoeuvre.

The coup of 25 July, though it did not in the end save the monarchy, bought it time (almost three years), and introduced an element of ambiguity into the process of political renewal. The 'Kingdom of the South' had a formal legitimacy which was paradoxically enhanced by the birth of Mussolini's upstart Social Republic. In 1940 many French officials initially backed the authoritarian, collaborationist, Vichy regime because it embodied the continuity of the state; in Italy, in 1943, the same principle worked in favour of a monarchy which grudgingly accepted democracy and was in turn grudgingly recognized by Britain and the United States as an ally. So the complete collapse of the old state did not lead to a lasting repudiation of its methods and institutions. There was no general reform of administrative structures, nor any wholesale abolition of Fascist laws. A comparison with the far more radical reforms introduced by the Allies in Germany shows the importance of the kind of negative independence ensured by the fiction of Italy's 'co-belligerency'. The Rocco Penal Code and the restrictions on internal migration survived into the Republican period. A serious attempt was made to purge the administration and the universities of those most compromised with the regime, and to prosecute the authors of atrocities committed during the civil war of 1943–5. But the onset of the Cold War halted prosecutions, and most of those dismissed were reinstated. The position of Marshal Badoglio himself, arguably responsible for the use of poison gas in Ethiopia, was decisive in preventing any serious investigation of Italian war crimes. So the compromises of 1943 played an important role in prolonging the influence of a Fascist past which, at the same time, was not clearly acknowledged or discussed.

This is only one side of the story. The 'myth of the Resistance' has come under much criticism recently. Like all founding myths, it was undoubtedly manipulated for party ends and the limitations, errors, and crimes of the Resistance were overlooked. The significance of the fact that most of the south had experienced only a brief occupation by the Germans and had consequently not shared in the Resistance was minimized, so that once again the official values of Italy were those of the north. The solidarity of local communities with the Resistance has been exaggerated. Recent investigations of Nazi massacres has shown that the partisans were frequently blamed for provoking them. Nonetheless the Resistance, in both its political and military aspects (examined in more depth by Patrick McCarthy in the introduction to the next volume) was critical for the restoration of Italian self-respect. Foreign observers were frequently impressed by the alacrity and energy with which Italians seized the opportunity to revive political life, although this varied greatly according to region and size of community.

Against the idea of 'the death of the nation' it should be stressed that both the Resistance and the Fascists of the republic of Salò continued to invoke traditional patriotic values and symbols. The Fascist cult of Garibaldi was reshaped and appropriated by the Communists without too much difficulty.[2] Many army officers joined the Resistance and formed 'autonomous' units, motivated by patriotism rather than party. Nor is it true that the conflict of rival visions of national identity makes Italy anomalous. They were, on the contrary, the proof that enough common ground remained to be worth fighting over. It was the Cold War and, even more, the uneasy reconciliation which followed, which weakened the emotive force of appeals to Italian identity and history. Indeed, it could be argued that the mass politicization undertaken by the political parties between 1943 and 1947 made the idea of Italy more real for many Italians than it had been before. During the same period, all the parties in liberated Italy shared an ideology of national reconciliation and renewal which conditioned their actions.

A full social history of the years 1943–5 has yet to be written. It would have to set political events and movements in the context of the day-to-day struggle for survival, the black market, the effects of air bombardment, and the varied relationships of fear, hope, and dependency towards the occupying armies and authorities. When the Allies arrived in Naples, they were faced by scenes of almost unbelievable deprivation and degradation. The reactions of the journalist Alan Moorehead were typical: 'Hunger governed all. . . . What we are witnessing was . . . the moral collapse of a people. They had no pride any more or dignity. The animal struggle for existence governed everything. Food. That was the only thing that mattered.'[3] Many passages in the classic account of Norman Lewis, *Naples '44*, show a similar horrified fascination. Yet by the end of his stay contempt had been replaced by admiration for the ingenuity of the Neapolitans in coping with an impossible situation. The phenomena of the rise of a new class of more or less criminal profiteers, often in league with members of the occupying forces (it has been reckoned that in Naples as much as 60% of all Allied supplies ended up on the black market), and the opportunistic political conversions of many officials and

[2] See D. Forgacs, '*Nostra patria*: Revisions of the Risorgimento in the Cinema, 1925–1952', in A. R. Ascoli and K. von Henneberg (eds.), *Making and Remaking Italy* (Oxford and New York, 2001), pp. 257–74.

[3] D. W. Ellwood, *Italy 1943–1945* (Leicester, 1985), p. 49.

notables, aroused much unfavourable comment among foreign observers, and contributed to a mood of cynical pessimism among the Italians themselves. Yet, on the other side, many Italians showed an extraordinary capacity for human solidarity with the victims of war and persecution. Both Allied prisoners of war and Jews were sheltered by Italian families at great risk to themselves, and helped to escape by networks in which the Church often had an important role. Women, often by necessity, took on new initiatives and responsibilities which prepared the way for their political activism after the war. With its independence lost and consumption levels lower than at any time since unification, Italy still possessed in the resilience of its people the resource which made recovery possible.

Glossary

aeropittura: Aerial painting.

arditi: Shock troops.

ascaris: African colonial troops.

autorizzazione maritale: Civil Code requirement for husbands to authorize wives' property transactions.

Autostrade: Motorways.

biennio rosso: The 'two red years' (1919–1920).

Borgate: New working-class suburbs (of Rome).

braccianti: Agricultural labourers.

Brigate nere: Fascist paramilitary units of Salò Republic.

Capo di Stato maggiore: Chief of the General Staff.

carabinieri: Police, under dual military and civilian control.

Cinecittà: 'Cinema city'.

colonie: Holiday camps.

Crepuscolari: The 'twilight poets'.

Decima Mas: Special marine units of Salò Republic under command of Prince Valerio Borghese.

Destra Storica: The historic Right, the party of Cavour.

fasci: Axe and bundle of rods: emblems of Roman authority carried by lictor (v. littorio).

fasci di combattimento: Fascist combat groups (local branches of Fascist movement).

fasci femminili: Women's Fascist groups.

fascistizzazione: Takeover of institutions and associations by Fascists.

federali: Secretaries of Fascist Party provincial federations.

Federterra: Federation of agricultural workers.

fiancheggiatori: Fellow-travellers of Fascism.

gerarchi: Authorities of the Fascist regime.

Gioventù Italiana del Littorio: Fascist youth movement.

Giustizia e Libertà: 'Justice and Liberty'. Democratic anti-Fascist movement.

impegno: Commitment.

interventisti: Supporters of Italy's intervention in First World War.

Istituto Luce: Institute for production of documentary films and newsreels.

Italietta: 'Little Italy' (used by nationalists to refer to Italy under Giolitti).

Littoriali della cultura e dell'arte: Fascist Party competitions for writers and artists.

littorio: Fascist (see *fasci*).

Massaie rurali: Organization of rural housewives.

massimalisti: Supporters of maximum socialist programme.

mazzieri: Bands of thugs used by local politicians to intimidate opponents.

Mezzogiorno: Southern Italy.

non expedit: Papal instruction to Catholics not to participate in parliamentary elections.

podestà: Fascist head of municipal government.

Politecnico: Polytechnic.

prefect: State official in charge of province.

Rationalist movement: Movement for rational modern architecture.

Red Week: General strike and riots, 7–13 June 1914.

Resistance: Resistance to Nazi occupation and Fascism, 1943–1945.

ruralismo: Fascist exaltation of rural life.

squadristi/squadrismo: Armed Fascist squads and their violent actions.

stato nuovo: New state.

Statuto Albertino: Constitution granted to dominions of the House of Savoy by king Charles Albert in 1848.

Stile littorio: Fascist style.

Strapaese: 'Super-country' (cf. *ruralismo*).

Syndicalism: Doctrine asserting central role of workers' unions as opposed to parties.

terre irredente: 'unredeemed lands': Trent, Trieste, and other lands claimed by Italians from Austria after 1870.

Triennale delle arti decorative ed industriali moderne: Triennial Exhibition of modern decorative and industrial arts.

Ultramontanists: Supporters of papal supremacy.

Ventennio: The Fascist twenty years (1922–1943).

verismo: Realism.

Further reading

Introduction

The best general history of the period is still the classic if controversial work of D. Mack Smith, *Italy: A Modern History* (Ann Arbor, 1969). M. Clark, *Modern Italy 1871–1945* (London, 1996) is an excellent up-to-date survey.

R. Putnam, *Making Democracy Work: Civic Traditions in Modern Italy* (Princeton, 1993) offers a stimulating if highly debatable interpretation of the different development of 'civil society' in North and South. See also A. Lyttelton, 'Liberalism and Civil Society in Italy: From Hegemony to Mediation', in N. Bermeo and P. Nord (eds.), *Civil Society before Democracy: Lessons from Nineteenth-Century Europe* (Lanham, Md., 2000).

On emigration, R. Foerster, *The Italian Emigration of Our Times* (New York, 1968) is still useful. There are good general surveys by R. J. B. Bosworth, *Italy and the Wider World* (New York, 1996) and D. R. Gabaccia, *Italy's Many Diasporas* (London, 2000). See also D. Cinel, *The National Integration of Italian Return Migration, 1870–1929* (Cambridge, 1991).

The standard biography of Toscanini in English is H. Sachs, *Toscanini* (London, 1993). For Caruso, see M. Scott, *The Great Caruso* (London, 1988); E. Caruso, Jr. and A. Farkas, *Enrico Caruso: My Father and My Family* (Portland, Ore., 1990).

For the golden age of Italian silent cinema, see M. Landy, *Italian Film* (Cambridge, 2000), G. Nowell Smith (ed.), *The Oxford History of World Cinema*, and, in Italian, the indispensable work by G. P. Brunetta, *Storia del cinema italiano*, Vol. I. *Il cinema muto 1895–1929* (Rome, 1993).

Chapter 1

The most comprehensive general survey of the period is still C. Seton-Watson, *Italy from Liberalism to Fascism 1870–1925* (London, 1967). Work specifically on Giolitti in English is limited, although his memoirs are available and make good reading (G. Giolitti, *Memoirs of My Life* (London, 1923)). Economic developments can be followed in G. Toniolo, *An Economic History of Liberal Italy 1850–1918* (London, 1990) and in the important work of D. Forsyth, *The Crisis of Liberal Italy: Monetary and Financial Policy, 1914–1922* (Cambridge, 1993). On the specific issue of labour unrest in rural areas, see A. Cardoza, *Agrarian Elites and Italian Fascism: The Province of Bologna 1901–1926* (Princeton, 1982). The growth of nationalism is charted in A. J. De Grand, *The Italian Nationalist Association and the Rise of Fascism in Italy* (Lincoln, Nebr., 1978) and in R. Webster, *Industrial Imperialism in Italy*

1908–1915 (Berkeley and Los Angeles, 1975). Many of the articles in J. A. Davis (ed.), *Gramsci and Italy's Passive Revolution* (London, 1979) are relevant to the Italian experience in the decades before Fascism.

The impact of the First World War on Italy has received a great deal of attention over the past two decades. For some of the results of recent research, see the section on Italy in L. Haimson and G. Sapelli (eds.), *Strikes, Social Conflict and the First World War: An International Comparison* (Milan, 1992); G. Procacci, 'Popular Protest and Labour Conflicts in Italy, 1915–1918', *Social History*, 1 (1989); and P. Corner and G. Procacci, 'The Italian Experience of Total Mobilization, 1915–1920', in J. Horne (ed.), *State, Society and Mobilization in Europe during the First World War* (Cambridge, 1997).

Material on the post-war crisis of liberalism and the development of Fascism is easier to find. The *biennio rosso* has stimulated several studies; apart from the two works cited in the text, there is also G. Williams, *Proletarian Order* (London, 1976). A. Lyttelton, *The Seizure of Power: Fascism in Italy 1919–1929* (London and Princeton, 1987) remains the best single-volume study of the first years of Fascism. For studies of the growth of Fascism in various regions, see P. Corner, *Fascism in Ferrara 1915–1925* (London 1975), A. Kelikian, *Town and Country under Fascism: The Transformation of Brescia 1915–1926* (Oxford, 1986), F. Snowden, *The Fascist Revolution in Tuscany 1919–22* (Cambridge, 1989), and the work of Cardoza cited above.

The literature in Italian is obviously much more extensive. Readers will find excellent general surveys in G. Candeloro, *Storia dell'Italia moderna*, Vol. VII., *1896–1914* (Milan, 1974), in G. Carocci, *Storia d'Italia dall'Unità ad oggi*, (Milan, 1975) and in A. Aquarone, *L'Italia giolittiana* (Bologna, 1981). An important recent study on a key issue in Italian politics is G. Melis, *Storia dell'amministrazione italiana 1861–1993* (Bologna, 1996). For economic developments, see G. Barone, 'La modernizzazione italiana dalla crisi allo sviluppo', in G. Sabbatucci and V. Vidotto (eds.), *Storia d'Italia*, Vol. III (Rome, 1995). On the First World War, see the new synthesis by M. Isnenghi and G. Rochat, *La Grande Guerra 1914–1918* (Milan, 2000) and the essays in G. Procacci, *Dalla rassegnazione alla rivolta* (Rome, 2000). Comprehensive bibliographies, informative articles, and useful statistical appendices can all be found in Sabbatucci and Vidotto, Vol. III, cited above, and Vol. IV (Rome, 1997).

Chapter 2

Any guide to the Anglo-American literature on Church and state over the long view must begin with the classics. Arturo C. Jemolo's *Church and State in Italy 1850–1950* (Oxford, 1960) considers this fractious history from the perspective of liberal Catholicism. Daniel A. Binchy's account, *Church and State in Fascist Italy* (Oxford, 1941), starts with the nineteenth-century background to the Roman Question but focuses for the most part on the pontificate of Pius XI. Richard A. Webster's *Christian Democracy in Italy 1860–1960* (London, 1961) looks at Catholic groups as much as Popes and prime ministers. For an examination of separatist doctrines before conciliation, see S. William Halperin's *The Separation of Church and State in Italian Thought from Cavour to Mussolini* (Chicago, 1937) and *Italy and the Vatican at War* (Chicago, 1939).

Bolton King and Thomas Okey, in *Italy To-day* (New York, 1901), offer a contemporary account of Catholic politics and social work at the turn of the century. For a portrait of the lay and religious leadership in the *fin-de-siècle*, see Henry Lewis Hughes's book, authorized by the Vatican, *The Catholic Revival in Italy, 1815–1915* (London, 1935). Adrian Lyttelton's 'An Old Church and a New State: Italian Anticlericalism 1876–1915', *European Studies Review*, 13 (1983) gives a comprehensive yet succinct analysis of anticlericalism during its heyday. Raymond Grew's 'Catholicism in a Changing Italy', in Edward R. Tannenbaum and Emiliana P. Noether (eds.), *Modern Italy: A Topical History since 1861* (New York, 1974) surveys popular and political Catholicism from neo-Guelfism up through fascism. Alice Kelikian's 'Nuns, Entrepreneurs, and Church Welfare in Italy', in Olwen Hufton (ed.), *Women in the Religious Life* (Florence, 1996) examines convents in the service of rural industry from 1870 to the Second World War. Michael P. Carroll's *Veiled Threats: The Logic of Popular Catholicism in Italy* (Baltimore, 1996) subjects cults, popular devotions, and relics to sociological scrutiny.

On the internal structure of the Holy See, see Thomas J. Reese, *Inside the Vatican: The Politics and Organization of the Catholic Church* (Cambridge, Mass., 1996). Owen Chadwick's *A History of Popes: 1830–1914* (Oxford, 1998) and Carlo Falconi's *The Popes in the Twentieth Century: From Pius X to John XXIII* (Boston, 1968) provide excellent overviews of the papacy for the period under consideration in this chapter. Readers should consult Raphael Merry del Val, *Memories of Pope Pius X* (London, 1951) and Leonard von Matt and Nello Vian, *St. Pius X: A Pictorial History* (London, 1955) for Pius X. John F. Pollard's *The Unknown Pope: Benedict XV (1914–1922) and the Pursuit of Peace* (London, 1999) explores the short pontificate of Giacomo Della Chiesa. Philip Hughes, in *Pope Pius the Eleventh* (London, 1937), examines the tenure of Achille Ratti, the architect of conciliation.

On Catholicism and the regime, read Don Luigi's Sturzo's *Church and State* (New York, 1939). Much more than a portrait of Eugenio Pacelli, John Cornwell's *Hitler's Pope: The Secret History of Pius XII* (New York, 1999) gives a compelling description of papal politics in the 1930s and 1940s. John Pollard, *The Vatican and Italian Fascism 1929–1932* (Cambridge, 1985) follows Church–State relations from the Lateran accords to the fascist attack on Catholic Action. For the diplomatic impact of the conciliation, see Peter C.

Kent, *The Pope and the Duce: The International Impact of the Lateran Agreements* (New York, 1981). David Kertzer's *The Popes Against the Jews: The Vatican's Role in the Rise of Modern Anti-Semitism* (New York, 2001) and Susan Zuccotti's *Under His Very Windows: The Vatican and the Holocaust in Italy* (New Haven, 2001) deal with the Roman Church's anti-Judaism. Consult P. Vincent Bucci's *Chiesa e Stato: Church–State Relations in Italy within the Contemporary Constitutional Framework* (The Hague, 1969) about the incorporation of the Lateran accords into the constitution of the post-war republic.

Chapter 3

There are two excellent recent general economic histories of Italy in English for this period: G. Toniolo, *An Economic History of Liberal Italy, 1815–1918* (London and New York, 1990) and Vera Zamagni, *The Economic History of Italy, 1860–1990* (Oxford, 1993). For the late nineteenth century, see also the chapter on 'Economy, State and Society' in the previous volume in this series by John A. Davis (*Italy in the Nineteenth Century* (Oxford, 2000), pp. 235–55) and the older but still useful chapter by L. Cafagna on 'The Industrial Revolution in Italy, 1830–1914', in C. Cipolla (ed.), *The Fontana Economic History of Europe*, Vol. IV (London, 1973). A. Gerschenkron, *Economic Backwardness in Historical Perspective* (Cambridge, Mass., 1962) offers a classical interpretation of Italy's economic 'backwardness', but for a recent revisionist survey, see G. Federico, 'Italy 1860–1940: A Little Known Success Story', *Economic History Review*, 49 (1996).

For English language studies on more detailed aspects of Italy's economic development down to the First World War, see Pierluigi Ciocca and Gianni Toniolo, 'Industry and Finance in Italy, 1918–1940', *Journal of European Economic History*, 13: 2 (special issue) (1984), 113–36. J. S. Cohen, *Finance and Industrialization in Italy* (New York, 1977); Frank J. Coppa, *Planning, Protectionism and Politics in Liberal Italy: Economics and Politics in the Giolittian Age* (Washington, DC, 1978); M. Fratianni and F. Spinelli, 'Currency Competition, Fiscal Policy and the Money Supply Process in Italy from Unification to World War I', *Journal of European Economic History*, 14 (1985), 473–95; G. Toniolo, 'Effective Protection and Industrial Growth: The Case of Italian Engineering, 1896–1913', *Journal of European Economic History* (1978).

On the economic origins of the post-First World War political crisis and the origins of the Fascist seizure of power: Anthony Cardoza, *Agrarian Elites and Italian Fascism: The Province of Bologna, 1901–1925* (Princeton, 1982); Douglas Forsyth, *The Crisis of Liberal Italy: Monetary and Financial Policy, 1914–1922* (Cambridge, 1993); Alice A. Kelikian, *Town and Country under Fascism: The Transformation of Brescia 1915–1926* (Oxford, 1986); Charles Maier, *Recasting Bourgeois Europe: Stabilization in France, Germany and Italy in the Decade after World War I* (Princeton, 1975); A. Lyttelton, *The Seizure of Power* (London, 1974); R. Webster, *Industrial Imperialism in Italy, 1908–1915* (Berkeley, 1974). On Fascism and the economy, see also: Roland Sarti, *Fascism and the Industrial Leadership in Italy, 1919–1940: A Study in the Expansion of Private Power under Fascism* (Berkeley, 1971); J. S. Cohen, 'Was Italian Fascism a Developmental Dictatorship? Some Evidence to the Contrary', *Economic History Review*, 2nd ser., 41: 1 (1988), 95–113; A. J. Gregor, *Italian Fascism and Developmental Dictatorship* (Princeton, 1979); Douglas Forsyth, 'The Rise and Fall of German-Inspired Mixed Banking in Italy, 1894–1936', in Harold James, Håkan Lindgren, and Alice Teichova (eds.), *The Role of Banks in the Interwar Economy* (New York, 1991), pp. 179–205. Paul Corner, 'Women in Fascist Italy: Changing Family Roles in the Transition from an Agricultural to an Industrial Society', *European History Quarterly*, 23 (1993), 51–68; Angela Raspin, *The Italian War Economy, 1940–1943, with Particular Reference to Italian Relations with Germany* (New York, 1986). On the public debt, see also Francesco Giavazzi and Luigi Spaventa (eds.), *High Public Debt: The Italian Experience* (New York, 1988).

Chapter 4

The indispensable background for Italian foreign policy after unification is Federico Chabod, *Italian Foreign Policy: The Statecraft of the Founders* (Princeton, 1996). For an informative and sceptical view of the monarchy, see Denis Mack Smith, *Italy and Its Monarchy* (New Haven, 1989). The most useful general treatment of the Italian army before 1915 is John Gooch, *Army, State and Society in Italy, 1870–1915* (London, 1987). There is no general book in English on Italy during the First World War. For the cultural background to the war, see John Thayer, *Italy and the Great War: Politics and Culture* (Madison, 1964). R. J. B. Bosworth provides a sharply critical treatment of pre-war diplomacy in *Italy: The Least of the Great Powers: Italian Foreign Policy before the First World War* (London, 1979). On Italian nationalism, see Alexander De Grand, *The Italian Nationalist Association* (Lincoln, Nebr., 1978). Douglas Forsyth, *The Crisis of Liberal Italy: Monetary and Financial Policy, 1914–1922* (Cambridge, 1993) provides an excellent treatment of war-time financing and politics. Michael Ledeen, *The First Duce: D'Annunzio and Fiume* (Baltimore, 1977) recounts the Fiume episode and its influence on Mussolini. Emilio Gentile, *The Sacralization of Politics in Fascist Italy* (Cambridge, Mass., 1996) is the best analysis of Fascism's use of patriotism and the cult of the war.

Chapter 5

The fundamental work of Federico Chabod, *Italian Foreign Policy: The Statecraft of the Founders* (Princeton, 1996 [1951]), esp. Part I, Chapter 2, traces the distant origins of many of the ideas underlying Fascist foreign policy. No archivally grounded survey of that policy itself exists even in Italian, although the rich and sophisticated synthesis of Enzo Collotti, with Nicola Labanca and Teodoro Sala, *Fascismo e politica di potenza: Politica estera 1922–1939* (Milan, 2000) covers in style the period to the outbreak of war in Europe. The later segments of Renzo De Felice's gargantuan eight-volume *Mussolini* (Turin, 1965–97) offer sometimes eccentric coverage of key moments, but should be read in conjunction with MacGregor Knox, 'The Fascist Regime, its Foreign Policy and its Wars: An "anti-anti-Fascist" Orthodoxy?', *Contemporary European History*, 4: 3 (1995), 347–65. H. James Burgwyn, *Italian Foreign Policy in the Interwar Period, 1918–1940* (Westport, Conn, 1997) offers a recent if bewildered account. Chapter 3 of MacGregor Knox, *Common Destiny: Dictatorship, Foreign Policy, and War in Fascist Italy and Nazi Germany* (Cambridge, 2000) provides narrative and interpretation through 1936–7 based upon a wide range of sometimes novel sources. Vital primary sources are available in lame and often inaccurate English translations: Galeazzo Ciano, *Diary, 1937–1938* (London, 1952); *Ciano's Diary, 1939–1943* (London, 1947); and *Ciano's Diplomatic Papers* (London, 1948), which includes many of the key discussions with the Germans. Corresponding German documents and much else pertinent to Italian policy in 1933–41 can be found in *Documents on German Foreign Policy 1918–1945*, Series C and D (London, 1949–66).

Alan Cassels, *Mussolini's Early Diplomacy* (Princeton, 1970) and the same author's 'Mussolini and German Nationalism, 1922–25', *Journal of Modern History*, 35: 2 (1963), 137–57 remain fundamental on the 1920s. Angelo Del Boca, *The Ethiopian War, 1935–1941* (Chicago, 1969) is still the best account in English of Mussolini's first large war; John F. Coverdale, *Italian Intervention in the Spanish Civil War* (Princeton, 1975) offers an archivally based account of its sequel. Elizabeth Wiskemann's able chronicle of *The Rome-Berlin Axis*, rev. edn. (London, 1966) remains useful, as does Mario Toscano's semi-official *The Origins of the Pact of Steel* (Baltimore, 1967).

On the armed forces and the Second World War, readers with Italian should consult without fail the works of Lucio Ceva and Giorgio Rochat. Brian R. Sullivan, 'The Italian Armed Forces, 1918–40', in Allan R. Millett and Williamson Murray (eds.), *Military Effectiveness*, Vol. II. *The Interwar Period* (Boston, 1988) and 'The Italian Soldier in Combat, June 1940–September 1943', in Paul Addison and Angus Calder (eds.), *Time to Kill* (London, 1997) offer vital analysis. MacGregor Knox, *Mussolini Unleashed, 1939–1941* (Cambridge, 1982) covers diplomacy, strategic planning, decision-making, internal politics, and combat through 1941. The same author's *Hitler's Italian Allies: Royal Armed Forces, Fascist Regime, and the War of 1940–43* (Cambridge, 2000) dissects the performance of armed forces, industry, and regime. Finally,

F. W. Deakin, *The Brutal Friendship: Mussolini, Hitler and the Fall of Italian Fascism*, rev. edn. (Harmondsworth, 1966) and Elena Agarossi, *A Nation Collapses: The Italian Surrender of September 1943* (Cambridge, 1999) offer—respectively—a vivid panorama of the regime's collapse and merciless analysis of Italy's final débâcle.

Chapter 6

The readings mentioned here are strictly limited to internal policy. English-language studies on the internal politics of Fascism, the Fascist party, the organization of the totalitarian state, and the institutions of the regime are not numerous.

For the place of Fascism in the context of general Italian history, useful general works of reference, with a full bibliography, are: G. Candeloro, *Storia dell'Italia moderna*, Vol. X. *Il fascismo e le sue guerre* (Milan, 1981); id., *Storia dell'Italia moderna*, Vol. XI. *La seconda guerra mondiale, il crollo del fascismo, la Resistenza* (Milan, 1984); G. Sabbatucci and V. Vidotto (eds.), *Storia d'Italia*, Vol. IV. *Guerre e fascismo* (Rome-Bari, 1997); S. Colarizi, *Storia del Novecento italiano* (Milan, 2000).

Among those general histories of Fascism which best represent different interpretations, still useful are the concise syntheses of F. Chabod, *A History of Italian Fascism* (London, 1963) and G. Carocci, *Italian Fascism* (Harmondsworth, 1975), the first an expression of the liberal interpretation, the second of the Marxist. More up-to-date syntheses are E. Santarelli, *Storia del fascismo*, 3rd edn. (Rome, 1981); A. J. De Grand, *Fascism: its Origins and Development* (Lincoln, Nebr., 1982); A. Cassels, *Fascist Italy*, 2nd edn. (Arlington Heights, Ill., 1985); P. Morgan, *Italian Fascism 1919–1945* (New York, 1995); and P. Dogliani, *L'Italia fascista 1922–1940* (Milan, 1999). E. Gentile, *Fascismo e antifascismo: I partiti italiani fra le due guerre* (Florence, 2000) is an analysis of Italian political parties between 1919 and 1940, which combines the history of Fascism and of anti-fascism. R. Griffin, *The Nature of Fascism* (Oxford, 1991); Stanley G. Payne, *A History of Fascism 1914–1945* (Madison, Wisconsin, 1995); R. Eatwell, *Fascism: A History* (London, 1995); and R. Bessel (ed.), *Fascist Italy and Nazi Germany: Comparison and Contrasts* (Cambridge, 1996) relate the history of Italian Fascism to attempts to define so-called 'generic fascism'. A classic work of reference for the chief interpretations of the Fascist phenomenon is R. De Felice, *Interpretations of Fascism* (Cambridge, Mass., 1977); see also W. Laqueur (ed.), *Fascism: A Reader's Guide* (London, 1979).

For a critical review of the research and the historiographic debate in the last decades, see G. Sabbatucci, 'Fascist Institutions: Recent Problems and Interpretations', *Journal of Italian History*, 2 (1979), 75–92; E. Gentile, 'Fascism in Italian Historiography: In Search of an Individual Historical Identity', *Journal of Contemporary History*, 2 (1986), 179–208; B. W. Painter,

'Renzo De Felice and the History of Italian Fascism', *American Historical Review*, 2 (1990), 301–405; N. Zapponi, 'Fascism in Italian Historiography 1986–93', *Journal of Contemporary History*, 2 (1994), 547–68; A. Del Boca, M. Legnani, and M. G. Rossi (eds.), *Il regime fascista* (Rome-Bari, 1995); A. De Bernardi, *La dittatura fascista* (Milan, 2001). Notwithstanding the apparent abundance of the works examined, the volume of R. J. B. Bosworth, *The Italian Dictatorship: Problems and Perspectives in the Interpretation of Mussolini and Fascism* (London, 1998) contains serious errors of fact, inventions, and omissions, and gives an incomplete and distorted representation of the results of research and the historical debate, while it ignores the contributions of the leading representatives of Marxist historiography.

Useful works of reference are: P. V. Cannistraro (ed.), *Historical Dictionary of Fascist Italy* (Westport, Conn., 1982) and A. De Bernardi and S. Guarracino (eds.), *Il fascismo* (Milan, 1998).

Studies of internal politics

For a general analysis of the problem of fascism and totalitarianism, seen from different perspectives, see: L. Shapiro, *Totalitarianism* (London, 1972); A. Gleason, *Totalitarianism* (New York, 1995); J. J. Linz, *Totalitarian and Authoritarian Regimes* (London, 2000); E. Gentile, *La via italiana al totalitarismo: Partito e Stato nel regime fascista*, new edn. (Rome, 2001); id., *The Struggle for Modernity: Nationalism, Futurism, and Fascism* (Westport, Conn., forthcoming).

The interpretations of the role and personality of Mussolini within Fascism are in sharp conflict. The controversial and lengthy biography of R. De Felice, *Mussolini* (Turin, 1965–97) is fundamental. I. Kirkpatrick, *Mussolini: A Study of a Demagogue* (London, 1964); D. Mack Smith, *Mussolini* (London, 1981); J. Ridley, *Mussolini: A Biography* (New York, 1998) are shorter biographies in English. The most recent and the best single-volume biography is P. Milza, *Mussolini* (Paris, 1999). Mussolini's role as a leader is examined by E. Gentile, 'Mussolini's Charisma', *Modern Italy*, 2 (1998), 219–35.

For the other personalities of Fascism, F. Cordova (ed.), *Uomini e volti del fascismo* (Rome, 1980) contains a gallery of brief biographies. Works in English include: H. Fornari, *Mussolini's Gadfly: Roberto Farinacci* (Nashville, 1971); C. G. Segre, *Italo Balbo: A Fascist Life* (Berkeley, 1987); J. Tinghino, *Edmondo Rossoni: From Revolutionary Syndicalism to Fascism* (New York, 1991); R. Mosley, *Mussolini's Shadow: The Double Life of Count Galeazzo Ciano* (New Haven, 2000).

On the period of the conquest of power down to the stabilization of the regime, the best analysis in English is still A. Lyttelton, *The Seizure of Power: Fascism in Italy 1919–1929*, 2nd edn. (London, 1987). For regional studies of the origins of Fascism, see the bibliography for Paul Corner's chapter and E. Gentile, *Storia del partito fascisto 1919–1922* (Rome–Bari, 1989). The heredity of *squadrismo* under the Fascist regime is explored by R. Suzzi Valli, 'The Myth of Squadrismo in the Fascist Regime', *Journal of Contemporary History*, 2 (2000), 131–50.

On the role of the Fascist Party in the transformation of the regime and in the construction of the totalitarian state, see E. Gentile, 'The Problem of the Party in Italian Fascism', *Journal of Contemporary History*, 2 (1984); id., 'Le parti dans le régime fasciste italien', *Annales économies Sociétés Civilisations*, 3 (1988), 567–91. A thorough study of the relationship between the monarchy and Fascism is still lacking, but see D. Mack Smith, *Italy and its Monarchy* (New Haven, 1989) and the relevant sections of the biography of Mussolini by De Felice. The function of the prefect under the Fascist regime is briefly examined by P. Morgan, 'The Prefects and Party–State Relations in Fascist Italy', *Journal of Modern Italian Studies*, 3 (1998), 241–72. The volume of S. Lupo, *Il fascismo: La politica in un regime totalitario* (Rome, 2000) offers an analysis of the internal life of the Fascist regime and the conflicts between the *gerarchi*. On the relationship between the Fascist Party and the syndicates, the most recent study is O. Dahl, *Syndicalism, Fascism and Post-Fascism in Italy 1900–1950* (Oslo, 1999), to which should be added D. D. Roberts, *The Syndicalist Tradition and Italian Fascism* (Manchester, 1979), although both works are prevalently concerned with the ideological aspects. An overall picture, although not up to date, of the politics of repression and the anti-Fascist opposition is contained in C. F. Delzell, *Mussolini's Enemy: The Italian Anti-fascist Resistance*, new edn. (New York, 1974); on anti-Fascism, see further F. Rosengarten, *The Italian Anti-Fascist Press 1919–1945* (Cleveland, 1968), L. Caplair, *Under the Shadow of War: Fascism, Antifascism, and Marxists 1918–1939* (New York, 1987), D. Ward, *Antifascisms: Cultural Politics in Italy 1943–1946* (Madison, 1996), and S. G. Pugliese, *Carlo Rosselli: Socialist Heretic and Antifascist Exile* (Cambridge, Mass., 1999).

Various aspects of the organization of the masses, of the fascistization of the new generations, and of public opinion are analysed from different points of view in: V. De Grazia, *The Culture of Consent: Mass Organization of Leisure in Fascist Italy* (Cambridge, 1981); L. Passerini, *Fascism in Popular Memory* (Cambridge, 1987); De Grazia, *How Fascism Ruled Women: Italy, 1922–1945* (Berkeley, 1991); M. Fraddosio, 'Donne e fascismo. Ricerche e problemi di interpretazione', *Storia contemporanea*, 1 (1986), 95–135; id., 'La donna e la guerra. Aspetti della mobilitazione femminile nel fascismo: dalla mobilitazione civile alle origini del Saf nella Repubblica sociale italiana', *Storia contemporanea*, 6 (1989), 1105–81; T. H. Koon, *Believe, Obey, Fight: Political Socialization of Youth in Fascist Italy, 1922–1943* (Chapel Hill, NC, 1985); N. Zapponi, 'Il partito della gioventù. Le organizzazioni giovanili del fascismo

1926–1943', *Storia contemporanea*, (1982), 569–633; L. La Rovere, 'Fascist Groups in the Italian University: An Organization at the Service of the Totalitarian State', *Journal of Contemporary History*, 3 (1999); S. Colarizi, *L'opinione degli italiani sotto il fascismo 1929–1943* (Rome–Bari, 1991); D. Thompson, *State and Control in Fascist Italy: Culture and Conformity 1925–1943* (Manchester, 1991).

The characteristics of Fascism as a political religion are analysed by E. Gentile, *The Sacralization of Politics in Fascist Italy* (Cambridge, Mass., 1997) and id., *Le religioni della politica* (Rome-Bari, 2001). For the relationship between the regime and the Church, see R. A. Webster, *Christian Democracy in Italy 1860–1960* (London, 1961), P. C. Kent, *The Pope and the Duce* (London, 1981), J. F. Pollard, *The Vatican and Italian Fascism 1929–1932* (Cambridge, 1985).

On racism and anti-Semitism: R. De Felice, *The Jews in Fascist Italy: A History* (New York, 2001); M. Michaelis, *Mussolini and the Jews* (Oxford, 1978); S. Zuccotti, *The Italians and the Holocaust* (New York, 1987).

On the period of the Social Republic, F. W. Deakin, *The Brutal Friendship* (London, 1962) is still useful. For a more in-depth analysis, see, as well as the last volume of De Felice's biography, L. Ganapini, *La repubblica delle camicie nere* (Milan, 1999) and D. Gagliani, *Brigate Nere: Mussolini e la militarizzazione del partito fascista repubblicano* (Turin, 1999), which follow the revival and development of the totalitarian experiment down to the final catastrophe.

Chapter 7

The experience of Italian society under Fascism has received growing attention over the last decades. An excellent example of new social history is L. Passerini, *Fascism in Popular Memory: The Cultural Experience of the Turin Working Class* (Cambridge, 1987). Although dating back to the late 1920s, C. Gower Chapman's anthropological study *Milocca: A Sicilian Village* (Cambridge, Mass., 1971), also remains of great interest.

The best study of women under Fascism is V. De Grazia, *How Fascism Ruled Women: Italy, 1922–1945* (Berkeley, 1992). For women in the workforce, see P. R. Wilson, *The Clockwork Factory: Women and Work in Fascist Italy* (Oxford, 1993). The male gender role has received less attention. An interesting and thought-provoking contribution is B. Spackman, *Fascist Virilities: Rhetoric, Ideology and Social Fantasy in Italy* (Minneapolis, 1996).

Aspects of Fascist demography have been studied by C. Ipsen, *Dictating Demography: The Problem of Population in Fascist Italy* (Cambridge, 1996), and, in a comparative perspective, M. S. Quine, *Population Politics in Twentieth Century Europe: Fascist Dictatorships and Liberal Democracies* (London, 1995).

For the role of Fascist mass organizations, see De Grazia, *The Culture of Consent: Mass Organization of Leisure in Fascist Italy* (Cambridge, 1981) and T. Koon, *Believe Obey Fight: Political Socialization of Youth in Fascist Italy 1922–1943* (Chapel Hill and London, 1985).

The various aspects of the contribution of intellectuals and artists to the creation of consensus have been studied by M. S. Stone, *The Patron State: Culture and Politics in Fascist Italy* (Princeton, 1998). For the impact of mass culture on Italian society, see J. Hay, *Popular Film Culture in Fascist Italy* (Bloomington, Ind., 1987). The most recent analysis of Fascism's attempt to strike a balance between modernity and tradition is R. Ben-Ghiat, *Fascist Modernities: Italy, 1922–1945* (Berkeley, 2001).

A survey of recent studies about sport can be found in P. McCarthy, 'Sport and Society in Italy Today', *Journal of Modern Italian Studies*, 5: 3 (2000).

For translations of sources, see J. P. Pollard, *The Fascist Experience in Italy* (London, 1998) and J. T. Schnapp (ed.), *A Primer of Italian Fascism* (Lincoln, Nebr., 2000).

Although less extensive than might be expected, much literature about the Fascist experience is obviously available in Italian. P. Dogliani, *L'Italia fascista 1922–1940* (Milan, 1999) offers an excellent introduction. Many of the articles in M. Isnenghi, *L'Italia del Fascio* (Florence, 1996) are relevant as well. The best single-volume study of women's history is M. De Giorgio, *Le italiane dall'Unità a oggi: Modelli culturali e comportamenti sociali* (Rome–Bari, 1992). Urban development under Fascism has received much attention over the last few decades. For architecture, see G. Ciucci, *Gli architetti e il fascismo: architettura e città (1922–1944)* (Turin, 1989), and more specifically about interior design, M. Boot and M. Casciato (eds.), *La casalinga riflessiva: La cucina razionale come mito domestico negli anni '20 e '30* (Rome, 1983).

An interesting contribution to the history of the radio is G. Isola, *Abbassa la tua radio, per favore . . . Storia dell'ascolto radiofoniconell Italia fascista* (Florence, 1990).

The best introduction to the problems of youth under Fascism remains R. Zangrandi, *Il lungo viaggio attraverso il fascismo: Contributo alla storia di una generazione* (Milan, 1976).

Chapter 8

Although there are few Anglo-American surveys of art under Fascism, scholarship outside Italy has taken the lead in directly addressing the relationship between individual artists and the regime. The revisionist approach began in architectural history with Diane Ghirardo's 'Italian Architects and Fascist Politics: An Evaluation of the Rationalists' Role in Regime Building', *Journal of the Society of Architectural Historians*, 39 (May 1980), and 'Politics of a Masterpiece: The Vicenda of the Decoration of the Façade of the Casa del Fascio,

Como, 1936–39', *The Art Bulletin*, 62 (Sept. 1980). Richard Etlin's *Modernism in Italian Architecture, 1890–1940* (Cambridge, Mass., 1991) provides the most thorough account of building under the regime, including the effects of the Racial Laws on the architectural community. For the Fascist legacy on urban planning and Mussolini's imperial ambitions, the classic remains Spiro Kostof, *The Third Rome 1870–1950: Traffic and Glory* (Berkeley, 1973).

For case studies of artists and cultural politics, see Emily Braun, *Mario Sironi and Italian Modernism: Art and Politics under Fascism* (New York, 2000), which also considers the Italian experience in the context of the European avant-garde. Braun revises post-Second World War interpretations of the Fascist period in 'The Scuola Romana: Fact or Fiction?', *Art in America*, 76 (Mar. 1988), and 'Speaking Volumes: Giorgio Morandi's Still Lifes and the Cultural Politics of Strapaese', *Modernism/modernity* (Sept. 1995). Marcia Vetrocq in 'National Style and the Agenda for Abstract Painting in Postwar Italy', *Art History*, 12 (Dec. 1989) documents the effects of Fascism on postwar cultural debates. For women artists under Fascism, see the collected essays in Robin Pickering-Iazzi (ed.), *Mothers of Invention: Women, Italian Fascism, and Culture* (Minneapolis, 1995), and the exhibition catalogue, *La futurista: Benedetta Cappa Marinetti*, Moore College of Art and Design, Philadelphia, 1998. For the Corrente group, see Bette Talvacchia, 'Politics Considered as a Category of Culture: The Anti-Fascist Corrente Group', *Art History*, 8 (Sept. 1985) and Ruth Ben-Ghiat, *Fascist Modernities* (Berkeley, 2000). The latter, while not concerned with the visual arts, is useful for its discussion of realist aesthetics.

The literature on Futurism in English is abundant, though art historic bias still favours the pre-war movement. For the group's relationship to Fascism, see Gunther Berghaus, *Futurism and Politics* (Providence, RI, 1996). *Aeropittura* is surveyed in Bruno Mantura, Patrizia Rosazza-Ferraris, and Livia Velani, *Futurism in Flight* (Accademia Italiana, London, 1990). There are few contextual studies that compare art of the *Ventennio* to that of other nations and totalitarian regimes, although such approaches determine what imagery and styles are specific to Fascism. See, in particular, Igor Golomstock, *Totalitarian Art in the Soviet Union, Third Reich, Fascist Italy and the People's Republic of China* (London, 1990); the amply illustrated exhibition catalogue by Dawn Ades, Tim Benton, David Elliot, and Ian Boyd White (eds.), *Art and Power: Europe under the Dictators, 1930–45* (Hayward Gallery, London, 1995); and the essays in Matthew Affron and Mark Antliff (eds.), *Fascist Visions: Art and Ideology in France and Italy* (Princeton, 1997). Diane Ghirardo, *Building New Communities: New Deal America and Fascist Italy* (Princeton, 1989) focuses on shared styles of state patronage and building types.

The fundamental study on the regime's cultural politics remains Philip V. Cannistraro's *La Fabbrica del Consenso* (Bari, 1975). The extraordinary influence of Sarfatti on Mussolini's policies is documented in Cannistraro and Brian R. Sullivan, *Il Duce's Other Woman* (New York, 1993). Marla Stone in *The Patron State: Culture and Politics in Fascist Italy* (Princeton, 1998) further details the regime's cultural bureaucracy with a focus on state exhibitions. Contemporary opinions by leading cultural figures are translated in Jeffrey Schnapp and Barbara Spackman (eds.), 'Selections from the Great Debate on Fascist Culture: Critica Fascista, 1926–27', *Stanford Italian Review* 8 (1990). For a solid interpretation of Fascist culture informed by critical theory see Simonetta Falasca-Zamponi, *Fascist Spectacle: The Aesthetics of Power in Mussolini's Italy* (Berkeley, 1997). The Exhibition of the Fascist Revolution is treated in depth by Libero Andreotti, 'The Aesthetics of War', *Journal of Architectural Education*, 45 (Feb. 1992) and Jeffrey Schnapp, 'Epic Demonstrations', in Richard Golsan (ed.), *Fascism, Aesthetics, and Culture* (Hanover, NH, 1992).

Chapter 9

During the past decade several major publishing houses have issued surveys in English of Italian literature and of individual writers, including Peter Brand and Lino Pertile (eds.), *The Cambridge History of Italian Literature*, rev. edn. (Cambridge, 1999) and Peter Hainsworth and David Robey (eds.), *The Oxford Companion to Italian Literature* (Oxford, 2002). More detailed bibliographical information is available in these two volumes.

For general studies on twentieth-century Italian Literature, see Giorgio Luti, *Introduzione alla letteratura italiana del Novecento* (Rome, 1985); Giuliano Manacorda, *Storia della letteratura italiana fra le due guerre (1919–1943)* (Rome, 1980); and Carlo Salinari, *Preludio e fine del neorealismo* (Naples, 1968).

Individual authors and topics

Listed below is a selection of (mainly) translated works and critical studies which may be useful in providing further insight into the subjects discussed in this chapter.

Calvino, Italo, *Our ancestors*, trans. A. Colquhoun (London, 1950); *If on a Winter's Night*, trans. W. Weaver (London, 1993); and M. L. McLaughlin, *Italo Calvino* (Edinburgh, 1998).

Campana, Dino, *Orphic songs*, trans. I. L. Solomon (New York, 1968).

Cardarelli, Vincenzo, *Opere*, ed. C. Martignoni (Milan, 1981); and C. Burdett, *Vincenzo Cardarelli and his Contemporaries: Fascist Politics and Literary Culture* (Oxford, 1999).

Carducci, Giosuè, *A Selection from the Poems*, trans. E. A. Tribe (London, 1921); and U. Carpi (ed.), *Carducci Poeta* (Pisa, 1985).

Croce, Benedetto, *Philosophy, Poetry, History: An Anthology of Essays*, trans. C. Sprigge (London, 1965); and G. N. G. Orsini, *Benedetto Croce, Philosopher of Art and Literary Critic* (Carbondale, Ill., 1961).

D'Annunzio, Gabriele: There are no adequate or unbowdlerized translations of D'Annunzio's novels, but see his anthology of short stories, *Tales of My Native Town*, trans. G. Mantellini (London, 1922); *La figlia di Iorio: An English transcript*, trans. W. H. Woodward (London, 1926); *Alcyone*, trans. J. G. Nicols (Manchester, 1988); and John Woodhouse, *Gabriele D'Annunzio: Defiant Archangel* (Oxford, 2001).

Deledda, Grazia, *The Mother*, trans. M. Steegman (Dunwoody, 1974); and A. Dolfi, *Grazia Deledda* (Milan, 1979).

Futurism (see also Marinetti, F. T.), *Manifestos*, ed. V. Apollonio (New York, 1971); and M. Martin, *Futurist Art and Theory (1909–1915)* (Oxford, 1968).

Gentile, Giovanni, *The Theory of Mind as Pure Act*, trans. G. Gullace (Urbana, Ill., 1960); and H. S. Harris, *The Social Philosophy of Giovanni Gentile* (Urbana, Ill., 1960; Oxford, 1969).

Gozzano, Guido, *Poesie e prose*, ed. A. De Marchi (Milan, 1961); and A. Vallone, *I Crepuscolari* (Palermo, 1970).

Gramsci, Antonio, *Selections from the Prison Notebooks*, trans. Q. Hoare and G. N. Smith (New York, 1975); and A. Davidson, *Antonio Gramsci: Towards an Intellectual Biography* (London, 1977).

Lampedusa, Giuseppe Tomasi Di, *The Leopard*, trans. A. Colquhoun (London, 1961); and D. Gilmore, *The Last Leopard: A Life of Giuseppe di Lampedusa* (London, 1988).

Levi, Carlo, *Christ stopped at Eboli*, trans. F. Frenaye (New York, 1947); and V. Napolillo, *Carlo Levi: Dall'antifascismo al mito contadino* (Cosenza, 1986).

Levi, Primo, *If this is a Man & The Truce*, trans. S. Woolf (London, 1987); and F. Vincenti, *Invito alla lettura di Primo Levi* (Milan, 1973).

Marinetti, Filippo Tomaso, see Futurism for the *Manifestos*. See also L. De Maria, *Per conoscere Marinetti e il futurismo* (Milan, 1981).

Montale, Eugenio, *The Storm and Other Poems*, trans. E. Farnsworth (Chicago, 1970); G. Nascimbeni, *Eugenio Montale* (Milan, 1969), and Joseph Cary, *Three Modern Italian Poets: Saba, Ungaretti, Montale* (New York 1992).

Moravia, Alberto, *The Time of Indifference*, trans. A. Davidson (St Albans, 1975); and D. Heiney, *Three Italian Novelists: Moravia, Pavese, Vittorini* (Ann Arbor, 1968).

Palazzeschi, Aldo, *Man of Smoke*, trans. N. J. Perella and R. Stefanini (New

York, 1992); and A. J. Tamburri, *Of saltimbanchi and incendiari: Aldo Palazzeschi and Avant-gardism in Italy* (Rutherford and London, 1990).

Pascoli, Giovanni, *Poems of Giovanni Pascoli*, trans. E. Stein (New Haven, 1923); and G. Capovilla, *La formazione letteraria del Pascoli* (Bologna, 1988).

Pavese, Cesare, *The Moon and the Bonfires*, trans. L. Sinclair (London, 1978); and D. Heiney, *Three Italian Novelists* (Ann Arbor, 1968).

Pirandello, Luigi, *Collected Plays*, ed. R. Rietty (Paris, London, New York, 1987 (continuing)); and G. Giudice, *Pirandello: a Biography* (Oxford, 1975).

Pratolini, Vasco, *Family Chronicle*, trans. M. King (London, 1991); and Giancarlo Bertoncini, *Vasco Pratolini* (Rome, 1987).

Quasimodo, Salvatore, *To Give and to Have, and Other Poems*, trans. E. Farnsworth (Chicago, 1975); and Michele Tondo, *Salvatore Quasimodo* (Milan, 1975).

Saba, Umberto, *Italian Sampler: An Anthology of Italian Verse*, trans. T. Bergin (Montreal, 1964); and Joseph Cary, *Three Modern Italian Poets: Saba, Ungaretti, Montale* (New York, 1992).

Silone, Ignazio, *Fontamara*, trans. E. Mosbacher (London, 1983); and Luce D'Eramo, *L'opera di Ignazio Silone* (Milan, 1971).

Svevo, Italo, *Confessions of Zeno*, trans. B. de Zoete (New York, 1958); and J. A. Gatt-Rutter, *Italo Svevo: A Double Life* (Oxford, 1988).

Ungaretti, Giuseppe, *Selected Poems of Giuseppe Ungaretti*, trans. A. Mandelbaum (Ithaca, NY and London, 1975); and Joseph Cary, *Three Modern Italian Poets: Saba, Ungaretti, Montale* (New York, 1992).

Vittorini, Elio, *The Red Carnation*, trans. A. Bowyer (Westport, Conn., 1975); Sandro Briosi, *Vittorini* (Florence, 1970); and J. H. Potter, *Elio Vittorini* (Boston, 1979).

Chapter 10

The best overviews of social and political thought during this period are Alberto Asor Rosa's scholarly volume on *La Cultura* in the *Storia d'Italia dall'unità ad oggi*, Vol. IV, Part 2 (Turin, 1975) and Norberto Bobbio's masterly *Ideological Profile of Twentieth Century Italy* (Princeton, 1995). Richard Bellamy provides an account of the six main thinkers of the age in *Modern Italian Social Theory: Ideology and Politics from Pareto to the Present* (Cambridge, 1987), four of whom are also the subject of Joseph V. Femia's collection *The Machiavellian Legacy: Essays in Italian Political Thought* (Basingstoke, 1998). E. E. Jacobitti links Croce to the Italian idealist tradition in *Revolutionary Humanism and Historicism in Modern Italy* (New Haven, 1981). The later period is covered by D. D. Roberts, *Benedetto Croce and the Uses of Historicism* (Berkeley, 1987). The best account of Gentile remains H. S. Harris, *The Social Philosophy of Giovanni Gentile* (Urbana, Ill., 1960). Studies of Gramsci are legion, but four of the best are W. L. Adamson, *Hegemony and Revolution: A Study of Antonio Gramsci's Political and Cultural Theory* (Berkeley, 1980); Richard Bellamy and Darrow Schecter, *Gramsci and the Italian State* (Manchester, 1993); Martin Clark, *Antonio Gramsci and the Revolution that Failed* (New Haven, 1977); and J. V. Femia, *Gramsci's Political Thought* (Oxford, 1981). Finally the origins and career of Fascist thought are traced in Walter Adamson, *Avant-Garde Florence: From Modernism to Fascism* (Cambridge, Mass., 1993); D. D. Roberts, *The Syndicalist Tradition and Italian Fascism* (Manchester, 1979); A. Lyttelton (ed.), *Italian Fascisms: From Pareto to Gentile* (New York, 1977); and the Italian chapters of E. Nolte, *Three Faces of Fascism* (London, 1965).

Epilogue

On the Italian surrender, see E. Agarossi, *A Nation Collapses: The Italian Surrender of September 1943*, tr. H. Fergusson (Cambridge, 1999).

The thesis of the 'death of the nation' was launched by E. Galli Della Loggia, *La morte della patria: la crisi dell'idea di nazione tra resistenza, antifascismo e repubblica* (Rome-Bari, 1996). For a more balanced (and better documented) view, see E. Gentile, *La Grande Italia: ascesa e declino del mito della nazione nel ventesimo secolo* (Milan, 1997). For the continuity of the state, see C. Pavone, *Scritti su fascismo, antifascismo e continuità dello stato* (Turin, 1995). For the purges, see R. P. Domenico, *Italian Fascists on Trial 1943–1948* (Chapel Hill, NC, and London, 1991) and, in more depth, H. Woller, *I conti con il fascismo: L'epurazione in Italia 1943–1948* (Bologna, 1997).

The definitive study of the politics of the Allied occupation is D. W. Ellwood, *Italy 1943–1945* (Leicester, 1985), and of the German occupation, L. Klinkhammer, *L'occupazione tedesca in Italia 1943–1945* (Turin, 1993). R. Lamb, *War in Italy 1943–1945: A Brutal Story* (London, 1993) is a vivid if not always reliable account. There is a fine monograph on the Italians and Allied prisoners of war by R. Absalom, *A Strange Alliance: Aspects of Escape and Survival in Italy 1943–45* (Florence, 1991). Two classics among the many English memoirs are N. Lewis, *Naples '44* (London, 1978), and E. Newby, *Love and War in the Apennines* (Harmondsworth, 1978).

Chronology

1900 JUNE   Opposition gains in elections.
      JULY   King Umberto I assassinated. Victor Emanuel III succeeds.

1901 FEB.   Zanardelli and Giolitti form government.

1903 JAN.   Benedetto Croce founds journal *La critica*.
      AUG.   Pius X succeeds Leo XIII as Pope.
      OCT.   Giolitti becomes prime minister.

1904 SEPT.   General strike.
      NOV.   Pius X sanctions Catholic participation in elections.
           Pirandello, *Il fu Mattia Pascal*.
           Puccini, *Tosca*.
           D'Annunzio, *La figlia di Iorio*

1906 JUNE   Simplon Tunnel opened.
      SEPT.   Confederazione Generale del Lavoro (CGL) founded.
           Carducci wins Nobel prize for literature and Camillo Golgi for medicine.

1907   Pius X condemns modernism.
           Ernesto Moneta wins Nobel peace prize.

1908 DEC.   Publication of review *La Voce*, edited by Giovanni Prezzolini.
           Messina earthquake: 80,000 victims.
           Marconi wins Nobel prize for physics.
           First *Giro d'Italia* (cycling).
           Foundation of Olivetti typewriter company.

1909 FEB.   Marinetti publishes Futurist manifesto in Paris.

1910 DEC.   Italian Nationalist Association founded.
           Balla, Boccioni, and Carrà publish Manifesto of Futurist Painting.

1911 MAR.   Giolitti returns to power.
      NOV.   Italy declares war on Turkey and invades Libya.

1912 MAY   Universal male suffrage granted.
      JULY   Socialist Congress of Reggio Emilia. Mussolini becomes editor of *Avanti!*.
      OCT.   Treaty of Lausanne ends war between Italy and Turkey, which cedes Libya.
      NOV.   Italy renews Triple Alliance.

1913 OCT.   General elections. Catholic electoral association supports liberal candidates (Patto Gentiloni).
Papini founds review *Lacerba.*

1914 MAR.   Giolitti resigns as prime minister, and is succeeded by Antonio Salandra.

JUNE   Red Week.

AUG.   Outbreak of Great War: Italy declares neutrality Pius X dies: succeeded by Benedict XV.

NOV.   Mussolini founds *Il Popolo d'Italia* and is expelled from Socialist Party.
Giovanni Pastrone, *Cabiria.*

1915 APR.   Treaty of London with Great Britain, France, and Russia.

MAY 24   Italy declares war on Austria.

1916 MAY   Austrian counter-offensive in the Trentino.

JUNE   Formation of national unity government under Paolo Boselli.

AUG.   Capture of Gorizia.
Italy declares war on Germany.

1917 AUG.   Mass strikes against the war in Turin.

OCT.   Italian defeat at Caporetto.
Orlando becomes prime minister.

1918 JUNE   Italians resist Austrian offensive on the Piave.

OCT.   Italian victory at Vittorio Veneto.
Occupation of Trent and Trieste.

NOV. 4   Armistice of Villa Giusti ends war with Austria.

1919 JAN.   Partito Popolare founded.

MAR.   Mussolini founds *fasci di combattimento.*

JUNE   Nitti becomes prime minister. Peace Treaty of St Germain with Austria.

SEPT.   D'Annunzio seizes Fiume.

OCT.   Socialist Party joins Communist Third International.

NOV.   General elections held under system of proportional representation. Socialists (156) and Popolari (100) win half of seats.

1920 JUNE   Giolitti becomes prime minister.

JULY   Fascists burn headquarters of Slav organizations in Trieste.

SEPT.   Factory occupations.

OCT.   Fascists force resignation of Socialist administration in Bologna. Start of offensive by Fascist armed squads in Po Valley (*squadrismo*).

NOV.   Rapallo Treaty with Yugoslavia.

	DEC.	End of D'Annunzio's occupation of Fiume.
1921	JAN.	Congress of Livorno. Socialist Party splits. Left, led by Bordiga and Gramsci, founds Communist Party (PCd'I).
	MAY	General elections. Fascists join government candidates in National Bloc lists.
	AUG.	'Pact of pacification' between Fascists and Socialists.
	NOV.	Foundation of Fascist Party (PNF).

D'Annunzio, *Notturno.*
Pirandello, *Sei personaggi in cerca d'autore.*
First radio transmissions.

1922	JAN.	Pius XI succeeds Benedict XV as Pope.
	AUG.	General strike called by Alliance of Labour crushed.
	OCT. 28–9	Fascist March on Rome.

King Victor Emanuel refuses to sign decree instituting martial law.
Mussolini appointed head of coalition government.

	DEC.	Foundation of Fascist Grand Council.
1923	JAN.	Law legalizes Fascist Militia (MVSN).
	APR.	Gentile education reform.
	AUG.	Italian fleet bombards Corfu.
	NOV.	Acerbo electoral law: two-thirds of seats to go to winning coalition.

Svevo, *La coscienza di Zeno.*

1924	JAN.	Italy annexes Fiume.
	APR.	Fascist victory in general elections.
	JUNE	Murder of Socialist deputy Giacomo Matteotti.

Opposition parties withdraw from Parliament.

1925	JAN. 3	Mussolini speech takes personal responsibility for Fascist violence.

Police measures against opposition groups.

	APR.	Gentile, Manifesto of Fascist Intellectuals.
	MAY	Croce, Manifesto of Anti-Fascist Intellectuals.
	OCT.	Pact of Palazzo Vidoni between Confederation of Industry and Fascist unions.

Montale, *Ossi di seppia.*

1926	JAN.	Communist Party's Third Congress in Lyons adopts Gramsci's theses.
	APR.	Law on labour relations.

Foundation of Opera Nazionale Balilla.
Foundation of Istituto Cinematografico Luce.

NOV.   *Leggi fascistissime*: opposition parties outlawed.
Institution of Special Tribunal for the Defence of the State.
Grazia Deledda wins Nobel prize for literature.
Exhibition of *Novecento italiano*.
Puccini, *Turandot*.

1927 APR.   Charter of Labour.
Anti-Fascist Concentration founded in Paris.

DEC.   Revaluation of the lira (*Quota Novanta*).

1928 MAY   Electoral law: deputies to be chosen from single national list.

DEC.   Grand Council law.
Law on land reclamation (*bonifica integrale*).

1929 FEB.   Lateran Pacts signed by Mussolini and Pius XI.

MAR.   Plebiscite.
Foundation of Giustizia e Libertà.
Moravia, *Gli indifferenti*.

1930 MAR.   Institution of National Council of Corporations.
Silone, *Fontamara*.

1931 SEPT.   End of conflict between Fascism and Catholic Action.
Pius XI forced to accept restrictions on youth organizations.

NOV.   Creation of IMI.

1932 OCT.   Mostra della Rivoluzione Fascista.
The Fiat *Balilla* car.
Foro Mussolini.

1933 JAN.   IRI founded.

JUNE   Four Power Pact.

JULY   Balbo's seaplane squadron flies to Chicago.

AUG.   The liner *Rex* crosses the Atlantic.

1934 JUNE   Hitler meets Mussolini in Italy.

JULY   Mussolini moves troops to Brenner pass following attempted Nazi coup in Vienna.
Italy wins football World Cup.
Pirandello wins Nobel prize.

1935 APR.   Stresa Conference.

OCT.   Italy invades Ethiopia.
League of Nations votes economic sanctions.

1936 MAY   Conquest of Addis Ababa, Victor Emanuel proclaimed Emperor of Abyssinia.

	JUNE	Galeazzo Ciano becomes foreign minister.
	AUG.	Italian intervention in Spanish Civil War.
	OCT.	Rome–Berlin Axis.
1937	APR.	Inauguration of Cinecittà.
	MAY	Ministry of Popular Culture founded.
	JUNE	Assassination of Rosselli brothers.
	SEPT.	Mussolini visits Germany.
	NOV.	Anti-Comintern pact with Germany and Japan.
	DEC.	Italy leaves League of Nations.
1938	MAR.	Mussolini accepts Hitler's annexation of Austria.
	MAY	Hitler's second visit to Italy.
	SEPT.	Racial Laws.
		Mussolini at Munich Conference.
		Italy wins World Cup again.
		Bartali wins Tour de France.
		Enrico Fermi wins Nobel prize for physics and emigrates to USA.
		Croce, *La storia come pensiero e come azione.*
1939	MAR.	Pius XI succeeded by Pius XII.
	APR.	Italy occupies Albania.
	MAY	Pact of Steel with Germany.
	SEPT.	War between Germany, Britain, and France. Italy declares 'non-belligerency'.
1940	JUNE	Italy declares war on France and Britain.
	OCT.	Italy invades Greece.
	NOV.	British air force sinks Italian battleships in Taranto.
	DEC.	British counter-offensive in Libya.
1941	MAR.	Battle of Cape Matapan.
	APR.	Fall of Addis Ababa.
	MAY	The Italian Viceroy, Duke Amedeo d'Aosta, surrenders at Amba Alagi.
	JULY	Italian Expeditionary Force sent to Russia.
		Guttuso, *Crocefissione.*
1942	NOV.	Battle of El Alamein.
	DEC.	Russians defeat Italian Eighth Army in Stalingrad offensive.
		Visconti, *Ossessione.*
1943	JAN.	Loss of Tripoli.
	MAR.	Mass strikes in northern Italy.

MAY   Italian army surrenders in Tunisia.

JULY   Allies land in Sicily.
Fall of Mussolini.
Marshal Badoglio forms government.

SEPT.   Armistice with Allies.
Germans occupy Rome: Victor Emanuel and Badoglio escape to Brindisi.
Mussolini founds Italian Social Republic.
Foundation of Committee of National Liberation.

1944 MAR.   Togliatti's Salerno speech: Communist Party cooperates with Badoglio government.

JUNE   Allies liberate Rome.

1945 APR.   Final Allied offensive.
Partisan insurrection in northern Italy.
Mussolini shot.

Map section

Map 1 Italy in 1918

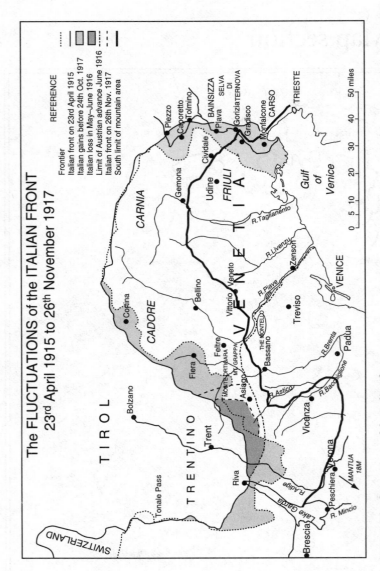

Map 2 The fluctuations of the Italian front

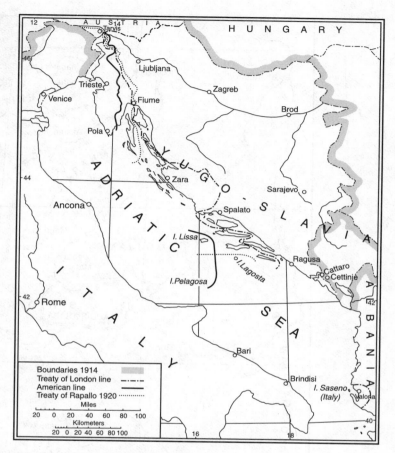

Map 3 The Adriatic Settlement of 1920

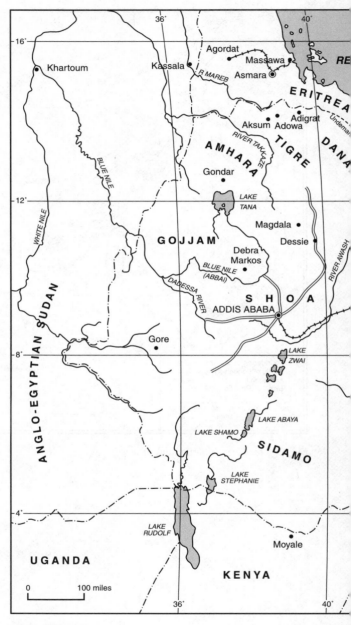

Map 4 Ethiopia 1935

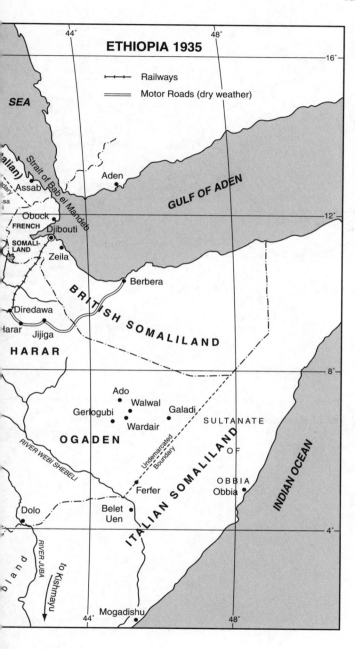

ETHIOPIA 1935

Railways

Motor Roads (dry weather)

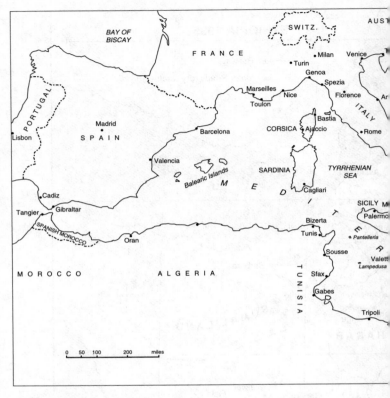

Map 5 The Mediteranean Sea

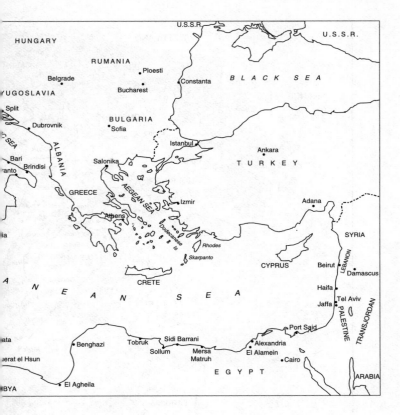

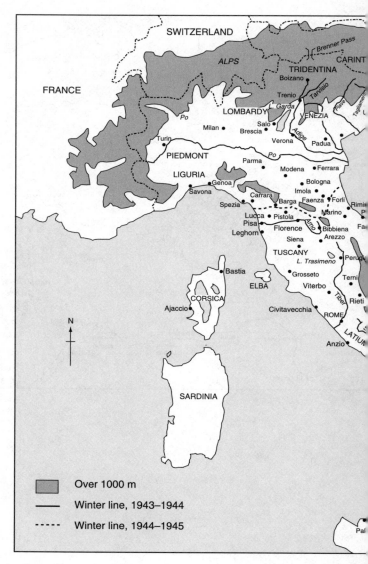

Map 6 Italy, 1943–5

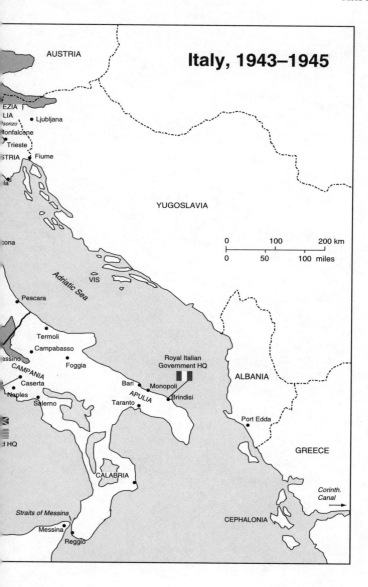

Italy, 1943–1945

Index